"Choudhuri and McCarthy's book should be on every group worker's Group Process Observation fills a large gap in the literature related to addressed role of process observation in group work. The highly acces by renowned group work experts who effectively bridge the research ...es with illustrative case examples. I look forward to synthesizing the book i... ...oth my content and clinical courses across my work with master's and doctoral students, as well as within my group work in professional development and servant leadership."

— **Melissa Luke, PhD, LMHC, NCC, ACS**, *Dean's Professor, Department of Counseling & Human Services, Syracuse University*

"Scholars, educators, students, and group workers will finally have a resource that explores the use of process observations in a variety of group settings and structures. Process observations are invaluable tools for understanding how the process of interactions impacts the functioning of a group. However, before this book, there was no resource that covered all aspects of process observations, from skills needed to ethical concerns. This book belongs on the shelf of group workers in all fields and will be of particular value to group facilitators using process observers as well as practitioners who do or aspire to include process observation as part of their professional repertoire."

— **Sheri Bauman, Ph.D.**, *Professor Emerita, College of Education, University of Arizona*

"Wow! If you are looking to learn about process observation in groups, this is the book! The editors and authors cover the entire subject of process observation. You will be thrilled if you are wanting to learn what process observation is; how it is done; when it is done, and the different kinds of process observation. A much needed book for the field of group counseling."

— **Ed Jacobs**, *West Virgina University*

Fundamentals of Group Process Observation

This edited collection covers the role of the process observer – a position that enhances the effectiveness of group functioning by observing the process, summarizing the behavior of the group so that the group can learn and, if needed, improve its functioning.

There is little guidance on best practices for this role, and in most settings, process observers are forced to rely on whatever previous training they have received in group work to fulfil their role. The first of its kind, this book offers a wealth of resources for the role of group process observer organized in a systematic way. Each contributor focuses on a specific aspect of group process observation, identifying what is currently known on the topic, suggesting best practices, and providing the reader with tools, structures, and guidelines for effective process observation.

Students and educators of group-work courses will find this book integral as it covers the existing gap in literature on group-process observation.

Devika Dibya Choudhuri has served as President of the Association for Specialists in Group Work and as a process observer. Her research interests include group work for diversity, equity, and inclusion, trauma-informed counselor pedagogy, ethics and supervision.

Christopher J. McCarthy is a past editor of the *Journal for Specialists in Group Work* and a past president of the Association for Specialists in Group Work, as well as an ASGW Fellow. His research interests include group interventions stress and coping in educational contexts, and career development.

Fundamentals of Group Process Observation

Edited by
Devika Dibya Choudhuri and
Christopher J. McCarthy

Routledge
Taylor & Francis Group
NEW YORK AND LONDON

Designed cover image: © Getty Image

First published 2023
by Routledge
605 Third Avenue, New York, NY 10158

and by Routledge
4 Park Square, Milton Park, Abingdon, Oxon, OX14 4RN

Routledge is an imprint of the Taylor & Francis Group, an informa business

ISBN: 978-1-032-25183-7 (hbk)
ISBN: 978-1-032-25180-6 (pbk)
ISBN: 978-1-003-28195-5 (ebk)

DOI: 10.4324/9781003281955

Typeset in Perpetua
by codeMantra

We both have chosen to dedicate this book to a mentor who influenced our passion for group work.

Contents

Preface

The genesis for this book was our participation in a group tasked with revising the Association for Specialists in Group Work's (ASGW) Guiding Principles for Group Work (McCarthy et al., 2022). Section D of that document (Facilitation of Group Work) refers to the importance of reflective practice, i.e., considering the relationship between the group leader, what is happening in each group session, and among the group members. Section D also refers to processing and meaning-making, namely that group leaders are aware of, and make use of, what is happening in their groups. We all had in mind Process Observation (PO) as essential to reflexive practice and of course-processing sessions, but process observation never made it into the standards. It was something we all did, but there was little scholarship on it, and codifying it in our standards seemed premature.

The other reason came from informal conversations with colleagues about the fact that process observation is used frequently in group counselor training and when group leaders get stuck leading their groups. But PO lives mostly in the shadows, with recommended best practices passed on informally by group trainers and teachers. It seemed well past time to create a book culled from the collective knowledge of experts in the field, so that process observation could more fully take its place among the accepted practices of effective group work.

We started with group process among the book contributors – regularly scheduled zoom meetings with leaders in the group work field and prospective authors to participate in ongoing meetings about defining the construct, critical aspects to cover, and ways to professionalize the role of process observer and bring it into the sunlight. As the book progressed, the group meetings became more collaborative and every chapter author had access to other authors' work. We collected literature referencing process observation for all to use, as well as developed common case vignettes that would serve as a connecting thread across chapters. In our conclusion to the book, we discuss some of our own observations about this process and its implications for future scholarship.

So what is process observation?

Process observation at its essence refers to a person who serves as an observer, recorder, analyst, interpreter, and reporter of what happens in a group with the goal of helping that group improve its functioning (Barnlund, 1955). Of course, in order to be effective, group-process observation requires a number of different skills, including knowledge about group process, the behavior of members in a group, the typical roles that people often take in group, and how individual differences in identity (ethnicity/race, gender, ability status, age, to name but a few) interact in the dynamics of a group.

Process observation is not just limited to group interventions – it is also a commonly used tool for trainees and students who may observe a group counseling session to learn more about group dynamics (Weiss and Rutan, 2016). Process can be observed in other settings, such as education – an administrator may observe a teacher in a class (classes are a type of group!) to help that instructor improve their teaching methods, and student teachers are required to have a training experience working under the observation of a master teacher (Kohut et al., 2007). Additionally, process observation can be used in supervision of counseling/therapy, where a more seasoned clinician observes the work of a trainee (Crespelle, 1988).

In formal terms, the group PO is usually not a member of the group itself but in some cases the group facilitator, leader, or even a third-party supervisor. Informally however, a member of the group can serve as a PO, playing the role of both participant and observer. So you can see, the role of the PO is quite complex!

Structure of this book

This book is organized into four parts, the what, how, where, and when of PO as we currently know it. You will encounter the group expertise of many different authors in the various chapters, which we view as essential, since PO currently has little foundation in the published literature. Our contributors all have extensive backgrounds in using PO, and they have all attempted to make this book as practical as possible by including case examples and exhibits that you can use in process observation.

Part I, Essentials of Process Observation, answers the question "what is process observation"? Chapter 1, co-authored with Dr. Jane Okech, provides an indepth overview of PO, while Chapter 2, also written by Dr. Okech, focuses on group-process observer skills that are grounded in evidence-based group-work literature. We wrote Chapter 3 to examine the complex ethical issues inherent in PO, while in Chapter 4 we offer a step-by-step review of how to select a PO for your group.

Part II covers the "how" of PO – in other words, how can one be an *effective* PO? Chapter 5, written by Dr. Rachel Vannata, is titled, "Processing the Process," and examines best practices for how a PO can share their observations with group leaders and members. Chapter 6, written by Dr. Katy Schroeder, introduces readers to Group Focal Conflict Theory and how central concepts of this theory can be applied to process observation in groups. This section concludes with a review of diversity, equity, and inclusion principles essential to PO.

Part III covers "where" PO takes place. First, Dr. Maria Riva describes PO in counseling and psychotherapy groups, which are the prototypical type of group for many leaders. This is followed by two chapters, lead authored by Dr. Theresa Coogan, on PO in task and psychoeducational groups. This section of the book concludes with chapters by Dr. Christine Suniti Bhat on PO in education and business settings and by Dr. Lorraine Guth, Dr. Marty Jencius, and Dr. A. Michael Hutchins on PO in higher education training settings.

Part IV of the book addresses some of the "when" of PO with a chapter on its history by graduate students Madison Blaydes and Keshav Goud, followed by a review of previous research by Dr. Shing Yee Bay, Dr. Yiying Xiong, and Dr. Kristopher M. Goodrich. Dr. Sam Steen and Dr. Priscilla Prasath then look at how technology in group work changes the conduct of process observation, both enriching and limiting, in their chapter on technology and PO. We provide a conclusion at the end of the book suggesting what we know about PO and imagine what the future holds.

Below we have provided a list of terms used in this book. Also, a note about the style we used. Because we engaged in a collaborative group process, we use "we" to refer to ourselves as authors. We use "you" to refer to you, the reader.

Terminology

Group leader = person(s) leading the group. At times, groups can have more than one leader or sometimes be leaderless, with no specific person formally identified.
Process observer (PO) = the person in that role.

Group process observation (GPO) = refers to the activities associated with the role of PO. GPO is the perspective of looking on and into the patterns of the group interaction. Observation can be wholly from an external perspective or with one foot inside the group.

Group = a collection of individuals characterized by a shared experience of being in relationship with one another.

Members = Participants who comprise the group and are present enough to contribute to the group dynamics.

Diversity, Equity, and Inclusion (DEI) = refers to the variance amongst historical and lived experience, identity, and perspective amongst persons; systemic ways of historical exclusion or marginalization of persons who are deemed as less socially worthy due to their group identities; and attempts to address those inequities by intentionally revising, recreating, and renewing efforts to create a sense of value and belonging for all.

Black, Indigenous, and other People of Color (BIPOC) = Refers to individuals historically marginalized by society and stands for Black, Indigenous, and other People of Color (Mental Health America, 2022).

References

Barnlund, D. C. (1955). The use of group observers. *Communication Education*, *4*(*1*), 46–48.

Crespelle, I. (1988). An active observation model for therapists in training. *Transactional Analysis Journal*, *18*(*3*), 249–253.

Kohut, G. F., Burnap, C., & Yon, M. G. (2007). Peer observation of teaching: Perceptions of the observer and the observed. *College Teaching*, *55*(*1*), 19–25.

McCarthy, C. J., Bauman, S., Choudhuri, D. D., Coker, A., Justice, C., Kraus, K. L., Luke, M., Rubel, D. & Shaw, L. (2022). Association for Specialists in Group Work Guiding Principles for Group Work. *The Journal for Specialists in Group Work*, *47*(*1*), 10–21, DOI: 10.1080/01933922.2021.1950882

Weiss, A. C., & Rutan, J. S. (2016). The benefits of group therapy observation for therapists-in-training. *International Journal of Group Psychotherapy*, *66*(*2*), 246–260.

Acknowledgments

Dibya

I was always taken by the power of groups, but I want to dedicate this book to Dr. Richard Pearson, a faculty member at Syracuse University who showed an eager graduate student the power of a process observer as he shared his report at a meeting of the North Atlantic Region of the Association for Counselor Education and Supervision. What had simply been an event acquired depth and complexity, spotlighting phases and dynamics to become a process that had meaning. I am so glad to be able to offer this book as a contribution to the field he showed me.

Chris

I dedicate this book to Dr. Jo Anna White, a now retired faculty member at Georgia State University who first introduced me to the fascinating world of group work. Dr. White introduced me to the Association for Specialists in Group Work and appointed me to teach group counseling as a doctoral student. She was an inspiration to me for the healing power of groups and how I might contribute to the field as a faculty member and practitioner.

We also acknowledge a debt of gratitude to the Association for Specialists in Group Work, our home association, and one that many of our chapter authors also call home.

Contributors

Devika Dibya Choudhuri (she/ella)
Department of Leadership & Counseling at Eastern Michigan University at Ypsilanti, MI, USA.

Dr. Choudhuri is a Professor of Counseling. She has served as president of the Association for Specialists in Group Work and as a process observer for the Board. Her research interests include group work for diversity, equity, and inclusion, counselor pedagogy, ethics and supervision. She can be reached at dchoudhur@emich.edu.

Christopher J. McCarthy (he/him)
Department of Educational Psychology at the University of Texas at Austin, USA.

Dr. McCarthy is a past editor of the Journal for Specialists in Group Work and a past president of the Association for Specialists in Group Work, as well as an ASGW Fellow. His research interests include group interventions, stress and coping in educational contexts, and career development. He can be contacted at cjmccarthy@austin.utexas.edu.

Shing Yee Bay (he/him/his)
Department of Counselor Education at the University of New Mexico, Albuquerque, NM, USA.

Shing Yee Bay is a doctoral student in Counselor Education. His research interests include international students issues, social justice and advocacy issues, and counselor education. He can be reached at bays027@unm.edu.

Christine Suniti Bhat (she/her)
Department of Counseling & Higher Education at Ohio University, Athens, OH, USA.

Dr. Bhatt is Professor and Chair in Counselor Education, and was a Process Observer for two former presidents of the Association for Specialists in Group Work (ASGW) as well as a past president of ASGW herself. She currently serves on the ACA Governing Council as the ASGW representative. Dr Bhatt's recent scholarship has focused on group counseling, leadership, mentoring, and cyberbullying prevention. Contact information: bhatc@ohio.edu

Madison Blaydes (she/her)
Department of Educational Psychology at the University of Texas at Austin, USA.

Madison is a Ph.D. student in Counseling Psychology. Her research interests include stress, coping, trauma, and group interventions in school settings. She can be contacted at blaydes@utexas.edu

Theresa Coogan (she/her)
Dr. Coogan is a licensed school counselor and clinical mental health counselor. She served as a full-time counselor educator, training master's and doctoral students preparing to enter different counseling specialties for nearly 15 years. Her full-time focus now is working on team cultures in large corporations, applying aspects of group work and dynamics. Dr. Coogan has served the Association for Specialists in Group Work (ASGW) in several roles including Treasurer, Process Observer, and Co-Chair of the Conference Committee.

Chris Godwin (he/him)
Assistant Dean/Chair of Professional Education, Campbell University, Buies Creek, NC, USA.

Dr. Godwin is current president of the North Carolina Association of Colleges for Teacher Educators. His research interests include effective teacher education practices, rural education, and differentiated instruction. He can be contacted at godwinc@campbell.edu.

Kristopher M. Goodrich (he/him/his)
Department of Counselor Education at the University of New Mexico, Albuquerque, NM, USA.

Dr. Goodrich is Associate Dean for Research and Distance Education. He has served as President of the Association for Lesbian, Gay, Bisexual, and Transgender Issues in Counseling (ALGBTIC, recently renamed as the Society for Sexual, Affectional, Intersex, and Gender Expansive identities), Association for Counselor Education and Supervision (ACES), and, at the state-level, as President of the New Mexico Counseling Association (NMCA). Since July 2017, he has served as the editor-in-chief of the *Journal for Specialists in Group Work* (JSGW).

Keshav Rai Goud (he/him)
Department of Educational Psychology at the University of Texas at Austin, USA.

Keshav is a master's student in Counselor Education and a scholarship recipient of the Austin Group Psychotherapy Society. He has also taught postgraduate courses on group dynamics in India and Nigeria. His research interests include group processes, psychodynamic theory, existential philosophy, and creative-relational inquiry. Contact information: keshavraigoud@utexas.edu

Lorraine J. Guth (she/her)
Department of Counseling at Indiana University of Pennsylvania in Indiana, PA, USA.

Dr. Guth served as President, Process Observer, and Special Initiatives Committee Chair for the Association for Specialists in Group Work (ASGW). She is an ASGW Fellow. Her research focuses on group work, multiculturalism, social justice, sexuality, international counseling, and technology in counselor education. She can be contacted at lguth@iup.edu

A. Michael Hutchins (he/him)
Dr. Hutchins is a retired group work practitioner, educator, and consultant from Tucson, Arizona. He is an ASGW, ACA and SAIGE Fellow. He is a Past-President of ASGW and was the founding President of CSJ and was an ACA Governing Council member and process observer. He can be reached at amhutchins2@gmail.com

Marty Jencius (he/him)
Department of Counselor Education and Supervision at Kent State University in Kent, OH USA

Dr. Marty Jencius is an Associate Professor at Kent State where he teaches group work and process observation. He is past president of the Association for Counselor Education and Supervision and past ACA Governing Council Representative. His scholarly interests include the application of technology in teaching or practice and subjectivity (Q-Methodology) in counselor education. He can be contacted at mjencius@kent.edu

Jane E. Atieno Okech, Ph.D. (she/her)
Department of Counseling, Human Development and Family Science at the University of Vermont.

Dr. Okech is a Professor of Counseling, and is also the Editor Elect of *The Journal for Specialists in Group Work (JSGW)*. Her research and scholarly activity primarily focuses on the advancement of proficiencies in the practice of group psychotherapy and specifically clinical supervision with diverse cultural populations. She can be contacted at Jokech@uvm.edu

Priscilla Prasath, Ph.D. (she/her)
Department of Counseling, College of Education and Human Development, University of Texas at San Antonio (UTSA), USA.

Dr. Prasath is an Assistant Professor of Counseling, who currently serves as the secretary of Association for Specialists in Group Work (ASGW) (2022–25) and had previously served as the strategic communications committee chair and the awards chair. Her research focus is on promoting well-being and mental health through development of positive psychological assets and strengths among culturally and developmentally diverse adult population groups. With the goal to foster well-being and positive mental health, in her scholarship and practice, Dr. Pris Prasath utilizes group counseling, leadership development, training, and creativity. Contact information: priscilla.prasath@utsa.edu

Maria T. Riva (she/her)
Department of Counseling Psychology at the University of Denver, CO, USA.

Dr. Riva is a Professor and Training Director in Counseling, and has been actively involved in Group Psychology and Group Psychotherapy (Division 49 of APA) and the Association for Specialists in Group Work (ASGW). She is a Fellow of both organizations. She is on the Editorial Boards of *Group Dynamics*; *International Journal of Group Psychotherapy*; and *Training and Education in Professional Psychology*. She has published numerous articles on group topics including group supervision and group dynamics. She can be contacted at maria.riva@du.edu

Katy Schroeder (she/her)
Department of Counselor Education at the University of Iowa in Iowa City, IA, USA.

Dr. Schroeder is an Assistant Professor of Clinical Mental Health Counseling. She currently serves on the editorial board of the *Journal for Specialists in Group Work*, and she also serves on the research committee for the Association for Specialists in Group Work. Her research interests include group work and the human–animal bond, with a special focus on the inclusion of horses in counseling and psychotherapy group work practice. She can be contacted at Kathryn-schroeder-1@uiowa.edu

Sam Steen (he/him)
Counselor Education Program at George Mason University, Fairfax, VA USA.

Dr. Steen is the Director of the Diversity in Research Action Consortium, a past Associate Editor for the *Journal for Specialists in Group Work* and past *Group Worker* Newsletter Editor for the Association for Specialists in Group Work. His research interests include culturally sustaining group interventions, using groups to foster racial equity in schools, and cultivating Black students' racial and academic identity development. He can be contacted at ssteen@gmu.edu.

Rachel Vannatta (she/her)
Dr. Rachel Vannatta is a Senior Training Specialist at the University of Maryland School of Social Work, Institute for Innovation and Implementation. Dr. Vannatta was a counselor educator where she taught group counseling, counseling skills, and theories of counseling. Her research interests include teaching group work, social emotional development in children from birth through five, and perinatal mental health issues. She can be reached at: rachel.cody@gmail.com.

Yiying Xiong (she/her)
Department of Counseling and Educational Studies, Johns Hopkins University, Maryland, USA.

Dr. Xiong had served as the research committee chair of the Association for Specialists in Group Work (ASGW). Dr. Yiying Xiong's research focuses on promoting international students' mental health and academic success and utilizing group counseling and mindfulness practice with diverse populations. She has also investigated best practices in group counseling training and published on those topics. She can be contacted at yxiong@jhu.edu.

Part I

Essentials of Process Observation

Chapter 1

Introduction to Process Observation in Groups

Devika Dibya Choudhuri, Eastern Michigan University
Christopher J. McCarthy, University of Texas at Austin
Jane E. Atieno Okech, University of Vermont

Introduction to Process Observation in Groups

All of us have been in group situations – at work, with friends, or among family – where something meaningful, upsetting, or disruptive was happening, but was not talked about or addressed. It can feel risky to call out such a situation. You could offend someone, you could be "wrong," or you could be retaliated against. Even well-functioning groups that have established trust with each other can run into trouble sometimes. Having another person who is at least somewhat "outside" the group, whose job it is to observe and evaluate the group's functioning, can be vital (Bieschke et al., 1998).

Techniques for Process Observation were first used in the mid-20th century in fields such as organizational development, anthropology, and sociology (Kaplan, 1987), but the person in this role was not necessarily called a Process Observer (PO). Yalom (1995) popularized the role of Process Observation in group settings for the training of psychiatry residents, in which the PO attended group meetings, took notes, and debriefed with the leader. Later refinements included having the PO debrief in the presence of members to reduce the sense that the PO was intruding on the group life, and to act as more of a participant in the life of the group. Many organizations and groups are now choosing to appoint someone to enhance the effectiveness of group functioning.

While PO's have long been utilized by professionals in the fields of group work, psychology, education, and organizational development, there is very little published guidance or research on the role, tasks, and functions of POs. Given this reality, the PO is often forced to rely on whatever previous training they have received and the experience of others. This is surprising, since Process Observation has been around for decades. Fortunately, there is some published scholarship and expert knowledge available, and we believe the time has come for a book using the collective experience of group workers who have functioned in this role for years. This chapter is organized into three parts. First, in Part I, we will pose and answer several fundamental questions about group process observation (GPO) as an introduction. Then in Part II: "Settings for Process Observation", will go over a step-by-step approach to fundamental considerations in effective GPO. Finally, in Part III, "Past, Present, and Future of Process Observation" we use a case example to illustrate some of the complexities that occur in GPO. It is these complexities that will be the focus of the rest of the book.

DOI: 10.4324/9781003281955-2

Section I: Fundamental Aspects of PO

Purpose

The purpose of a PO is literally to observe and report the dynamics of the group. Yalom and Leszcz (2020) describe process as "the nature of the relationships between interacting individuals-members and therapists" (p.185). Observation of process in this context therefore means noticing events in terms of their dynamics of interpersonal engagement; verbal and non-verbal communication; and recognizing incidences of initiation, patterns of interaction, the meanings of such interactions and their outcomes. Finally, Process Observation includes recognizing and being able to characterize the development of a group's culture as manifested in group norms and member roles, evolving nature of group cohesion, and group outcomes. The role and function of a PO is thus multidimensional, further complexity being added by the expectations of the group leader or the context in which the PO works, and influenced by interactions with group members.

Research supports the value of professional training and skill development for POs (Losada & Manolov, 2015). It's therefore not surprising that most formal POs are professionally trained counselors who specialize in the practice of group work. While it is a critical skill for group leaders who facilitate all types of groups, including counseling, psychotherapy groups, task, and psycho-education groups, there is little systematic training in Process Observation.

Role

Though the exact role of the PO can vary considerably depending on how a group is structured, the PO's job is essentially to monitor and track a group's interactions and offer input to improve its effectiveness. The role of the PO varies by the degree of their involvement in the group, that is, whether their role is purely that of an observer, a participant-observer or a participant who also observes. The practice of GPO as a non-group member is more common and will be the focus of this chapter. By non-group member, we mean a person who does not technically belong to a group and who is not there for counseling, guidance, or whatever goals the group has set for its members. This can lead to an ambiguity of role with ethical and legal consequences that is discussed in more detail elsewhere (Chapter 3: "Ethical and Professional Issues"). In formal terms, the PO is therefore not a member of the group itself but in some cases the group facilitator, leader, or even a third-party supervisor. Informally however, a member of the group can serve as a PO, playing the role of both participant and observer. Very few individuals can perform both roles (being a member and an observer) without their perception of the group's process being influenced by their membership experiences and their participation in the group dynamics.

Typically, in a group meeting, the PO is not a regular participant, but rather takes notes about the group's functioning, identifying how and where the process worked well and where it did not. POs can also be charged with providing commentary on the group, sometimes during the meeting, or with a few minutes at the end. The goal is usually to summarize the behavior of the group so that the group can learn and, if needed, improve its functioning. As you can imagine, the degree of involvement will depend on the goals, the purpose, and the developmental nature of the group. The more autonomous a group, the more they can directly use and benefit from the POs feedback. On the other hand, groups that include those with severe mental illness, very young members, or specialized skill sets such as drama troupe, may be better served by the therapist, the counselor, or the director receiving and using the feedback (this is discussed in greater detail in Chapter 5: "Processing the Process").

We find a comparison of the role of a PO to that of a pilot and first officer helpful. As Patrick Smith describes in his book *Ask the Pilot* (Smith, 2004), planes are always staffed by two fully qualified pilots, one designated as the captain, and one designated as the first officer. While the captain is in command of the aircraft, both the captain and first officer may alternate flying the plane. The person not flying the plane, is then busily engaged in monitoring the planes' systems, communicating with ground control, checking fuel and navigation, and many other functions essential to safe flight. This takes considerable teamwork and communication, and the relationship between the pilots (group leader and PO) and the aircraft (the group) can be tested when something goes wrong.

Concentrating on the "content" of the group takes focus and energy, and it can be difficult to monitor the "process" of the group at the same time. This process can consist of concerns such as how the members are interacting; who seems engaged versus checked out; how diversity and equity are considered and addressed. While a co-leader can often take on the process role, a PO can offer the unique perspective of someone not directly involved in leading the group, which can be particularly helpful when the group experiences turbulence.

Settings for PO

Group counseling is the prototypical setting in which Process Observation takes place, but it can also be a tool for counseling trainees, who may observe a group counseling session simply to learn more about group dynamics (Weiss & Rutan, 2016). Additionally, process observation can be used in supervision of counseling/therapy, where a more seasoned clinician observes the work of trainees (Crespelle, 1988). However, GPO can occur in any setting that involves groups of people working together – an administrator may observe a faculty member teaching a class (classes are a type of group!) to help that instructor improve their teaching methods (Kohut et al., 2007), and many student teachers are required to have an experience where they are observed by the Master teacher in the classroom to be teacher-certified (Lucas, 2018). POs can be used in healthcare or business settings to observe meetings to promote teamwork, boost productivity, and address dynamics that may impede the team (Finn, Chiappa, Puig, & Hunt, 2011).

Many organizations, ranging from businesses to academic entities, increasingly recognize the value in including skilled POs in committee work to enhance their success at meeting target goals and to support leadership development (Armentrout & Wiedeman, 2017). As more professional and academic organizations recognize the role of intersectionality between individual identities, their values, and beliefs, their performance at work, and the complexity of tasks completed in groups, more organizations realize the value that POs can bring in enhancing the effectiveness of various types of groups as they work towards meeting identified group and organization strategic goals. GPO can also occur in qualitative research with a researcher serving as a participant observer (Debaere, 2014).

To sum up, POs are increasingly seen as the key to:

- keeping a group accountable to its identified individual, communal, and organizational goals;
- holding leaders accountable to their responsibility to act in the best interest of the group members by being ethical and culturally responsive;

- holding group leaders accountable for prioritizing group goals and objectives in their choices of interventions.

Section II: Getting Started as a Process Observer, Step-by-Step

So far in this chapter, we've introduced a number of key elements of the role of a PO. Our purpose so far has been to establish at a very general level the importance of this role, why it can be useful, and considerations for establishing an effective PO relationship with your group. We next provide a systematic review of the critical elements that make up preparation for PO.

Process Observation Preparation Skills

The preparation process for observing a group requires a unique skill set that has implications for a PO engaging in effective, ethical, and culturally responsive Process Observation roles and responsibilities. The preparation skills set includes the initial steps a PO would take to be effectively ready to meet the objectives of their assigned role and responsibilities. While the preparation includes completing contractual agreements with an employer, this section will focus on the clinical and professional preparation skills. Preparation skills in many ways mirror many of the steps any group leader would take in preparing to lead a group. These preparation skills and strategies are grounded in group conceptualization theory and skills, an understanding of group dynamics and processes, as well as the understanding that these processes and group activities may look different depending on the type of group one will be observing. Other critical factors impacting preparation skills include the purpose of the group, the composition of the group, nature of the group, and the purpose of the Process Observation. The implementation of these skills are deeply influenced by one's cultural worldview as well as one's level of proficiency regarding interpersonal and intrapersonal awareness and skills. A clinical supervisor needs to have skills in clinical practice, but this level of knowledge is insufficient to do better. Just as supervisors need to also have knowledge of supervision to be effective supervisors who don't simply counsel through their supervisee, POs need to have an understanding and knowledge of GPO over and above group counseling skills.

Examine Personal Values, Beliefs, and Attitudes

All POs need to engage in an ongoing, in-depth examination of their values, beliefs, and attitudes towards different types of groups, group members, group leaders, and group foci (Guth et al., 2018; Okech & Rubel, 2007). This awareness of one's own preferences for observation or member concerns and group styles of communication may have a significant influence on the attitude with which one approaches a Process Observation task, the nature of interaction with group members and leaders, and the content of one's assessment and reports regarding the GPO (Okech et al., 2022). Most trained group counselors have undergone the intense process of examining their personal reactions as part of their professional training. This process includes examining one's worldview and identities, such as race, gender, sexuality, etc., as well as reflecting on their patterns of observations, interventions, assessment, recommendations, and reports on their roles and responsibilities. During such processes the observer needs to pay attention to emerging biases and patterns of preferences and assess their basis. For example, are one's patterns of viewing the group's processes or member roles based on one's own personal fears and concerns? One's own worldview based on race, gender, or sexuality? Or are one's patterns strongly influenced by religious and spiritual values and beliefs? This level of introspection on one's performance as a PO, and the ensuing personal knowledge, awareness, and cultural insight, may be a significant element in every aspect of the role.

Establish the Purpose of Process Observation

The PO needs to clearly establish the purpose of the GPO. The purpose can range from the goals and objectives of the leader, group members, or the organization that offers the groups. Group leaders or organizations that house their groups seek the services of POs for different reasons. Sometimes, it is simply to gain more awareness of the dynamics of the groups they serve and the impact of their leadership. A PO may also be sought if a leader is struggling with a group and facing challenges leading the group towards its stated goals and objectives, or if they have challenges managing the behavior and interaction patterns of a specific group member or a sub-group in the group. It is also possible to seek a PO because one is leading a specialized group for the first time, and one wants to ensure that they are meeting members' needs, or one has previously encountered ethical concerns with their leadership and the PO is part of a personal remediation procedure. Another reason could be to observe the dynamics of co-leadership in meeting group leadership objectives (Okech, 2003).

Most POs' roles entail supporting a group's progression towards its stated goals and objectives, and even in such cases, understanding the core objective of the leader or organizer is key. It is therefore critical that a PO seeks clear instructions regarding the expectations of their role and responsibilities, including expected level of engagement with group members, the leaders and/or their supervisor where applicable. It is also necessary to clarify any expectations regarding documentation, assessment, and reporting requirements. The ability to seek clarity before committing to serve is an important professional skill in all practices but is particularly important for a PO due to the dynamic and impactful role they play in the groups they observe.

Determine the Purpose of the Group

The PO needs to scrutinize the purpose of the group, that is, the group's goals and objectives. This way, the PO can be prepared for the core subject matter and engage in some literature review if the topic is highly specialized, thus gaining knowledge of the topic and enhancing the depth of understanding of the potential group's process regarding the subject matter. For example, is it a group focused on grief and loss, gender or racial identity development, trauma in general or specific traumatic experience? An observer who understands the core dynamics and stages of grief for example, is likely to have better insight into the interpersonal dynamics of a group focused on grief and loss.

Determine the Type of Group

The PO needs to examine the type of group they will be observing (Kline, 2003). For example, is it a counseling or psychotherapy group?

They must understand that interpersonal processing of dynamics of engagement as well as feedback exchange will be a critical part of the group's interaction process. If the group is a psycho-educational group, the PO may need the group syllabus or curriculum, associated assessment procedures, and the structure of the group. Understanding that most psychoeducational groups follow a teaching model may help the PO prepare for observing learning and teaching approaches, group management skills, as well as the leader and group interactions around an identified curriculum. Observations may include focus on the group leader's teaching and discussion facilitation skills or leaders' management of disruptive group behavior. Additionally, if the group is a task group, understanding the goal-oriented nature of such a group, including expectations for interactions to mainly revolve around exploring and meeting group goals and timelines will influence the observations around the leader's ability to keep the group on task, progression towards goals, the dynamics of the group in navigating contentious issues, and time management among other considerations (Bell & Morse, 2013). Finally, establishing whether the group will be opened or closed is also critical to understanding the dynamics of the group's process. Knowing the type of the group one will be observing, and whether it is an opened or closed group is key to effective process identification, analysis, and reporting.

Understand the Demographic Composition of the Group

The PO needs to learn the demographic composition of the group to prepare for potential issues associated with the group's membership and the opportunities and challenges that a leader is likely to encounter in the process of leading such a group. A group's composition focus includes information on members' gender, age, race, sexual orientation, ability statuses, and social locations of group members among other descriptors. Asking questions about a group's composition reflects a PO's understanding of the social-microcosmic nature of groups (Yalom & Leszcz, 2020). Such an understanding would lead an observer to know the importance of preparation to respond to social and cultural dynamics in society emerging within the group and influencing the group's interpersonal dynamics, group discussion content, pace of group cohesion development, and group process in general. The skill of recognizing group composition factors and their potential influence of group content and interaction patterns is key to effective group process conceptualization, analysis, and reporting.

Understand the Nature of the Group

The PO needs to know if the group is made up of voluntary members or if it is a mandatory group. Such membership dynamics are likely to impact the attitudes of members towards each other, the group leader, and the PO (Hachtel, Vogel, & Huber, 2019). Literature suggests that leaders of mandatory groups experience more resistance to change and the therapeutic process from members, than those of groups made up of voluntary members (Snyder & Anderson, 2009). Understanding the nature of group membership and the potential opportunities and challenges that they raise is key to effective analysis of group interactive patterns, particularly in the early stages of group development, group member interactive patterns with the group leader, and approach to group participation in general. All these factors influence accurate conceptualization and assessment of the dynamics of group process, the culture of a group, and its progression towards its stated goals.

Clarify Structural Issues About the Group

Finally, PO preparation skills include paying attention to structural issues about the group they will be observing. Structural issues in this context pertain to ethical and administrative procedures and protocols that facilitate effective group formation, function, and processes. Attention to group structural procedures includes ensuring that an informed consent process has been completed by group members, that they have consented to process observation of the group, that they are aware of the role the PO will be playing in the group, including the extent and type of engagement members and group leaders/co-leaders might have with the PO. Secondly, basic factors such as the size of the group, modality of group sessions, location of the group's sessions if offered in-person, length of the sessions, and expectations of attendance are key to the PO making accurate assessments about members' participation and commitment to the group, as well as leader's executive functioning and responsiveness to emerging group concerns and processes.

Active Group Process Observation Skills

The active observation skills set is at the core of the POs role, responsibilities, and impact on the groups and leaders that they observe (Keiding, 2011). This active aspect of the PO's role can take various forms:

(a) that of a silent observer in the room,
(b) an engaged observer within the room,
(c) an observer outside the room observing the session from behind a glass screen,
(d) an observer watching an audio-visual recording of a session.

There are two common roles practiced by POs. One is of the silent observer in the physical or virtual space who minimally interacts with the group or its leader during the session. The other is the actively engaged observer who periodically steps in to highlight certain dynamics while they are in process so that the group leader and members can acknowledge them and address them in the moment. It is therefore critical that a PO seeks clear instructions regarding the expectations of their role while the group is in session and to be prepared to interact with the group as expected. The core components of GPO can be categorized as follows: group conceptualization, active group observation, assessment of observations, documentation of observations and reporting skills (see Figure 1.1).

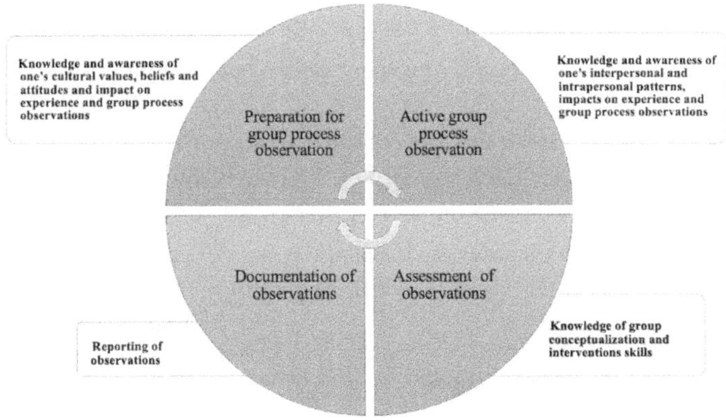

Figure 1.1 Components of group process observation
Source: Dr Jane Atieno Okech.

The first quadrant is preparation, which rests on the knowledge, awareness, and skills that the PO brings with them, which includes cultural and social justice awareness of self and others, group intervention theories, and expertise in group dynamics. The second quadrant focuses on active group process observation, which is based on the PO being able to use their intra- and interpersonal awareness and knowledge lens while simultaneously bracketing this knowledge so as not to contaminate what is observed. Quadrant three emerges from the active group process to assess what has been observed. This rests on the POs knowledge of group conceptualization skills so that they can accurately assess group dynamics, draw conclusions, intervene (if required), and make recommendations for outcomes aligned with the group's goals and objectives. Finally, the fourth quadrant focuses on documentation and reporting of group process assessment, where a knowledge of group intervention skills is needed to maximize efficacy, as well as provide reports that are useful for the group. With these basic elements in mind, we will next use a case example to further develop some of the complexities inherent in the work of a PO.

Section III: Structural, Ethical, and Process Issues that Can Arise in Process Observation: A Case Example

We have already noted that a PO should be skilled in the fundamentals of group dynamics, and may take an active role in planning with the leader, but during the group itself they take a more observational role (Zieman et al., 1981). In some cases, the PO may be given the authority to intervene if group dynamics are problematic or group goals are not being met, while in others, the role simply involves a report post-group (Barnlund, 1955), either to the group as a whole or to the leader(s). Planning the terms of the engagement is a crucial first step. Below are some initial questions the PO and group leader should consider together before Process Observation takes place:

1. *What questions about the life of the group is the PO being asked to consider, and how do these questions relate to the purpose of the group?*
2. *What kind of informed consent about the PO's role in the group will be given to group members?*
3. *What will be the nature of the PO's involvement in the life of the group – will they attend one, some, or all of the meetings? Will they participate in group discussions?*
4. *Will the PO be asked to help with any aspect of the group beyond observing the process, such as planning group activities?*
5. *How will the PO give feedback to the group leader and its members? Is it oral as part of the session; only given at discrete intervals in the life of the group; or written and recorded as part of the group notes?*

The case below of a group demonstrates the complex structural, ethical, and process issues that can arise in Process Observation. Each segment of the case below contains questions for consideration about the role and function of the PO in this group. We do not expect you to have all the answers of course! In the remainder of this chapter, we will use this case example to further describe some of the responsibilities and roles filled by a PO.

Process Observation Case example

Kiara, a Black middle-aged cisfemale therapist in the agency who is a seasoned group facilitator, is leading an eight-week group on Mindfulness where eight adult members from the community are attending. While experienced, Kiara has not led this type of group before, and given the popularity of mindfulness approaches, she is worried that some members will be more expert than her, while others will be newcomers to the topic. She also wishes to further refine her skills at attending to member diversity in this type of group and thinks a PO could be helpful in that regard as well. She has asked Ash, a senior White facilitator in the agency who uses they/them pronouns, to be a PO. Kiara has already pre-screened all the members and has a sense of their personal goals for the group.

- *Based on this brief introduction, what do you think Kiara should be telling Ash about the group and in how much detail before they decide about being a PO?*
- *Should Kiara describe her goals for the group, the demographics and goals of the attending members, or all of the above to Ash?*
- *If the decision to invite a PO in was a part of Kiara's plan, should she have informed all the members during the pre-screening?*

Kiara briefly reviews the goals of the group and provides a brief sketch of the membership to Ash. She also shares her goals of being as much of a mindfulness expert as possible while attending to member diversity in the group. Ash tells Kiara that they will be glad to observe the group and asks if they will be observing from behind the two-way reflecting mirror, or sitting with the group. Ash also asks if Kiara expects them to attend all the sessions, meet prior and post to the group to plan and debrief with Kiara, and whether she would prefer the feedback expressed to the group, communicated to her alone, and whether the feedback needs to be in writing or orally. Ash discloses that they are not familiar with mindfulness groups either, but plan to do some research to prepare.

- *Ash asks Kiara some important questions about the nature of their involvement in the group.*
- *Based on what you have read so far, what do you think might be the most useful way for Ash to observe? Is usefulness based on Kiara's needs or the members, or the combination of Kiara's facilitation of the group?*
- *What forms of feedback might be most beneficial, particularly given Kiara's interest in being an effective leader for a mindfulness group and in attending to member diversity?*

Ash and Kiara ultimately decide Ash should join the group in person from the first meeting but be an observer only. On opening, Kiara introduces herself and then asks the members to briefly introduce themselves. Ash remains silent, and as the members look curiously at them, Kiara introduces Ash as the PO and invites Ash to introduce themself to the group. Group members respond in various ways, but Tom, a middle-aged African American man asks, "So, are you a part of the group or are you like an evaluator? I want to know what you're going to be doing here, and by the way, do we even get a vote in deciding if you can be here?" Kiara at this point says, while smiling, "I asked Ash to be here as the group leader, so it's okay. I can tell you from my experience, their presence will be really helpful, you'll see."

- *What do you think of Kiara's response to Tom?*
- *How should Ash be positioned vis-à-vis the group; introduced as part of the structure of the group early on, or as Kiara did, at the end?*
- *How should Ash introduce themself?*
- *To what degree should their self-disclosure be focused on personal information versus their function in the group? Should Ash answer challenges to their presence, or do they allow Kiara to handle it as the leader?*

Later in the first session, Kiara has members talk in dyads, then quads, and finally as a whole group about their goals, both for themselves and the group. Ash essentially stays in one place and even when the group breaks up, does not join any of the small groups. After the halfway point, Kiara facilitates a common mindfulness exercise in which members focus on the experience of eating a raisin, reflecting on the various sensations they experience, and then process the experience with the group. In the last 15 minutes, Kiara asks Ash to share their observational feedback with the group. Ash describes the various processes they observed while looking around the group and making eye contact with everyone, including noting that Tom's challenge did not get addressed, that several members seemed to feel uncomfortable with Ash's presence, and that at least a third of the members did not appear to be following the mindfulness exercise and wondered aloud if they had received any benefit from it.

- *What do you think of Ash's separation from the rest of the group – should it have been so marked, or would it have been better to join in with members more?*
- *How important is it that Ash did not observe interaction in the sub-groups?*
- *What was significant about the feedback Ash shared; was it the most useful for the group purpose given the group's early stage of development?*
- *What other feedback might Ash have shared?*

Tom is one of the first to respond to Ash, remarking with a laugh, "Now I get it...you sort of keep us in check, and you can call out anybody for anything. I want to do that!" Kiara seemed somewhat defensive as she said, "I don't think Ash is calling anyone out, Tom. But let's engage with some of that, shall we? Did anyone here not get anything out of the raisin exercise?" Margarita, a young Latina member responded, saying, "I guess that's right. I hate raisins and I wished you'd allowed us to use something else – -I wasn't going to put that crap in my mouth." Sandra, an older White woman, responded sharply, "Well I thought it was a great exercise and that Kiara did really well. We should be thanking her for taking the time, not complaining about meaningless details." A couple of other members remarked that they wanted to focus more on their personal mindfulness goals, and Kiara moved the conversation to assignments for the group members to think about for the next session. As members left, Julian, a young Asian transman, stopped on their way out to say to Ash, "I'm really grateful you're here – I feel much safer knowing someone is watching out for us."

- *At this point, what do you think the members' understanding of the PO is?*
- *What do you think about Kiara's understanding of the PO role, and how it is helping the group?*
- *Might the PO role evolve and develop just as the group does, or is it a fixed element that provides structure and stability?*

We hope the questions for processing that followed each segment of the vignette were helpful in demonstrating some of the many aspects of group functioning a PO might contemplate before observation begins. In the sections below, we expand on some of these important considerations.

Competence Necessary for PO

Process Observation requires knowledge about group dynamics, group leadership skills, group stages and group leadership. A PO is often selected for their perceived expertise or congruence with the goals or style of the group leader. Kiara, in the example above, was already a seasoned group leader, but was embarking on leading a mindfulness group for the first time, and was wishing to further hone her leadership of diverse group members. Hanson (1972, 1981) laid out a tool for observation of group processes that is still useful today, stating, "Group process or dynamics deals with such items as morale, feeling, tone, atmosphere, influence, participation, styles of leadership, leadership struggles, conflict, competition, cooperation, etc." (Hanson, 1972, p. 1). For Ash to be effective as a PO, it was important that they, at a minimum, have experience and knowledge about groupwork and these processes.

An understanding of group development theory and how groups function during different stages of group development is critical to understanding group dynamics and process (Kline, 2003). For example, the most well known and most researched classic group development theories are Tuckman's model, Bion's theory, Bennis and Shepard, Schutz, and Tuckman and Jensen (see Kline, 2003). These theories provide varied but important perspectives on systematic and predictable ways in which groups develop over time, the transitions they undergo through stages or phases of development, the challenges they encounter and the circumstances that predict their success or failures at meeting their goals. Group development theories also describe member behavior during different phases of the group's development and give an indication of how member behavior evolves and impacts group process as it develops over time (Kline, 2003). How Ash, Kiara, and the individual members experience the first session of the group isn't necessarily indicative of the relationships that will develop the interactions, conflicts, and connections over time.

Equally important for the PO is the understanding of group dynamics during the period of stage transition and stage intersection phases of group development. This knowledge and understanding is necessary for the PO to exercise a key skill of being able to conceptualize developmentally appropriate group behavior and to distinguish it from problematic group behavior. Knowledge of appropriate interventions is helpful, as the PO needs to be able to make recommendations that could enhance the group leaders' interventions with a group that might be stuck on one stage of development or struggling with resolving a group-as-a-whole concern before it can progress towards meeting its group goals and objectives.

A POs conceptualization skills can be enhanced by their knowledge and understanding of a variety of group intervention theories, e.g., group systems theory, interpersonal theory, focal conflict theory. These are theories that have evolved specifically for application in groups and are designed to take into consideration group dynamics and group process, as well as group levels of interactions including the individual level, interpersonal level, and the group as a whole level (Kline, 2003; Okech & Rubel, 2007). Equally important is understanding the intersections of diversity and multicultural factors in groups, issues pertaining to the group's stage of development, and the leader's skill at addressing emerging concerns and facilitating effective interpersonal interactions among members on such issues. This conceptualization foundation and associated skills are key to enhancing the accuracy and effectiveness of one's observations, interventions, reports, and recommendations to the group members and/or its leader(s).

POs need to have training in how to both be in group and not in group, i.e. be sensitive to the dynamics and yet separated enough to notice and observe them without intervening unless it is ethically necessary. Similar to the systemic view in structural family therapy (Minuchin, 1981), it may be necessary for the PO to "join" the group, but not belong to it. From the vignette above, Ash did this by attending group meetings, but not joining in discussions. This is done to enhance the PO's ability to observe, learn, and ultimately enhance the group process, without getting individually caught up in the group. A necessity for being able to do this is to have flexible boundaries that are neither diffuse nor rigid; the group does not feel enmeshed and overinvested with the PO nor that they are regarded as some sort of specimen under observation. However, it is important to note that groups are composed of individuals with differing histories, personalities, intersecting identities and needs, and a group rarely responds as a block.

In the vignette, there is some conflict already occurring, and Tom appears to have taken on the role of the challenger, while Sandra is clearly protective of the status quo and hierarchy and of Kiara. It is far too early in the group for Ash to comment on this, as it would not be helpful because the group could not deal with it. However, Ash could have a conversational debrief with Kiara post-group, where they might share that Process Observation with her. As the leader, it then becomes up to her to decide how she might want to facilitate.

Process of Process Observations

The person in this role observes the group process and provides timely feedback to the leader(s) and, often, the members as well. This report is not a summary of the meeting, but a description of the observed process. Some examples of what might be shared are:

- *How well discussion flowed and the extent to which all participants were engaged and contributing.*
- *Any conflicts that arose and how they were handled.*
- *Any side conversations or other distractions.*
- *The emotional tone of the meeting: Was it tense, supportive, etc.?*
- *Was the agenda accurate, followed, and sufficient time given to elements?*
- *Were participants well prepared?*
- *Was interpersonal communication appropriate and thoughtful?*

When describing the meeting process to the group, it can be useful for the comments to be appropriate for the general dynamics of the meeting, meeting design and management, and/or the group's developmental stage rather than targeting any one individual or group of individuals. The PO is separate from the facilitator or the recorder precisely to keep these functions separate. The goal of having a PO is to help keep the group's meetings functioning well and encourage group members to share responsibility for the tone and productivity of the meeting. This will be explored in detail in Chapter 5 ("Processing the Process")

Ethics of Process Observation

In the practice of group work as in any interpersonal human endeavor with differing levels of power and vulnerability, ethics are of immense importance. Ethical values pertain to human conduct and the recognition that we have obligations towards others (ACA, 2014), a commitment made by all professional counsellors, which captures the essence of how groups work. The role of PO is no different in having both a general and a particular set of ethics that pertain.

As a PO, the individual may have little input into the structure, format, purpose, or direction of the group. Taking up the invitation to be a PO, as Ash did, does require some ethical considerations and commitments. These are both separate from the group and residing in the person of the PO as well as in the process of observing the group and giving feedback.

The first aspect of ethical obligations of being a PO are largely indistinguishable from any helping professional and are a guide to self-regulation. These include the professional and ethical practice of the role with consistency, dependability, and a shared and clear set of expectations. Competence and scope of practice have yet to be adequately defined for this role, but are necessary adjuncts to be successful. Ash disclosed to Kiera that they were not well-versed in mindfulness. Is that an area of competence Ash is lacking, or is it less necessary than competence in the role of PO? The risk of doing harm increases in direct proportion to the lack of consideration. For instance, if Kiara was running a counseling group for sexual assault survivors, understanding of the sensitive processes of such groups might be far more necessary for a PO to have prior to entering.

In addition, the GPO is also an ethical practice. One useful framework is abiding by the six guiding ethical principles of non-maleficence, beneficence, autonomy, justice, fidelity, and veracity in the helping fields. Autonomy focuses on an individual's right to make their own decisions based on their values and beliefs; in this case on both a group and individual level. Beneficence is promoting the well-being of others, and the POs attention to possible dynamics that hinder or assist this. Non-maleficence is avoiding actions that would cause or create a risk of harm, such as confidentiality and protecting members' privacy in the task of being a PO. Fidelity pertains to honoring commitments and obligations, where Ash continues to attend the group and be consistent in honoring their duties to the group. Justice focuses on providing equitable and fair treatment; where even if Kiara originally asked for their presence, Ash owes the whole group their due diligence. Finally, veracity pertains to being truthful. Ash records and observes the processes as they perceive them and does not theorize beyond their knowledge or observation. It does not require that Ash share all observations but that keeping some back is as much an assessment of value of the observation to the group, as is the group's readiness to hear it.

Diversity, Equity, and Inclusion Knowledge and Skills in PO

POs, like all members of helping professions, are expected to have the knowledge and skills to work with members of diverse identities, as well as an understanding of their areas of competence when offering services. A PO's conceptualization skills are enhanced with their knowledge, awareness, and understanding of issues of diversity and multiculturalism within the context of the group and their manifestation within the group's process. This understanding includes appreciation of the knowledge and demographic composition of the group and its potential impact on the group's dynamics (Rubel & Okech, 2010). Knowledge of how individual members' identity intersects with other group members, the leader(s), and the purpose of the group is essential to PO and an area that could be easily overlooked if the PO takes a "color-blind" attitude toward their role. The PO must also have an awareness of how power and privilege manifest in group dynamics and the subtle and explicit ways that membership, contribution, engagement, and responses are cues to marginalization and inequity (Conyne, 1998).

Understanding the social-cultural context of the group and potential interactions around issues of race and racism, gender and gender identity, immigration status and nationality, etcetera, is essential for effective understanding of the patterns of interactions, the content of the group's interactions, dynamics of interaction among group members and the leader, and the group's advancement towards its goals (Rubel & Okech, 2018). A PO who recognizes the criticality of understanding heterogeneous groups and effective conceptualization and intervention with such groups can accurately assess group dynamics and process, leader interventions and impact, and provide service that is culturally responsive.

In the vignette above, Kiara has specifically asked Ash for assistance attending to multicultural factors in the group, and it would be important for Ash to have as clear an idea as possible about specific types of feedback Kiara is hoping to receive. Given that the group topic is mindfulness,

Kiara and Ash might both want to talk about research on mindfulness and how this form of group has been used with diverse populations. Each individual member has their personal goals for the group and this might also influence multicultural factors depending on member experiences and expectations.

Ash might observe for ways in which members use their positions as marginalized or privileged in society in the group. When Sandra "scolds" Margarita for "complaining" about the mindful eating activity, it would be useful for Ash to have noticed if this is a pattern Sandra has of using her "older" position to shut down disagreement. While ostensibly protecting Kiara from critique, is she also using her race privilege to "take care of" Kiara at the expense of a young Latina? Group members who have racial or age privilege can sometimes act as second-string *quasi* facilitators, policing the group and gaining status. While coming across as protective of the facilitator, it can also subtly siphon power from them since apparently they are in need of protection. It is also worth noting whether Tom has taken on the role of Challenger because it is his personality, his position as an older African American man *vis-à-vis* Kiara, or in an attempt to bring a greater degree of "realness" to the rarefied nature of mindfulness groups.

Positionality of Process Observer

The positionality of the PO in relation to the group is important to clarify. GPO may take place at one point in time, or over the life of a group. If the group is recorded, it is even possible for the PO to observe a group asynchronously. As shown in our vignette above, members will likely react to the presence of an observer, so it is important to clarify the PO's role in the group. It is also important to consider the impact of the PO on the development of the group. For the PO, it is important to consider what effect they may have on the very process they are observing. A study by Stinchfield, Hill, and Bowers (2019) found that a structured process of providing reflective feedback in group supervision positively impacted engagement, commitment, and investment in growth-producing ways. On the other hand, if the position of the PO is too closely aligned with the group, it can be powerful in unanticipated ways (Humphrey & Barmack, 2010). For instance, if the PO is perceived as aligned with one or more of the members through prior relationships, how much will members generally rely on the objectivity of the PO?

Conclusion

Groupwork is an important and powerful modality in helping, educational, and business settings, and in order to harness the potential of this intervention, a skilled PO can be an important ally. Currently there is scant established literature on effective Process Observation, and we have endeavored to map some of the contours of PO in this chapter.

References

American Counseling Association (APA). (2014). *ACA code of ethics*. Retrieved from https://www.counseling.org/knowledge-center/ethics.

Armentrout, J., & Wiedeman, T. (2017). Using an observation and feedback model, *Training Industry Magazine - Experiential Learning*, Retrieved from https://www.nxtbook.com/nxtbooks/trainingindustry/tiq_20170708/index.php#/p/30.

Barnlund, D. C. (1955). The use of group observers. *Communication Education*, *4(1)*, 46–48.

Bell, S., & Morse, S. (2013). An approach to comparing external and internal methods for analyzing group dynamic. *Group Dynamics: Theory, Research, and Practice*, *17(4)*, 281–298. https://doi.org/10.1037/a0034623.

Bieschke, K. J., Matthews, C., Wade, J., & Pricken, P. A. (1998). Evaluation of the process observer method: Group leader, member, and observer perspectives. *The Journal for Specialists in Group Work*, *23(1)*, 50–65. https://doi.org/10.1080/01933929808411381.

Conyne, R. K. (1998) What to look for in groups: Helping trainees become more sensitive to multicultural issues. *Journal for Specialists in Group Work*, *23(1)*, 22–32.

Crespelle, I. (1988). An active observation model for therapists in training. *Transactional Analysis Journal*, *18(3)*, 249–253.

Debaere, V. (2014). Beyond the "black box" of the Therapeutic Community for substance abusers: A participant observation study on the treatment process. *Addiction Research & Theory*, *22(3)*, 251–262. doi: org/10.3109/16066359.2013.834892.

Finn, K., Chiappa, V., Puig, A., & Hunt, D. (2011). How to become a better clinical teacher: A collaborative peer observation process. *Medical Teacher*, *33(2)*, 151–155.

Guth, L. J., Nitza, A., Pollard, B. L., Puig, A. M., Chan, C. D., Bailey, H., & Signh, A. A. (2018). Ten strategies to intentionally transform hate, facilitate courageous conversations, and enhance community building. Association for Specialists in group Work, retrieved from https://docs.wixstatic.com/ugd/513c96_fe59b-76c04b040f8bb17f653b3092b10.pdf.

Hachtel, H., Vogel, T., & Huber, C. G. (2019). Mandated treatment and its impact on Therapeutic Process and Outcome Factors. *Front Psychiatry 10(219)*. doi:10.3389/fpsyt.2019.00219.

Hanson, F. (1972). What to look for in groups: An observation guide. In J. Pfeiffer & J. Jones (Eds.), *The 1972 annual handbook for group facilitators* (pp. 21–24). Pfeiffer.

Hanson, P. G. (1981). *Learning through groups: A trainer's basic guide*. Pfeiffer & Co.

Humphrey, V. & Barmack, B. (2010). Transcendence, transmission, and transformation: the transcendent function in infant observation. *Analytical Psychology*, *55(3)*, 321–388.

Kaplan, B. (1987). Online process observation. *Proceeding of the Human Factors Society*.

Keiding, T. B. (2011). Observing Participating Observation - A Re-description Based on Systems Theory. *Historical Social Research / Historische Sozialforschung*, *36(1(135)*), 106–123. http://www.jstor.org/stable/41151259.

Kline, W. B. (2003). *Interactive group counseling and therapy*. Upper Saddle River, New Jersey: Merrill Prentice Hall.

Kohut, G. F., Burnap, C., & Yon, M. G. (2007). Peer observation of teaching: Perceptions of the observer and the observed. *College Teaching*, *55(1)*, 19–25.

Losada, J. L., & Manolov, R. (2015). The process of basic training, applied training, maintaining the performance of an observer. *Quality & Quantity*, *49(1)*, 339–347.

Lucas, C. (2018). More than I expected: Reflections on being observed and reviewed as a pharmacy teacher. *Currents in Pharmacy Teaching and Learning*, *10(6)*, 803–806.

Minuchin, S. (1981). *Family therapy techniques*. Cambridge, MA: Harvard University Press.

Okech, J. E. A., Ort, J., Steen, S., & Goodrich, K. (2022). New group work practice manuscripts: Recommendations for manuscript development. *Journal for Specialists in Group Work*, *47(1)*, 1–9. doi:10.1080/01933922.2022.2014744.

Okech, J. E. A., Pimpleton, A., Vannata, R., & Champe, J. (2016). Intercultural conflict in groups. *The Journal for Specialists in Group Work*, *41 (4)*, 350–369. doi:10.1080/01933922.2016.1232769.

Okech, J. E. A., Pimpleton, A., Vannata, R., & Champe, J. (2015). Intercultural communication: an application to group work. *The Journal for Specialists in Group Work*, *40*, 268–293. doi:10.1080/01933922.2015.1056568.

Okech, J. E. A. (2003). A grounded theory of group co-leader relationships. *Dissertation Abstracts International*, *62(02A)*, 0320 (University Microfilms No. AAI3082996).

Okech, J. E. A., & Rubel, D. (2007). Diversity competent group work supervision: An application of the supervision of group work model (SGW). *Journal for Specialists in Group Work*, *32(3)*, 245–266. doi:10.1080/01933920701431651.

Rubel, D. & Okech, J. E. A. (2018). Diversity and Multicultural Group Counseling. In D. Capuzzi & M. Stauffer (Eds.), *Foundations of Group Counseling*. (pp 111–131). Denver: Pearson.

Rubel, D. & Okech, J. E. A. (2010). Diversity Issues in Group Work. In D. Capuzzi, D. Gross, & M. Stauffer (Eds.), *Introduction to group work*. (5th ed., pp. 219–247). Denver: Love.

Smith, P. (2004). *Ask the pilot: Everything you need to know about air travel*. Berkeley Publishing: New York, NY.

Snyder, C. M. J., & Anderson, S. A. (2009). An examination of mandated versus voluntary referral as a determinant of clinical outcome. *Journal of Marital and Family Therapy*, *35(3)*, 278–292.

Stinchfield, T., Hill, N., and Bowers, R. (2019). Integrative reflective model of group supervision: Practicum Student experiences. *Counselor Education and supervision*, *58*(*2*), 141–157. DOI: org.ezproxy.emich.edu/10.1002/ceas.12137.

Weiss, A. C., & Rutan, J. S. (2016). The benefits of group therapy observation for therapists-in-training. *International Journal of Group Psychotherapy*, *66*(*2*), 246–260.

Yalom, I. D. (1995). *The theory and practice of group psychotherapy* (4th ed.). Basic Books.

Yalom, I., & Leszcz, M. (2020). *The theory and practice of group psychotherapy* (6th ed.). New York: Basic Books.

Zieman, G. L., Romano, P. A., Blanco, K., & Linnell, T. (1981). The process-observer in group therapy. *Group*, *5*(*4*), 37–47. https://doi.org/10.1007/bf01456612.

Chapter 2

Effective Observation

Skills of Process Observation

Jane E. Atieno Okech, University of Vermont

Effective Observation: Skills of Process Observation

All groups can benefit from the presence of a process observer (PO), and research has found the presence of a skilled PO to be minimally disruptive to groups (Bieschke et al., 1998). Skilled POs can be strategic and intentional about their level of engagement with groups, as well as the timing and nature of their engagement. Such intentionality is extremely beneficial to groups, group leaders, and their members (Hogan, Harris, & Cassidy, 2006). Skilled POs also understand the intersectionality of social and cultural identity and their impact on group dynamics and process. They recognize that gender, sexuality, race, and ethnicity do not exist in isolation from each other and from other categories of social and cultural identity. This understanding is critical to effective group process conceptualization, the understanding of the interpersonal processes in groups and effective group Process Observation.

The benefits of a PO extend from their impact on both homogenous and heterogenous groups and the unique conceptualization and intervention skills the different types of groups require. Homogenous groups tend to consist of members of primarily the same social and cultural identities. Such groups, including their leader, may struggle with the perception of commonality, and divergent views might not have room to develop or be explored. These groups can benefit from the presence of a PO who can support the group's effort to identify its norms, individual roles, their impact on group patterns of interactions, and implications for group outcome.

Equally beneficial is a PO of heterogenous groups. Heterogenous groups may consist of members of different social and cultural identities. Group research shows that there is a higher potential for misunderstanding and conflict to occur in heterogenous groups (Okech et al., 2015, 2016). Such groups may also struggle with developing group cohesion, that is, a sense of trust and confidence in each other that is critical to the success of groups.

Heterogenous groups can benefit most from a PO. The Group Process Observation (GPO) may enhance the capacity of both heterogenous and homogenous group members to deepen their understanding of each other, evaluate their interpersonal communication styles, intercultural communication dynamics, and address group processes that are hindering equal participation of members in an in-depth exploration of pertinent topics. The group PO's ability to meet their responsibilities and perform their roles effectively is directly linked to how proficient they are at conceptualizing groups, grounding their interventions on their conceptualization, and acquiring and executing effective group process observation skills (Losada & Manolov, 2015).

Effective GPO skills emanate from the intersections of effective group process conceptualization and active GPO skills. Group process conceptualization can be defined as how the PO thinks about what they observe, and how these thoughts help make sense of what's going on within the group. Effective conceptualization ensures that the PO can accurately assess group dynamics,

DOI: 10.4324/9781003281955-3

draw conclusions, intervene (if required), and make recommendations for outcomes aligned with the group's goals and objectives. GPO conceptualizations are most effective if grounded on three core foundational approaches to understanding group processes, their evolution, and impact. The foundational approaches are group development theory, group intervention theories, and principles of Diversity, Equity, and Inclusion (DEI) in groups.

Group development theories help us to understand "when and how issues common to group members surface, how these issues temporarily resolve, and how these issues recycle" (Kline, 2003, p. 69) during different stages of group development, which is critical to understanding group dynamics and process. For example, the most well known and most researched classic group development theories are Tuckman's model, Bion's theory, Bennis and Shepard, Schutz, and Tuckman and Jensen (see Kline, 2003). These theories provide varied but important perspectives on systematic and predictable ways in which groups develop over time, the transitions they undergo through stages or phases of development, the challenges they encounter, and the circumstances that predict their success or failures at meeting their goals. Every PO needs to read this literature to enhance their understanding of the transitional processes groups undergo as they develop over time.

Knowledge of group intervention theories is key to understanding "the dynamics of members' interactions, how leaders use these interactions therapeutically, the conditions necessary for change, how members change, and the roles of group leaders" (Kline, 2003, p. 69). For example, group intervention theories include group systems theory, interpersonal theory, focal conflict theory, and so on. These theories were either developed for groups (e.g., group systems theory) or have evolved over time for application in groups (e.g., interpersonal theory and focal conflict theory). These theories were designed to take into consideration group dynamics and group process, as well as group levels of interactions including the individual level, interpersonal level, and the group as a whole level (Connors & Caple, 2005; Kline, 2003; Okech & Rubel, 2007). Given that a key responsibility of the PO includes reporting on group dynamics and group process, this conceptualization foundation and associated skills are key to enhancing the accuracy and effectiveness of a PO's Process Observations, interventions, reports, and recommendations to the group members and/or its leader.

A PO's understanding of the principles of DEI in groups can be enhanced with their knowledge, awareness, and understanding of how social and cultural identity differences and historical relationships and experiences among different social and cultural groups manifest within the context of the group, as well as how they influence group interactions and outcome (Rubel & Okech, 2010). These principles include (a) understanding the social-cultural context of the group and potential manifestation of those issues within the group. For example, how they might manifest in the group through interactions around issues of race and racism, gender and gender identity, immigration status and nationality, and so on. (b) Understanding group member social and cultural identity and how it might influence their participation in the group. For example, how identity might influence the choices a member makes about what to share or not to share about their identity, and who to trust or not trust based on that member's identity. These two principles are essential to a PO's effective understanding of the group's patterns of interactions, the content of the group's interactions, dynamics of interaction among group members and the leader, and the group's advancement towards its goals (Rubel & Okech, 2018). A PO who recognizes the criticality of understanding the social and cultural context of a group and its implications for group member interactions is more likely than not to accurately assess group dynamics and process, leader interventions and impact, and provide service that is culturally responsive.

Finally, the active GPO skills set is at the core of the process observer's role, responsibilities, and impact on the groups and leaders that they observe (Keiding, 2011). The active group process observation skills can be defined as observable or audible, direct, and tangible interventions carried out by a GPO during the group session and after its conclusion. The rest of this chapter will provide a comprehensive examination of effective active group process observation skills. Several examples including the following case study will be referenced throughout this chapter to illustrate suggested group process observer skills.

Case Study

A peer supervision group of licensed clinical mental counselors has been meeting for several months, on a biweekly basis, for a two-hour time block on Saturday mornings. While the group started with eight members, it has recently had two original members drop out. Most of the members knew of each other either by practicing in a similar agency, graduating from the same counseling program, or having done their supervision for licensure under the same supervisor. They developed the group through word of mouth and identified the key objectives of the group to focus on consultations with each other about their clinical concerns, ethical dilemmas, and personal and professional development. The current membership consists of:

- *Marcia, a 42-year-old, White, Irish-American, Buddhist, lesbian cisfemale who has been practicing for three years.*
- *Kiara, a 37-year-old African American, Christian, heterosexual cisfemale, who has been practicing for four years.*
- *John, a 29-year-old White, heterosexual cisman, who received his full license last year.*
- *Gerda, a 35-year-old White, lesbian cisfemale of German heritage who has been practicing for five years.*
- *Ajay, a 39-year-old South Asian, Hindu transman who has been practicing for 11 years*
- *Carla, a 40-year-old White, Christian cisfemale of Italian-American heritage who has been practicing the longest at 14 years.*

Recently, two members dropped out who both identified as heterosexual Christian cismen in their early 40s, one Latino and one White. Both had different reasons but were increasingly distant before they left. Since these members left, the group is finding itself adrift, with meetings where members seem reluctant to bring up ethical concerns or discuss professional and personal struggles with clients. Carla, the most experienced clinician in the group suggested that they get a process observer to assist the group in finding its way back to the core purpose of the group. The group devoted a meeting to discussing a process observer, the benefits and costs associated with it, and eventually approved the hire of Tracy, a 54-year-old African American, heterosexual cisfemale, who has been practicing for ten years and has extensive experience leading homogenous and heterogenous groups, and supervising graduate students.

Active Group Process Observation Skills

The active group observation focus is highly influenced by the GPO preparation steps described in Chapter 1 and group process conceptualization skills described in the introductory sections of this chapter, specifically, the PO's knowledge, understanding, and expertise in utilizing various

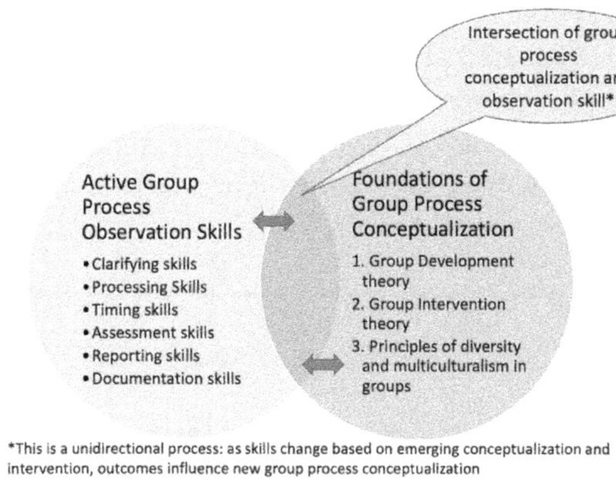

Figure 2.1 Skills of Group Process Observation
Source: Dr Jane Atieno Okech.

types of group development and group intervention theories, and the principles of DEI in groups. This section explores the practice of active group observation. A PO's active observation skills may be expanded by specific requests submitted by a group leader, group members (if invited to provide input), or a group supervisor (where appropriate). Essential active GPO skills include demonstrating knowledge, understanding, and practice of the following, (a) clarifying group process skills, (b) processing skills, (c) timing skills, (d) assessment skills, (e) reporting skills, and (f) documentation skills (see Figure 2.1).

Clarifying Skills

Clarifying Group Goals and Objectives

A key skill for the PO is the ability to discern the extent to which the group is meeting its objectives and being able to share observations that can help the group advance towards meeting its goals. A PO can attain this goal by paying close attention to the content of the group discussion, questions asked, and concerns raised by group members during the initial phases of the group or whenever the question of meeting group objectives and goals comes up. The PO should focus on establishing whether group members have a clear understanding of their individual and group objectives and goals. Additionally, the PO should pay attention to the pattern of group-member interactions with each other and with their leader as they explore group objectives. The following questions provide direct guidance on the processes the observer can pay attention to when seeking clarity on the group's intersection with its objectives. For example, did there appear to be a general understanding of the group's objectives and consensus among members of the same? Or do members appear confused about the group's and/or their personal goals for the group? The leader's response to member dynamics is key to observe, as well as how members respond to each other. For example, how well did the leader respond to the questions or concerns raised regarding group goals and objectives? Or how well was each member able to articulate their own personal goals and their hopes for the group? Are these ongoing challenges or were they resolved?

The following is an example of an interaction that could have occurred during the early meeting of the case study group:

MARCIA: I am so confused about the purpose of this group! I wonder why I stay on!

KIARA: Me too! Can someone clarify why we are here and how I can benefit from being in this group?

TRACY (PO): I have noticed that the question about the purpose of this group keeps on coming up when members are feeling frustrated with the focus of the group. My understanding is that the key objective of the group is to focus on consultations with each other about ethical, professional, clinical, and personal concerns emerging from your work.

In this example, the PO shares their observation of a pattern of interaction around the group objectives and goals, and also shares their understanding of the purpose of the group. See checklist in Appendix 1 for an expanded list of questions that a PO can use to enhance their understanding of the group's clarity on their group objective and goals.

Clarifying Patterns of Group Interactions

It's important for the PO to pay attention to the pattern of group member interpersonal interactions. This includes paying attention to the role their social and cultural identity play in the content of their interpersonal interactions. For example, in the case study, group membership reflects diverse social and cultural identities including race, ethnicity, gender, sexuality, etc. It's not clear if members have discussed their identities and how it interacts with their work as counselors and the fears and experiences they bring with themselves to the group. Tracy (PO) will need to pay attention to the group's patterns of interaction around their social and cultural identities, and the impact of those interactions on their progress towards meeting group objectives.

Based on observation of interaction patterns, what is the pattern of engagement and interaction within the group? Are all members engaged or are some more engaged than others? Is there a silent member or an overactive group member that the leader needs to manage? What is the participation level for the group as a whole? For example, after considering these questions, Tracy (PO) in the case study might state that, "I have noticed that while all of you participated in discussions regarding concerns with not getting enough input to support your work with clients, when the topic of personal risks and vulnerability came up, the group has for the third time changed the topic and went back to discussing clients in your caseloads." Also, consider if the group is generally well engaged or is the group struggling to engage with each other in addressing the focus of the group? Tracy (PO) might observe that, "I have noticed that while the group discussed the importance of everyone participating at length, no one has directly addressed Ajay's silence in the group."

It is essential that the PO working with groups with or without leaders considers how the group leader or other members contribute towards leveling group member participation and how they perform with regards to encouraging group participation. Additionally, the PO needs to consider how the group leader or other members are supporting the development of interpersonal connection among members. For example, Tracy (PO) in the case study might observe that, "I have noticed that while your group does not have a designated leader, for the last three weeks, Carla has initiated the beginning of each session and also provided the concluding summary reflection at the end of the session." Finally, it is essential that the PO considers if race, gender, or sexual identity are playing a role in member interactions within the group or the reactions of the leader or other members in the group. Naming these intercultural dynamics and the impact on the group's pattern of interaction is a critical part of culturally responsive practice. See Appendix 1 for the list of questions that can enhance this skill during the observation process.

Clarifying the Nature of Group Discussions

A crucial Process Observation skill is being able to focus on the content of the group's interactions and noticing if there is consistency in the discussion of the subject matter. It is also important to consider if the group's discussions are expanding conversation on the group core focus or deepening discussions on the group's core purpose. The PO needs to pay attention to the nature and quality of the discussion, for example, was the discussion arbitrary, meaningful, or insightful, and was it focused and cohesive? Were members able to conclude discussions on emerging concerns or were most discussions not concluded?

In the case study, Tracy might observe, "I have noticed that when the topic of redefining the norms of this group to ensure that it meets your goals for professional support and development came up, everyone got involved and offered suggestions about how that could be done." Additionally, the PO should consider whether members appear to be favoring certain subject matters while ignoring others, or if members are consistent in addressing all emerging concerns with the same focus, emotional investment, and consistency? Which topics are members avoiding discussing? Are topics related to social-cultural factors and identities emerging within the group? When they do, are they named, acknowledged, and engaged with, or are they ignored? (See checklist in Appendix 1.) Being culturally responsive requires being attentive to issues of diversity, equity, and inclusion as they emerge within the group and noticing intercultural dynamics and impact with this group. For example, in the case study, Tracy (PO) might say, "I have noticed the question of member sexual orientation and its impact on your relationships has come up several times today in both your interactions as members and in the content of the client cases that you have shared here today." Notice that the PO is making detailed observations of process without necessarily providing directions for actions. We will address circumstances when the PO can make recommendations later in the chapter.

Clarifying Group Interpersonal Dynamics

Based on Process Observations,

- what is the interpersonal dynamic of the group? That is, how are members interacting with each other and with the leader? Is the relational dynamic amicable and connective, empathic? Is it thoughtful and inviting? Or is it conflictual and disagreeable? When disagreements emerge, are they addressed or ignored?

For example, a PO might state that, "I have noticed that while members are thoughtful and cordial in interactions with each other, they seem abrupt and angry when interacting with the co-leaders. I wonder if this might have to do with unresolved issues regarding the informed consent process which has been at the center of all those interactions?"

- Other questions to consider could be, "Are members joining with each other, and if so, who is joining with whom? Is there an instigator in the group? Or a scapegoat in the group? Is there any social and cultural characteristic to these dynamics? And if so, are they influenced by gender, age, race, or religion?"

It is critical for the observer to be culturally astute and be able to recognize the dynamics of power, privilege, and oppression when they emerge within the groups they are observing. Are these dynamics persistent or are they circumstantial? Also critical is the observation and examination of how groups with leaders/co-leaders are responding during these moments of members connecting with each other or during moments of interpersonal conflict.

- Are leaders responding to interpersonal dynamics, such as sub-grouping based on discussion content, or sub-grouping driven by social cultural norms of alignment within the context in which the group is contextualized?

See the illustrative example below:

GERDA: I really want everyone to take risks and share their personal journey in the group. I was very scared and yet I found the courage to talk about my sexual orientation and my struggles with homophobic clients.

JOHN: I hear you! It was hard for me to share that I struggle being a White cismale in this field, given all the privileges everyone ascribes to me, and yet I am dying under the weight of student loans!

CARLA: Today's discussion was so heavy; I might not always agree with you, John, but I am so thankful that everyone is opening up and sharing more about their identity and how it intersects with the important work we do.

TRACY (PO): I have noticed that for the third week Ajay has not participated in social and cultural identity related group discussion and members continue to either ignore or leave Ajay out of discussions. Ajay is the only one who did not share today and yet the group is wrapping up. I'm wondering if it could have anything to do with his identity as the only trans man in the group?

In this example, Tracy (PO) has the unique opportunity to notice patterns and to gain insights into their etiology and impact because she, ideally, is not as emotionally involved in the group process as the group members are. If an observer finds themselves experiencing a strong emotional reaction to the group's interpersonal dynamics, content, and patterns of engagement, then they need to pay attention to their reaction and should seek consultation/supervision, as that reaction might impact the accuracy and effectiveness of their process observation role and responsibilities.

For example, twice Tracy (PO) has observed what appears to be a pattern of exclusion of Ajay, a 39-year-old South Asian, Hindu transman who she has described as not speaking in the group and is either being ignored or not included in group discussions. These are important observations, but also an opportunity to reflect on emerging concern about an individual group member and how to offer more direct observation that can lead to inclusion. For example, Tracy could have also responded more directly:

TRACY (PO): I have noticed that for the third week Ajay has not participated in social and cultural identity related group discussion and members continue to either ignore or leave Ajay out of discussions. Ajay is the only one who did not share today and yet the group is wrapping up. *I'm wondering if it could have anything to do with his identity as the only transman in the group?* Is this something the group can talk about given the shared value of all members participating and being included in the group?

Clarifying the Development of Group Cohesion

Literature shows that cohesive groups are more likely to meet their group goals and objectives than groups that do not attain cohesion (Yalom & Leszcz, 2020). Group cohesion is characterized by more authentic interpersonal interactions, risk taking, more evidence of trust within the group, as well as evident behavioral experimentation and change within the group, and reports of changes emerging from interactions outside the group. Therefore, based on observations, a PO should reflect on the following questions to help assess the group's progress towards cohesion: "Is the group developing a general sense of group cohesion or is the group made up of subgroups? If there are subgroups, are they occurring due to members' shared presenting concerns or social-cultural identities? What is causing the subgroups and how is the leader responding during such moments?"

An effective PO would notice these differences and their impact on the functioning of the group leader, as well as members evolving attitudes and interaction patterns within the group. For example, Tracy (PO) in the case study above might observe that, "I have noticed that since the group focused on discussing Ajay's sense of exclusion from group interactions due to his gender identity, that there is a greater sense of engagement by all members around their social and cultural identities." Another example, could be, "I have noticed that while members have shared deeply about their gender and sexual identity, there has been no discussion about Kiara's experience of race and racism, even though she has brought it up in the group multiple times." Note how in both examples the PO makes an observation of the process that is going on in the group and by design offers the group the opportunity to focus on the process and decide how to proceed. It is a powerful intervention with a respectful recognition of the power of the group to make its own choices about its process.

Processing Skills

Much has been written about processing skills in group work. Processing skills include the ability to examine relationships and their interactive patterns within a group, to recognize significant moments and patterns of behavior, and to bring it to the attention of group members and leaders (Kline 2003; Yalom & Leszcz, 2020). This skill is at the core of the POs' work and all other skills are embedded in it.

Kline specifically characterized processing skills as effective when they capture the emotional and cognitive content of an interaction and facilitate a meaning-making process for members and leaders. It is essential that a PO is astute in recognizing effective group processing skills and the necessity for processing. Processing that involves accurate naming of emotional content and that offers an opportunity for exploration of cognitive processes associated with the emotional content is likely to be effective at enhancing group leader and member learning and meaning attribution to their experiences. Kline cautioned against premature processing, as it could impede the group's development and leave members feeling inadequate. Skilled group leaders know this, and it is essential for PO's to know it as well.

Group work literature identifies four main times when processing is essential (Kline, 2003; Yalom & Leszcz, 2020) and they include:

(a) when a member is being targeted in the group, for example, a PO might say, "I have noticed that every time members are struggling with constructive feedback, they only direct their anger at Parminder. Is it possible for the group members to address why it appears easier to be angry with Parminder and not each other?"
(b) Members are avoiding an important recurring issue, for example, a PO might say, "I have noticed that for the last five weeks, members sharing their mistrust for the group comes up every time the leader asks members to consider offering each other feedback? Is it possible for the leader to address the mistrust among group members and how they can overcome it within the group?"
(c) An interaction is key to the group's transition, for example, a PO might say, "I have noticed that since Awino dropped out of the group, most of the group members have used her absence as a rationale for why they can no longer commit to the group. Is it possible for the group to discuss the impact of Awino's departure on their fears and concerns for the group, and how they can recommit to meeting their goals for the group?"

(d) When members are avoiding sharing their emotional reactions after a significant interaction, for example, a PO reflecting on significant moments in the group's process might say, "I noticed that it took Felix a lot of courage to ask for feedback on how the group is experiencing his commitment to the group. He then received feedback that indicated that fellow group members do not perceive him as being authentic, trustworthy, or committed to the group's goals. That is challenging feedback for anyone to hear and yet all he said was, 'okay,' and pulled back on his seat in silence. I have noticed that this is the second group member to respond this way after receiving challenging constructive feedback. Is it possible for you as the leader to address this pattern of group member response to constructive feedback?" POs who understand the foundation of GPO and the processing skills associated with it are more impactful in their roles and responsibilities.

Timing Skills

Timing is a critical Process Observation skill. In this context, timing means the choices the PO makes about when to intervene directly with group members or the leader. Effective processing skills include timing the processing appropriately. Typically timing that involves direct intervention is agreed upon as part of the role of the PO. Well-timed processing, for example when an incident has just occurred in the group, can be effective at drawing members' attention to a pattern of behavior and interaction within the group that is either working for them or getting in their way. Direct intervention by a process observer while the group is in session is rare in groups led by leaders/co-leaders and may only happen in the case where harm is occurring in the group that is either targeting a group member or directed at a leader. Regardless, circumstances that would warrant the direct intervention of a PO need to be agreed upon in advance.

Many leaderless groups, like the one in this chapter's case study, offer more latitude to POs and they intervene more frequently than is typical for groups that have leaders/co-leaders. The timing of offering feedback or reflections on a group session can also occur directly after a group session is complete. POs may offer feedback and reflection at this time to members or the leader, and may also choose to offer feedback much later. The approach of offering feedback soon after the session is most common practice among POs, and it has been found to be effective because of its proximity to the observed group's process and group events. The approach of offering observations while the group is in session also occurs frequently with leaderless groups like the one in the case study. You will notice that several times, the PO (Tracy) shared reflections of groups processes while in session. In the processing skills section, all the examples provided illustrated conversations between the PO and a group leader/co-leaders immediately after a session.

Assessment Skills

First and foremost, the key assessment skill for POs involves the assessment of oneself and one's impact on the group under observation (Keiding, 2011). Keiding argues that POs impact their groups whether they intend to or not. As a result, any assessment of the group members or leaders' performance must include reflections and assessment on the impact of the observer's presence and interventions with the group. This skill may require ongoing feedback from the subject of observation (members/leaders) and from peers who also engage in the practice of Process Observation (Losada & Manolov, 2015).

Another assessment skill is paying attention to the evolving group dynamics and process over time. For example, a PO could reflect on the following questions: "Have you noticed changes in the group's dynamics or the leader's performance since the initial session?" If the PO has been offering feedback after every session, "does it appear to be impacting the group's process? Is it influencing behavior and interactions among the members and between them and the leader?"

Assessing the impact of one's shared reflections of a group's Process Observations is an important tool for examining one's impact as a PO. A PO may also use a tool for assessing group process. For example, Bell and Morse (2013) recommend the BECM (Being, Engaging, Contextualizing and Managing) as a tool for assessing group dynamics by a PO. Rala et al. (2019) recommends utilizing Process Observation analysis as a means of understanding group process, member participation, and goal-oriented behaviors. Process Observation analysis may include reflections on the following questions:

1. Are your Process Observations positively influencing the group leader's interactions with group members?
2. Are your Process Observations positively influencing the group members' interactions with each other?
3. Are members addressing issues to do with their social and cultural identity? Who is initiating these conversations?
4. Are leaders actively paying attention to social and cultural identity concerns in the group? Are they initiating pertinent conversations with the group?
5. Are they directly addressing their group goals and objectives?
6. Are your Process Observations positively influencing the group leader/members' conceptualization of group process?
7. Are your Process Observations positively influencing the group leader/members' interventions with the group? Are they actively paying attention to diversity and multicultural concerns in the group?

Reporting skills

The principle of objectivity when aligned with knowledge of group dynamics and process, personal and cultural awareness, and thoughtful choice of language will enhance the reporting role of the PO. Objectivity can be enhanced by grounding one's reporting of group dynamics and process on group theory and developmental foundations, as well as direct observations of interactions within the group. Using specific language to capture observed events includes using quotations of direct language as it was used in the group to illustrate a process that is unfolding within the group.

Zieman et al. (1981) recommends that, "Among the important functions of the written summaries were reduction of initial anxiety, focusing the group on important issues, enhancement of continuity across sessions, and promoting therapeutic work between sessions," (p. 37). It's also essential to consider whether the report is submitted in written form or verbally. The same principles still apply. When submitting verbal reports or when asked to offer interpretations of observations, consider using language that directly links your submission to observations and your assumptions about those observations. Whether one is submitting verbal or written reports, consider the following questions and prompts:

1. What did you see or hear (report on verbal and non-verbal behavior)? Provide specific examples of words and phrases used.
2. Describe the interaction traffic patterns in the group, tone of voice, choice of language.

3. Describe patterns of connections, interruptions, conflict, miscommunication, complaints, and compliments.
4. Describe group norms and member roles.
5. Describe leader/co-leader style and approach, and evidence of that style and approach utilizing specific examples from the group session.
6. Identify any professional or ethical concerns.
7. Recommendations to leaders (see illustrations in the processing skills section above).

In order to capture group dynamics and enduring processes, observers should be sure to document and report leader pattern of interventions, individual, interpersonal, or group as a whole, and impact on group functioning (Okech & Rubel, 2007). Also, the PO must ensure that their report utilizes developmentally appropriate language that is accessible to group members in cases where feedback is offered directly to group members. Finally, provide recommendations that can help the group and/or its leaders advance towards their group goals and objectives. Each PO should ensure that the recommendations they offer are aligned with the original contractual specifications about the purpose and nature of their role (see Chapter 1's section on preparation for process observation role, pp. 000–000).

Documentation Skills

A unique skill set for reporting Process Observation insights is keeping the audience of the report in mind (Hogan, Harris, & Cassidy, 2006). It is advisable to keep reports to group members brief and concise, and the ones to the group leaders and/their supervisors more detailed and lengthier (Zieman et al, 1981). POs should always take ethical considerations with documentation and legal standards for access to therapeutic notes in the context of their work (American Counseling Association, 2014). Documentations can be submitted in two forms: (1) Written reports, these include completed Process Observation forms and written reports of group observations. (2) Audio-visual reports included are recorded observations of group process and are like the written report above, except that they are audio-visual or audio depending on the terms of one's contract with the group leader/organization. Regardless of the nature of reports and delivery mode, documentation of process has been found to be helpful to group members and leaders (Hogan, Harris, & Cassidy, 2006).

Summary and Conclusions

The process of becoming a skilled PO is complex and multidimensional. First and foremost, it is critical for the PO to be a trained group worker with the ability to work with different group types. This training is essential given that the foundation for effective Process Observation is based on knowledge and skill in the practice of group work, and specifically understanding of group dynamics and process. Equally important is the PO's personal awareness and skill working with diverse and multicultural groups. Personal awareness includes knowledge of one's social and cultural identity, impact on observation conceptualization and interventions, and awareness of personal values and belief and its impact on reactions to group leaders and members of different identities, social locations, and cultural backgrounds. Above all, the PO needs to be present. This means having the capacity for prolonged attentiveness, inquisitiveness, and intentional focus on the dynamics and process of a group. POs who love group work as a therapeutic modality and who derive personal and professional content from observing, analyzing, and supporting group leaders and members navigate group process and objectives, are more likely to be effective and to thrive in the role of a group PO.

References

American Counseling Association. (2014). ACA code of ethics. Retrieved from https://www.counseling.org/knowledge-center/ethics.

Bell, S., & Morse, S. (2013). An approach to comparing external and internal methods for analyzing group dynamic. *Group Dynamics: Theory, Research, and Practice*, *17(4)*, 281–298. https://doi.org/10.1037/a0034623.

Bieschke, K. J., Matthews, C., Wade, J., & Pricken, P. A. (1998). Evaluation of the process observer method: Group leader, member, and observer perspectives. *The Journal for Specialists in Group Work*, *23(1)*, 50–65. https://doi.org/10.1080/01933929808411381.

Connors, J. V., & Caple, R. B. (2005). A review of group systems theory. *The Journal for Specialists in Group Work*, *30(2)*, 93–110. https://doi.org/10.1080/01933920590925940.

Hogan, C., Harris, R. S., & Cassidy, J. M. (2006) The impact of process observers on interpersonal group therapy, *Journal of College Student Psychotherapy*, *21(1)*, 21–32, doi:10.1300/J035v21n01_03.

Keiding, T. B. (2011). Observing participating observation - A re-description based on systems theory. *Historical Social Research / Historische Sozialforschung*, *36(1(135))*, 106–123. http://www.jstor.org/stable/41151259.

Kline, W. B. (2003). *Interactive group counseling and therapy*. Upper Saddle River, New Jersey: Merrill Prentice Hall.

Losada, J. L., & Manolov, R. (2015). The process of basic training, applied training, maintaining the performance of an observer. *Quality & Quantity*, *49(1)*, 339–347.

Okech, J. E. A., Pimpleton, A., Vannata, R., & Champe, J. (2016). Intercultural conflict in groups. *The Journal for Specialists in Group Work*, *41(4)*, 350–369. doi:10.1080/01933922.2016.1232769.

Okech, J. E. A., Pimpleton, A., Vannata, R., & Champe, J. (2015). Intercultural communication: An application to group work. *The Journal for Specialists in Group Work*, *40*, 268–293. doi:10.1080/01933922.2015.1056568.

Okech, J. E. A., & Rubel, D. (2007). Diversity competent group work supervision: An application of the supervision of group work model (SGW). *Journal for Specialists in Group Work*, *32(3)*, 245–266. doi:10.1080/01933920701431651.

Okech, J. E. A. (2015). The ORAL model for feedback exchange. In M. Luke & K. Goodrich (Eds.). *Group work experts share their favorite supervision activities* Volume 2. (pp. 162–167). Alexandria, VA: Association for Specialists in Group Work.

Rala, C. J., Velasco, P. A., Abarico, J. R., & Tenerife, J. T. (2019). Tools in process observation analysis as a means of understanding group atmosphere, participation, and task behaviors. *Asian Journal of Research in Business and Management*, *1(2)*, 33–39.

Rubel, D. & Okech, J. E. A. (2018). Diversity and multicultural group counseling. In D. Capuzzi & M. Stauffer (Eds.), *Foundations of Group Counseling* (pp 111–131). Denver: Pearson.

Rubel, D. & Okech, J. E. A. (2010). Diversity issues in group work. In D. Capuzzi, D. Gross, & M. Stauffer (Eds.), *Introduction to group work* (5th ed., pp. 219–247). Denver: Love.

Yalom, I., & Leszcz, M. (2020). *The theory and practice of group psychotherapy* (6th ed.). New York: Basic Books.

Zieman, G. L., Romano, P. A., Blanco, K., & Linnell, T. (1981). The process-observer in group therapy. *Group*, *5(4)*, 37–47. https://doi.org/10.1007/bf01456612.

Chapter 3

Ethical and Professional Issues in Process Observation

Devika Dibya Choudhuri, Ph.D., Eastern Michigan University

Christopher J. McCarthy, Ph.D., University of Texas at Austin

In the practice of group work as in any interpersonal human endeavor with differing levels of power and vulnerability, ethics are of immense importance. Ethical values pertain to human conduct and the recognition that we have obligations towards others, which captures the essence of how groups work. The role of process observer is no different in having both a general and a particular set of ethics that pertain. In the following chapter, we will use the vignette of Ash as the process observer, to illuminate certain aspects of ethical and professional conduct.

The process observer (PO) may have little input into the structure, format, purpose, or direction of the group. Taking up the invitation to be a process observer, as Ash did, does require ethical reflection, considerations, and commitments. These reside simultaneously in the *person of the process observer* as well as in the *process of observing* the group and giving feedback. We will take these considerations in turn.

The Ethics of the Process Observer

The first aspect of ethical obligations of being a process observer should be largely indistinguishable from any helping professional and are a guide to self-regulation. These include performing within one's scope of practice, areas of competency, professional identity, and clarity of boundaries. Currently, the role of the PO is unlicensed and uncredentialed, so there tends to not be any relevant legal obligations for such a role. Typically, POs are invited to play such a role based on the inviter's knowledge of their skills, a reputation for doing group work, familiarity, and relationship with the group, or even current or former membership in the group. There is no serious audit of the competency, training, supervision, nor a delineation of such skills and competencies, or in fact any recourse if the PO does not meet the commitments. While there is empirical support for such training and performance (Losada & Maonolov, 2015), there is little general agreement in the literature given the variety of roles. Leaving such definition to other chapters in this text, here we will focus on the ethics required of a helping professional in the conduct of their work.

Acceptance and understanding of role

The role of PO must be accepted because it uses a set of skills and stance that is similar to that of a skilled group worker, but differently applied. The PO must also understand their capacity for performing in such a role with the group at hand. For instance, if the group that they were going to serve as PO was a group where they had been a member, it is ethically responsible to consider if they can separate their relationships with group members from their current role. In addition,

DOI: 10.4324/9781003281955-4

the PO must also clarify and manage the expectations and perceptions of the members. The PO may feel that they are able to be objective, but the members might believe that the PO is particularly close to a group member and will play favorites. In the vignette, if Ash had previously led a mindfulness group that was being replicated by Kiara, they might have some bias about how it should be done that might jeopardize their objectivity.

In cases where membership also comes with a sense of obligation, how will the PO pay attention to the demand to intervene or "correct" the direction of the group? While it may be the role of a member or a group leader, it may not be the role the PO now occupies. If the PO understands the role to be primarily one of observer (Bieschke et al., 1998), it is relatively easy to reflexively attend group meetings, sit on the margins, take process notes, and provide the leader and members with a debrief. On the other hand, a PO who understands their role to be one where they are an ongoing member of the group, will have a more complex role of both engaging with the group in process and dynamic, while simultaneously also being an observer. It is at once an insider/outsider dynamic that is an ongoing balancing act.

Professional Skills and Competencies

Since requests for a PO are rarely sent out as a recruiting call, it is the POs ethical responsibility to self-assess their skills and competencies in this area. While Ash is a senior facilitator in the agency and apparently has the requisite skills and competence, might their position in the agency be a source of confusion for Kiara? Can Kiara trust that Ash can observe without that evaluation impacting her reputation in the agency as a facilitator?

For prospective POs, other questions emerge:

- Do you believe you have sufficient experience in separating yourself from the group dynamic to be able to notice norms, themes, member roles, and interpersonal group processes that may involve your presence?
- Are you aware enough of different communication styles to be able to distinguish where content and process overlap?
- Finally, can you take such recognition and understanding and interpret it expressively to the group in ways that can positively impact the group outcomes?

This last is where the PO must be especially careful to not let their values of what is significant overly influence their message. When engaging with the group in process feedback, it is an intentional intervention that has consequences for the group dynamics, but also on individual members. If the group leader feels called out as inept, or a member feels singled out because of their interactions, their behavior and position in the group may change.

Self-Audit of Personal Values, Beliefs, and Attitudes

This audit must be both ongoing and carried out prior to each process observation, since different values and beliefs will be highlighted in different group contexts. It is an introspective constant process of examining one's own preferences in culturally based communication; member concerns, roles, and styles; awareness of one's comfort with level of intensity and conflict; as well as understanding both one's own identities of race, gender, sexuality, class, age, or disability, as well as how they influence the interpersonal context with others.

Preparation and Due Diligence for the Specific Engagement

Prior to accepting the role, the PO must do necessary research and have relevant information to be able to assess the necessary skills as well as the values that will play out specifically. For instance, it may seem that process observation of a team working on a marketing task should not be value-laden, but suppose the task is to market a Domestic Violence Intervention Program across different cultural groups in the community. The PO in this case may need to be adept at the usual skills and role of process observation, as well as become familiar with the ways in which gender, sexuality, class, and culture intersect in the team and in the group process that shapes the task. This diligence is necessary to be able to understand the general group process as well as develop insight into the ways in which the group purpose and focus shape the interpersonal dynamics.

Another aspect of the preparation is to learn the composition of the group, in terms of its members and their identities, statuses, roles, and context. A heterogenous group in terms of ethnicity and age, may be concurrently homogenous in gender and a common, shared issue of being inmates of men's prison. The PO must then account for the impact of incarceration and the presence of correctional officers on the group members' interactions. Does the PO have a personal history that they have not worked through sufficiently with incarceration? If the PO is sensitive to being in the prison, might it mean less attention to the group, and resulting disservice?

Professional Obligations

The PO must meet all the obligations of the license and credentials they hold while acting as a PO. If the PO is a mental health worker or school counselor, there may be ethical obligations that cannot be seconded to the role of PO. For instance, the duty of mandated reporting will continue even if the PO is not the leader with a group of adolescents who are going through family conflict. While of course the PO would discuss their observations and recommendations with the group leader, they must still make sure that the report is made if there is sufficient concern. If Margarita asks Ash to meet privately with her to report that she was going to leave the group because she frequently feels bullied by Sandra, and that it is not interrupted, what is Ash's responsibility? What if they take the concern to Kiara, who dismisses it as Sandra's "tough love" and Margarita's "flakiness" and lack of commitment?

Finally, PO's have an obligation to develop the necessary disclosures, contracts, informed consent documentation, that are needed to professionalize the engagement. These include:

- professional disclosure that describes the training, knowledge and expertise of the professional observer as well as the role played
- the benefits and risks of a professional observer presence, as well as alternatives. If there are costs and fees associated, these should also be recorded
- if there is any liability insurance, that is also noted.
- process observation description of the usual practices regarding the expectations of the PO, their commitment and attendance in the group, the level of desired engagement with the group, and the procedure of giving feedback
- the kinds of tasks expected of the PO (such as documenting the group meetings or when such reports will be due), the logistics of their involvement in terms of time, facilitation, and format fall in here
- the level of granularity depends on the context, but it will be important to have clarity regarding the PO's status vis-à-vis the group.

Questions to be addressed include:

Is the PO always present when the group meets?
Can the group ask for time apart from the PO?
May the group leader and PO have conversations apart from the group?
Is the PO considered aligned with the group leader or the member?
Does the group leader ask for feedback or can the PO give it when it is deemed appropriate?
Can group members interact with the PO during the group?
Does the PO facilitate the feedback process or simply deliver it?
Are group process notes given orally, in written form, and how detailed are they?
What are the storage and safety parameters for group process notes and how are they treated after being shared?
In case of emergencies or crises, can or should the PO take the place of the facilitator(s)?

Confidentiality and Its Exceptions

POs must highlight their professional obligation to maintain confidentiality about group process, as well as the limitations to such confidentiality. If licensed as a mental health worker, the usual exceptions of intent to harm self or others, and abuse of a minor or a vulnerable adult will apply. In addition, the PO should lay out the boundaries of the engagement such as multiple relationships with the group members or leader and a pause during the engagement of such ongoing relationships.

Ash might inform the group that while they and Kiara have often met for lunch as colleagues, they will not be meeting outside of the group for the duration of the eight weeks. Alternatively, if the group leader is guilty of malpractice, whether malfeasance in financial matters, abandonment of the group, or inappropriate relationship, the role of the PO may change. If Kiara is discovered to be in a romantic relationship with Sandra, the group may well implode. Should Ash step in or would it be better for another neutral facilitator to lead the group? If there are legal proceedings for any reason, the PO may be subpoenaed and will need to provide clarity on what they may share under what circumstances. This is ethically difficult because the PO might be a mental health specialist but have no legal standing of privileged communication in the context of the group.

Diversity, Equity, and Inclusion Statement (DEI)

A competent PO should lay out the foundational beliefs by which they practice, and their intersectional identities in the context of groupwork. Here Ash can denote preferred pronouns; how they will respond to cultural transmissions; attend to equity issues of how members communicate, are heard, responded to and how power differentials within the group as well as between the group and leader are negotiated, addressed, and reflected upon. Inclusion and access for membership, participation, and opportunity are key aspects. Rather than having to guess based on visual identity cues about Ash, members might have a clear understanding of Ash's position on such significant issues.

Assessment and Evaluation

A PO who wishes to learn and grow should use assessment at intervals during the engagement to ascertain whether they are meeting the obligations. In addition to formative assessment, some form of summative assessment is also helpful. Formative assessment can be conducted as a part of the process feedback and debrief in inquiring from group members how helpful the feedback was, what changes might be needed in procedures or structures to address the feedback, and selection of topics. Summative evaluations could be based on an overall report that the group members respond to and consider. If, ultimately, Kiara wishes to use the process observation to assist her own development as a group leader, a summative evaluation will be very helpful to her.

The Ethics of Process Observation (PO)

Beyond the person of the PO, is the ethics of group process observation (GPO) itself. Here, we can use the six guiding ethical principles described in the ACA (2014) *Code of Ethics*: non-maleficence, beneficence, autonomy, justice, fidelity, and veracity as a framework. In terms of the activity of process observation, these might present in the following ways.

Non-maleficence

The obligation not to inflict harm intentionally and to examine in good faith possible consequences of actions. Negligence in this case would be a departure from the standard of care due towards others. Ash should explicitly assess whether their presence in the group might lead to harm occurring, perhaps through increasing the risk of group members feeling less safe and unable to benefit from the group process; or alternately, feeling comfortable and oversharing to their detriment. If Julian feels safer in the group because of Ash's presence, he might share more than he otherwise would. If Ash maintains their obligations, they are in some part responsible for ensuring Julian's continued safety and lack of repercussions for disclosure.

Beneficence

The obligation to act for the benefit of others, this is an inclusive principle that spans the continuum from passively not inflicting harm to actively promoting good. In a group context, the process observer may choose to give feedback on group processes selectively, so that the intervention of a process comment may move the group to a more reflective process. By Ash commenting on Tom's challenge not being addressed, group members get permission to challenge the group without being punished. At the same time, by choosing not to focus on Kiara's response to Tom's challenge, Ash can safeguard Tom from being scapegoated.

Autonomy

This principle decrees that the freedom to choose and act is respected. To protect autonomy, the minimal requirements include being free from undue influence, having an adequate range of options, and having the capacity for decision making. In our vignette, members were voluntarily choosing to attend the mindfulness group, and if they had objections to Ash's presence, could voice those if they chose. But in groups that are less voluntary in nature, such as court-referred substance abuse groups, members may have limited attendance options so that they may have to forgo opportunities to have a livelihood. Having a process observer in this context might cause members to be concerned about why the PO is there, but members might experience little freedom to choose otherwise.

Justice

This principle involves liberty, fairness, equality, equity, and the common good. Distributive justice in groups is based on consistent, egalitarian, and equalitarian treatment, where all group members get equal resources, but the effects of the resources are also assessed to give to each what is required. In other words, Keith and Kortney as group members in our vignette, might require that they get similar screening, handouts, and notices of group meetings, Keith having a visual impairment might also need to get a phone call about scheduling, while Kortney's needs can be met with a mass email. A PO who colludes with the facilitator in regarding one member as problematic and deliberately doesn't attend to this person's process, might well be participating in scapegoating. It is notable that in the group vignette, Tom, Margarita, and Julian who might all identify as People of Color seemed to appreciate that Ash's presence afforded them more safety to speak honestly.

Hailes et al. (2020) proposed seven ethical guidelines across three domains of justice for engaging in social justice work within psychology. The first domain, interactional justice, focuses on fairness in interpersonal interactions. It includes three guidelines: (a) reflecting on relational power dynamics, addressing these dynamics, and emphasizing empowerment and a focus on strengths-based interventions. If in the group, Sandra's protection of Kiara by rebuking those who critiqued the process, resulted in the group moving to less fraught topics of personal goals, it would be an area of group dynamics for Ash to notice.

The second domain, distributive justice, pertains to fairness in distribution of outcomes, such as task leadership and recognition. Here, Julian, the Asian transman who says he feels safer due to Ash's presence, may be saying that the outcomes of the group process are not perceived as fair. The third domain is procedural justice, which focuses on fairness in the decision-making process. This includes two final guidelines: (a) interaction with social systems, and (b) increasing awareness about the effects of systems on the welfare of individuals and communities. When Tom in the group challenges Ash's presence, Kiara deflects by asserting her power as the group leader to bring Ash in. Essentially, she conveys to Tom that he does not get a say. Since this is likely an ongoing experience for Tom to be so invalidated, it is a testament to his resilience that he keeps trying.

Fidelity

Based on the duty to meet professional obligations and responsibilities, this requires that we do not place ourselves in positions where our interests can conflict with the duty to group members or exert undue influence. This is particularly sensitive for POs because they are often invited to serve as such by facilitators or leaders with whom they have a prior positive relationship as Ash has with Kiara. However, though the PO's fidelity should ultimately be towards the group, they may often align too much with the facilitator. Lack of clarity about goals and expectations contribute to this issue. Thus, it is important for PO's to have informed consent, to the extent that is possible, from the group (Lasser & Gottlieb, 2017). If Ash had upon receiving the invitation from Kiara, prepared a professional disclosure document that laid out their purpose, participation and position in the group that all group members received and had an opportunity to consider, there might have been far more clarity on how Ash's role was not a subsidiary of Kiara's.

Veracity

The honesty and authenticity of the process observer in that they can be trustworthy and reliable is contained in this principle. To a great extent in Western culture, contracts and written documents are perceived as evidence of veracity. However, other more oral cultures look at behavior and action as key indicators of trustworthiness. A diversity, equity, and inclusion statement might affirm that Ash holds those values, but Tom and Julian are more interested that Ash seems unafraid of commenting on processes that organize around differential power, or even acknowledging that not all members are comfortable with them. The level to which Ash is candid about their own stance and understanding of mindfulness will also shape the group's comfort with them. If Ash is ever found to be false, as in being seen having lunch with Kiara when they confirmed they would not, every action and behavior will be distrusted.

Multicultural Knowledge and Skills in PO

PO's, like all members of helping professions, are expected to have the knowledge and skills to work with members of diverse identities, as well as an understanding of their areas of competence when offering services. Knowledge of how individual members' identity intersects with other group members, the leader(s), and the purpose of the group is essential to PO and an area that could be easily overlooked if the PO takes a "color-blind" attitude toward their role. The PO must also have an awareness of how power and privilege manifest in group dynamics and the subtle and explicit ways that membership, contribution, engagement, and responses are cues to marginalization and inequity (Conyne, 1998).

Multicultural competence goes hand in hand with cultural humility. While PO's should have a general understanding and a keen awareness of group socio-political histories, they cannot generalize and stereotype the group members. Their understanding might be in error given the specific histories in the group. For instance, Sandra might be an older White ciswoman, but might have a familial relationship with Julian who happened to be her nephew. Margarita might be perceived as Latina, but being an immigrant from Brazil might have a very different history and relationship to the other LatinX member of the group who happens to be a Dominican-American man. Kiara might pass as White, but unknown to Ash, considers herself Black and is reactive to Tom because she once turned down a date with him and feels he is pushy. It behooves Ash to carefully and sensitively assess the dynamics across time and the various members to ascertain what factors are active in the mix.

Overall, understanding the ways coalitions form and may be maintained around social identities is a significant aspect of a POs work. Examining aspects of verbal and behavioral participation, influence within group processes, decision-making, task and maintenance functions, the extent to which the atmosphere is open or restricted around topics, levels of allowable conflict, involvement and engagement, is essential to understanding the multicultural aspects of the group (Conyne, 1998). A PO who has not done the requisite work on their own biases and areas of prejudice will not be able to bring the level of empathy and perception to bear on the group process, and may well miss the forest for the trees (Gutshell & Inzlicht, 2010).

Due to the lack of prior attention, this is only a beginning exploration of the ethical and professional issues inherent in conducting the work of a process observer. As the role becomes more professionalized, more issues will emerge, complexity will geometrically increase, and each of the points here will occasion much more nuanced discussion. In the meantime, this suffices to begin the endeavor to perform the tasks, roles, and obligations of a process observer consistently, using similar metrics, inclusively, and with equity and integrity.

References

American Counseling Association (ACA) (2014). *ACA code of ethics*. https://www.counseling.org/knowledge-center/ethics.

Bieschke, K. J., Matthews, C., Wade, J., and Pricken, P. A. (1998). Evaluation of the Process Observer method: Group leader, member, and observer perspectives. *Journal for Specialists in Group Work*, *23*(*1*), 50–65.

Conyne, R. K. (1998). What to look for in groups: Helping trainees become more sensitive to multicultural issues. *Journal of Specialists in Group Work*, *23(1)*, 22–32. https://doi.org/10.1080/01933929808411379.

Gutsell. J. N. and Inzlicht, M. (2010). Empathy constrained: Prejudice predicts reduced mental simulation of actions during observation of outgroups. *Journal of Experimental Social Psychology*, *45*(5), 841–845. https://doi.org/10.1016/j.jesp.2010.03.011.

Hailes, H. P., Ceccolini, C. J., Gutowski, E., & Liang, B. (2020). Ethical guidelines for social justice in psychology. *Professional Psychology: Research and Practice*. Advance online publication. http://dx.doi.org/10.1037/pro0000291.

Lasser, J., & Gottlieb, M. C. (2017). Facilitating informed consent: A multicultural perspective. *Ethics & Behavior*, *27(2)*, 106–117. https://doi.org/10.1080/10508422.2016.1174121.

Losada, J. L., & Manolov, R. (2015). The process of basic training, applied training, maintaining the performance of an observer. *Quality & Quantity*, *49(1)*, 339–347.

Chapter 4

Selecting and Using the Process Observer

Christopher J. McCarthy, University of Texas at Austin

Devika Dibya Choudhuri, Eastern Michigan University

Introduction

Given the paucity of literature on the general topic of Process Observation, it is not surprising that little is written about *choosing* a Process Observer (PO). There are many situations where the PO is already selected for the leader – for example, in training settings such as a graduate class on group counseling or an internship, Process Observation might be part of the milieu and thus an expectation of those in training. Yet selecting the right PO for your group is critically important, particularly given that most group leaders will likely have limited options for finding a PO.

When a group leader does need to *find* a PO, it can be challenging. The pool of available POs may come from personal connections with colleagues, employees of the same organization willing to devote time to being a PO, or because the group leader is able to hire a PO. The reality for most group leaders is often analogous to what Yalom and Leszcz (2020) described in selecting patients/members for psychotherapy groups: most leaders will be screening out those who are not appropriate for a given type of group – rarely does one have the luxury of picking and choosing group members from a large pool of candidates. Similarly, a group leader may have few choices in selecting a PO, or feel lucky to even have one. While likely facing constraints, it is still important to give careful consideration to selecting the right PO and this chapter highlights some of the factors to be considered in finding the right PO.

Overview

What considerations should guide a group leader in selecting the right PO for their group? First, we caution against the natural tendency to select someone based simply because we know and like them. While of course a leader will want to choose a PO they trust, one of the main strengths of having a PO is that they can bring another perspective to the group. Choosing a close colleague or friend runs the risk of having someone who shares similar perspectives observing the group: they can have the same blindspots as you when it comes to group process observation (GPO). This is a particularly important consideration with respect to diversity factors that may play out in a group – POs who share similar backgrounds and identities with group leaders may be less likely to notice and provide feedback about dynamics related to individual differences among group members. Therefore, it can be important for group leaders to step outside of their personal connections and comfort zone when selecting a PO.

We believe four considerations are paramount in choosing a PO: (1) the purpose of the group; (2) the expected role and function of the PO; 3) the competencies the PO will need in order to be effective in their role; and (4) the type of relationship that will be necessary between the PO, leaders, and group members given the considerations listed in points 1, 2, and 3. Each of these

DOI: 10.4324/9781003281955-5

four factors are inter-connected and build on each other, and we next describe each in turn, followed by a brief illustrative scenario that demonstrates ideas in this chapter. We close the chapter with a brief checklist of considerations for selecting a PO.

Consideration in Choosing a PO

Purpose of the Group

Ed Jacobs and colleagues (2016) noted that among the most important considerations in group work is its purpose. What is your group trying to accomplish for its members, and how is it designed to reach those goals? According to Jacobs et al., everything else about the group follows from that basic consideration, to which we add, selecting a PO.

Subsequent chapters in this book will provide specific information about the role of the PO in various types of group formats, but at this point we note that the goals of the group, whether it be educational, personal growth, or counseling, are paramount when selecting the right PO. If the purpose of your group is educational, for example, choosing a PO with expertise in the educational content of the group is likely an important consideration. However, if the goals of the group are personal growth or counseling, a PO with expertise in the dynamics of those particular groups will be important.

Integral to the type and purpose of the group is the format being utilized – in person groups might require a very different type of PO involvement from a group conducted virtually. And a central consideration in every group are diversity, equity, and inclusion (DEI) issues among the members and leader - the PO should be in a position to observe how privilege and power play out in your group regardless of whether this is a stated goal of the group.

Expected Role and Function of the PO

Following from the purpose of the group, the expected role and function you have in mind for the PO is another vital consideration. We say "expected" because of course the role of the PO is often dynamic, and may need to be negotiated over time as the PO works with the group. It is important, however, for you to have clarity at the beginning about what you hope to learn from the PO, and how the involvement of the PO will advance the goals of the group. A number of examples will hopefully serve to clarify this important step in selecting a PO.

As one example, a task group may be charged with strategic planning for a community center that serves people experiencing homelessness. However, as the group meets, disagreements arise about fundamental aspects of the center, including where it should be located, and what services are most important to the community. Planning such an enterprise would likely involve considerable expertise about building design, budgets, and the unique needs of those experiencing homelessness. Assuming the group is having trouble coming to consensus due to the sheer complexity of the project, a PO who has the expertise necessary to understand the complexities of what the group is trying to accomplish might be sought out to help keep the group on track.

Another example is a university counseling center group for students experiencing stress during the COVID-19 pandemic. The group is conducted by Zoom weekly by two members of the counseling center staff, who have noticed the energy level drop as the semester progresses. Is this because of increasing academic stress as the semester moves along, or are members not getting what they need from the group? And how well is the Zoom format working for members, given that much of their concerns stem from the lack of in-person connection with other students and faculty? In this case, another staff member from the counseling center might be asked to join the group for a few weeks as PO, in order to provide their perspective on dynamics in the group that are causing the lowered energy level.

In the first example, the PO is needed more for content knowledge, while in the second example, the PO is needed more for attention to process. Clarity about the role of the PO also helps them have appropriate boundaries about their role in the group. As one example, a PO in a therapy group should be able to resist "saving" the group when conflict arises. A PO who is uncomfortable with conflict may intervene prematurely, taking over from the facilitator, and end up suppressing conflict to the detriment of the group. On the other hand, a group that "plays it safe" might feel very harmonious and comfortable, but also does not grow. Being clear about what is to be learned from the PO's observations allows the leader to consider the competencies needed in a PO, which is discussed next.

Competencies Needed in a PO

The purpose of the group, and the type of feedback needed, can provide direction for you about the background needed in a PO. Should the PO have extensive information about a particular content area that would be needed for a task group, such as in the example we provided of a group planning a center for people experiencing homelessness? Or a more general knowledge of the dynamics in a counseling group, such as our second example of a university group for students?

As we noted in our introductory chapter, Process Observation requires knowledge about group dynamics, group leadership skills, group stages and group leadership. However, as noted in the previous section, matching the competencies of the PO to a given group is not a "one size fits all" proposition – it is essential that you identify what type of background is needed given your particular group and the specific information or feedback needed from the PO.

A key competency for the PO is to have a clear understanding of the degree to which the group is able to tolerate risk and conflict as a precursor to growth, without imposing such metrics on the group. It is also important that the PO and group leader(s) be on the same page about where the boundary lines are drawn – for example, might the leader check in with the PO in front of the group when conflict arises, perhaps as a way of de-escalating such situations? Or is the PO only an observer when the group is meeting. There is no set playbook for such matters, but again, it is important for you and the PO to be on the same page.

Expected relationship between the PO, leaders, and group members. While we place this step at the end, selecting a PO can be a recursive process, and the expected relationship with the PO will likely need to be considered at each stage of the PO selection process. However, after sifting through the various factors above, the relationship between you as the leader and the PO needs to be made as explicit as possible.

As noted above, a PO is often selected for their perceived expertise and/or congruence with your goals and style as the group leader. Once identified, a number of questions can be discussed to map the contours of the leader/PO relationship, which are explained in Table 4.1 at the end of the chapter. Each of the considerations listed in Appendix 1 revolve around several fundamental considerations:

- Identifying the relationship the PO will have with you as the group leader, the members, and if relevant, the organization or setting in which the group takes place.

- How will information be shared by the PO? Will members have access, or only you as the leader? Will any information be shared with outside entities, such as the clinic or school where the group is taking place?
- What is the positionality of the PO vis a vis the group? What aspects of the PO's identity will be most salient to the group, and how might that influence the observation process?

We next turn to a case study to highlight some of the important ideas reviewed in this chapter.

Case Study

A peer supervision group of counselors has been meeting for several months, on a biweekly basis, for a two hour time block on Saturday mornings. While the group started with eight people, it has recently had two original members leave the group. Most of the members knew of each other either by practicing in a similar agency, graduating from the same program, or having done their supervision for licensure under the same supervisor. They developed the group through word of mouth, as an egalitarian peer supervision space to consult with each other about their clinical concerns, ethical dilemmas, and professional issues. The current membership consists of:

- Marcia, a 42-year-old Irish-American Buddhist lesbian cisfemale who has been practicing for three years.
- Kiara, a 37-year-old African American Christian heterosexual ciswoman, who has been practicing for nine years.
- Josh/Jess, a 29-year-old biracial (Black/White) non-binary pansexual Agnostic, who received their full license last year.
- Gerda, a 35-year-old German lesbian ciswoman who identifies as a White Wiccan social worker and was introduced to the group because she has been in a relationship with Marcia.
- Jay, a 39-year-old South Asian Hindu transman, practicing for 11 years in total, but one year post transition.
- Carla, a 40-year-old Italian-American Catholic heterosexual ciswoman, who has been practicing the longest at 14 years.

Recently, two members dropped who both identified heterosexual Christian cismen in their early 40s, one Black (Mike) and one White (Dan). Both had different reasons but were increasingly distant before they left. Since these members left, the group is finding itself adrift, with meetings where members seem reluctant to bring cases or discuss professional or personal struggles with clients. One of the members suggests getting some assistance, and another suggests a PO. The members devote a meeting to discussing whether a PO should be engaged, which is being held over Zoom due to the rise in cases associated with the COVID-19 pandemic. Elements of the meeting are listed below:

1. The members discuss how a process observer might be helpful to get them "back on track." During this meeting, Kiara remarked that the exit of two members, Mike and Dan, has been chilling for the group. They said they left for their own reasons, but it

seemed clear that something was different about their participation before they left. They seemed distant and preoccupied. And they left at the same time – coincidence?

2. Jay commented on the timing of the group's discussions on diversity and the "pulling away" of Mike and Dan – just as the group seemed to be delving into issues of identity that informed their work, it seemed that Mike and Dan experienced more of a disconnect with the group.
3. Marica and Gerda both expressed a fear that the group would retreat to more superficial topics in order to keep things more safe for the members.
4. Carla, in response, thought the group might be better off without the two members – if they were uncomfortable being in the group, perhaps it was better they left. Kiara disagreed and said she felt that their leaving was a loss, while acknowledging that she felt closer to them than some others in the group.
5. Josh/Jess acknowledged the two members were free to leave, but talked about how helpful a PO was to their interpersonal growth group, and wondered if their group needed a PO to make sure it continued to grow. The group seemed to be at a turning point, and needed to decide if members wanted to add more people to the group.
6. Kiara volunteered to help identify a process observer for the group, but wanted to know what the group was looking for in a PO? Members expressed uncertainty about how to go about finding a PO and what their role should be.

Let us now return to the four considerations listed above to see what type of PO the group might consider.

(1) *Structure and Goals of the Group:* This is a self-lead growth and support group for seasoned counselors, which has been meeting for some time. This means that (1) it is likely that members are looking for an experienced counselor to serve as a PO and (2) the group will likely want to take a democratic approach to selecting a PO, and (3) given concerns about member leaving the group due to discussions about identity, a PO who can offer perspectives on the role of diversity in group dynamics will be important. Further, given the collaborative goals of the group, buy-in from all members about the PO chosen will be important.

(2) *Expected role and function of the PO*: The members are wondering how the exit of two counselors from the group will affect their dynamics. Some see their group life trajectory differently, and thus could use help from the PO to identify if the exit of two members signal a problem with the group, or was there a lack of fit between the two members and the rest of the group? Thus, it is likely the members will want a PO who can attend the group and provide feedback about its dynamics to all members.

(3) *PO Competencies:* The group will want to seek out a PO who is a seasoned counselor with extensive experience in group work. Further, the PO will need to be well-versed in multicultural group work and supervision. As a group of counselors, the expectations that the PO has a fundamental knowledge of counseling would be important for the group to take the person seriously.

(4) *Expected relationship between the PO, Leader, and Members* Given that the group is self-lead and has been meeting for some time, it seems likely the group will want a PO who can join with the group, observe their dynamics, and offer feedback in a timely manner.

So What's the Outcome?

The group decides on Xi, a Chinese American cisgender female counselor who has written on the topic of supervision, and is an experienced group counselor. The members decide to pay Xi to observe three sessions, and for the first meeting, rather than participate in the process in vivo, Xi will send notes to the members. The members agree to review the notes between meetings and start the second session by discussing their reactions. However, to keep the process ongoing, they agree to limit this to ten minutes. The same process will be followed in the next two meetings. Following those three meetings, the group realized the impact of having members leave the group, and how it affected their process. This realization led the group to delve more deeply into how issues of identity impacted their relationship with each other, and their work as counselors. They also decided it would benefit the group to add a few more members to the group, which they planned to discuss further in future sessions.

We offer Table 4.1, as a checklist of expectations for PO that builds on ideas discussed in this chapter.

Table 4.1 Checklist of questions and expectations for PO

Structure and Goals of the Group.

- What is the purpose of the group?
- What leadership style/theoretical orientation is used by the leader?
- What is the membership of the group, including criteria for inclusion/exclusion?
- What is the change model for the group, and how is this operationalized in each session?

Expected role and function of the PO.

- What is the leader's purpose in inviting a PO?
- What would the leader wish to know from the PO?
- What role, if any, will the PO have in planning group activities/sessions?
- How will the PO attend/observe the group? Is the PO present and visible with the members during the group? Or watching a recording?
- How many sessions will be observed?

Competencies Needed in PO.

- Training in group dynamics
- Familiarity with the type of group being observed
- Expertise in the topics addressed by the group

Expected relationship between the PO, Leader, and Members.

- How will the PO communicate with the leader and the members?
- What group norms and expectations have/will be established, and how can the PO contribute?
- Will the PO share openly with the group or only give feedback to the leader?
- How are diversity and equity issues present in the group, and how can the PO contribute to the creation of inclusive group processes?
- On what topics does the leader wish the PO to share openly with the group versus with only the leader?
  (For e.g. some observations on group process and tone are shared with all, while others on power, conflict, or oppressive dynamics are shared only with the leader to prevent harm)
- What unique ethical and legal dimensions pertain to the group and the role of the PO?

References

Jacobs, E., Schimmel, C. J., Masson, R. L., Harvill, & R. L. (2016). *Group Counseling: Strategies and Skills* (8th ed.). Boston, MA: Cengage Learning.

Yalom, I., & Leszcz, M. (2020). *The theory and practice of group psychotherapy* (6th ed.). New York: Basic Books.

Part II

Effective Process Observation

Chapter 5

Processing the Process

Giving Feedback and Facilitating Process Development

Rachel Vannatta, The Institute for Innovation and Implementation at the University of Maryland Baltimore School of Social Work

Having read up to this point in the book, we hope you have bought into the idea that group Process Observation (GPO) is something that can help nearly any type of group. In addition, you now have a strong foundational understanding of the preparation that is necessary either as the leader if you are leading a group and choosing a Process Observer (PO), or if you are preparing for taking on that role. Now, it is time to explore more about the *how* of providing feedback on group process in order to support the group's development.

Core Tenets

Connected to Your Role

In the first chapter, the authors identified that something important for the PO and leader to discuss is the expected role and function the PO will play in the group. In considering how you facilitate process development, your role and function in the group will inform how you will provide feedback and what feedback you will provide. For example, perhaps you are a PO of a task group, where your role is determined to be primarily one of helping the group remain on task. The group decided to add a PO to the meetings because it became increasingly difficult to get through the agenda, and numerous tangential conversations were occurring. As a result, the group was frequently sidetracked and members were feeling frustrated because there was very little forward momentum. Compare this scenario to one where you are working with a counseling group as a PO. The purpose of the group is to enhance interpersonal relationships, and the leader has asked you to specifically attend to the interpersonal relational patterns within the group. As you consider both of these scenarios, it is easy to identify that the type of feedback, and the processes you are attending to, are going to be quite different.

As a matter of logistics, timing of the feedback will also depend on the role and function of the PO. In some groups, the PO may step in throughout the session/meeting to provide feedback. For example, in the task group described above, it does not make much sense for the PO to wait until the end of the meeting to let the group know they went astray. In the counseling group described above, the feedback might come throughout the session as interpersonal interactions are occurring, or it might come at the end with an opportunity for members of the group to digest and respond to the feedback. In another example, consider a team meeting where a PO is assigned with the purpose of identifying some of the overall themes or patterns of the way in which the members of the team interact. In this scenario, it may make the most sense for the feedback to be delivered at the end of the meeting, when the entire process of the meeting has played out.

DOI: 10.4324/9781003281955-7

Connected to the Goal of the Group

Related to the importance of understanding your role in the group as the PO, the feedback you provide should also be connected to the goals of the group. Using the same two scenarios above, in the task group where the goal of the group is to get through an agenda in order to complete one or more tasks, the focus of your Process Observation will be on when the group is encountering obstacles (or having successes) in meeting this goal. On the other hand, in the counseling group, you probably would not be as concerned with providing feedback about how the leader and group have stuck to (or failed to stick to) the loose agenda of the session if the purpose of the group is to better understand interpersonal relational patterns.

Informed by an Understanding of What is Necessary to Share

Related to considering your role as the PO and the goal of the group, it is important to remember that not every observation you have needs to be shared. Because your entire role is to notice process issues, you will likely notice quite a lot! In nearly all groups, there are a plethora of explicit and implicit processes at the individual, interpersonal, and group levels. You will want to be thoughtful about the feedback you choose to share, keeping in mind what you and the leader discussed at the outset about your role, the goals of the group, and where the group is developmentally. When in doubt about whether or not an observation should be shared, a question you can ask yourself is, *how will sharing this feedback help the group to meet its goals?* If the answer is, *it won't*, or, *I am not sure*, it is best to hold off on providing that feedback. Chances are, if the process you are observing is something that is getting in the way of the group, it will come back up. If and when you notice a pattern and it becomes clearer that the observation needs to be shared, you can always identify it as a theme you have noticed.

Informed by an Understanding of Power

In the role of the PO, there is a certain amount of power you have in the room. This is due to the nature of the role of the PO – you are there observing and providing feedback, not the one(s) being observed and provided feedback to. In addition, any power and privilege you have in the "real world" as a result of your intersecting identities will also be present with you in the role of the PO. How the power and privilege of your intersecting identities plays out in the group will also depend on the power and privilege held by the members in your group. While it is impossible to consider all of the different combinations of PO intersecting identities and the power and privilege therein, combined with all of the group-member intersecting identities and the power and privilege therein, it is imperative that as the PO you consider what you bring into the room.

Nonevaluative

Perhaps the most important element to remember when offering your observations to the group is that they should be framed in a nonevaluative manner. Because no group functions perfectly, some of the feedback you provide will be around areas of tension, challenges, and conflict. If your role is noting some of the interpersonal process dynamics, group members may feel particularly on the spot if your feedback is about their style of relating. For both the member and the leader, process feedback can feel like a negative evaluation if it is not delivered with attention to the tone and framing of the feedback. Your role is not to judge the leader or members of the group, but to offer insight that might help the group function more effectively. One way to think about the tone and framing is to come from a perspective of curiosity. Starting your feedback with "*I noticed...*", or, "*I am wondering about...*" can help frame the feedback in a way that group members experience as helpful and interested, rather than evaluative.

Specific

In your life as a student, employee, partner, or friend, you have probably received your fair share of feedback. As you think about the feedback you have received, can you identify themes of what constituted helpful feedback (even if it was difficult to hear) versus feedback that was not helpful? In our experience, feedback that is very specific, and also avoids universalizing gneralizations (always, never, only) is the most helpful, even if the feedback is something that I do not want to hear. These two characteristics contribute to feedback being helpful, partially because it makes the feedback easier to internalize. Imagine if someone said to you, *you just never seem to listen to anybody*. Take a moment and first consider how it would feel to receive that feedback. For many people, hearing that would result in feeling defensive....you might think "*I never listen? Of course I listen!*" Compare this to "*I noticed when Ty started talking, you stared off into space and then started talking over him before he finished. It made me wonder if you were really listening to him as he spoke.*" The specificity of such feedback is hard to ignore, and by not making global statements about never listening, it makes the feedback easier to consider.

The same principles apply for delivering either whole-group process feedback or individual process feedback. The more specific you can be, the better, and there is no need to generalize one or two events to global behavior, by either the group or an individual. If you notice a pattern in regards to process, it can be described as such. For example, instead of, "*You all always avoid conflict as a group*," you might offer, "*I've noticed a theme developing over the last couple of meetings, and it seems like the group is wary of engaging in any kind of conflict. This came up last week, when the topic of a management change was brought up, and this week when broad concerns about the leadership were identified. In both situations, though there appeared to be a variety of strong feelings about the topic, these were aired in the group.*"

Anchored in Process, Not Content

This might be an obvious statement, but the PO must be careful to deliver process feedback, not a summary of the content of what was said or done during a session or meeting. As a leader, if you have selected a PO who has training and experience in Process Observation, this probably will not be an issue. But if you are either engaging a PO to observe your group, or you are a new PO, it is important to remember that there likely needs to be very little content discussed in your process feedback. The content can be briefly touched on for context, ("*when the group was discussing needing to make a change at the management level* (context), *I noticed that the conversation quickly stalled, and it seemed like no one was quite sure what to say next. It seemed like that topic both had some tension around it, and it was left unresolved* (process)"). Notice that there is no need to rehash all of the conversation that had occurred about needing to make the management change, and it will remove the temptation for groups to deflect reflecting on process to refocus on content.

Concludes With a Check in

Finally, it is good practice to check in and process the feedback that has been given. How you will process the feedback will depend on a number of things, including how it seems the person or group has received the feedback. That said, here are a few prompts that might help you get started in processing the process:

- What was it like for you (group) to hear my feedback on how you were working together?
- What was it like for you (individual) to hear my feedback?
- What stood out to you about the feedback you heard?
- How might you use the feedback you heard moving forward?
- What would you like to do differently as a group, given the feedback you heard?
- What feels unresolved from this discussion?

Case Example

A peer supervision group of counselors has been meeting for several months, on a biweekly basis, for a two-hour time block on Saturday mornings. While the group started as eight people, it has recently had two original members drop away. Most of the members knew of each other either by practicing in a similar agency, graduating from the same program, or having done their supervision for licensure under the same supervisor. They developed the group through word of mouth, as an egalitarian peer supervision space to consult with each other about their clinical concerns, ethical dilemmas, and professional issues. The current membership consists of:

- Marcia, a 42-year-old Irish-American, Buddhist, lesbian cisfemale who has been practicing for three years.
- Kiara, a 37-year-old African-American, Christian, heterosexual ciswoman, who has been practicing for nine years.
- Josh/Jess, a 29-year-old biracial (Black/White), non-binary, pansexual, Agnostic, who received their full license last year.
- Gerda, a 35-year-old German, lesbian ciswoman who identifies as a White Wiccan social worker and was introduced to the group because she has been in a relationship with Marcia.
- Jay, a 39-year-old South Asian, Hindu transman, practicing for 11 years in total, but one year post transition.
- Carla, a 40-year-old Italian-American, Catholic, heterosexual ciswoman, who has been practicing the longest at 14 years.

Recently, two members dropped who both identified heterosexual Christian cismen in their early 40s, one Black and one White. Both had different reasons but were increasingly distant before they left. Since these members left, the group is finding itself adrift, with meetings where members seem reluctant to bring cases or discuss professional or personal struggles with clients. Someone suggests getting some assistance, and someone else suggests a Process Observer. The members devote a meeting to discussing a Process Observer. The transcript below is a clip from the first meeting where they have invited Tonya, the new Process Observer, to attend.

KIARA: Let's just start with how all of our meetings start – with a check in about how things are going in our clinical work and anything in our life that is impacting our clinical work. Who wants to start?

MARCIA: I can start. I guess work things are going okay. Something I am having a hard time with is dealing with payment. I don't require payment at the time of service, and I have had to chase several people down on multiple occasions lately to pay their bill. It feels like a waste of time and I get annoyed having to ask people several times to pay what they owe. It sometimes feels like it creeps into the work because I have some residual frustration with these clients.

KIARA: Is that something you'd like time for today?

MARCIA: Sure, maybe a few minutes would be good. Personal life is fine, not much new to report and nothing that is substantially impacting my work. Jay, you want to go next?

JAY: Work is stressful for me. I think it's a combination of having to care for my ill mother and also having high acuity cases. I haven't been taking very good care of myself and I know that.

MARCIA: Do you want some time to talk more about that?

JAY: Not really. I know what I need to do, I just need to do it. I've scheduled a week off of work and gotten coverage for my mom next week, and that will help. Carla, do you want to check in?

CARLA: Sure (looking down). Everything is fine. Work is work. I'm tired but it's not impacting my clinical work at all. Who's next?

JOSH/JESS: Uh I guess I can go. Overall I'd say things are going really well. I am having a little bit of trouble with the parents of one of the kids I am working with, but the work with the kid is going great. The parents are really having a problem with how the kid is talking about their sexual identity. They are mad and sad and it almost seems like they are blaming me for "turning" their kid to identify as queer.

KIARA: (pointedly) Do you think you've encouraged the child to identify as queer?

JOSH/JESS: (cautiously) Um. I don't really know how to answer that question. I have encouraged the child to openly express to me, and to those they feel comfortable with, how they identify and I have been validating of their expressions to me (nervously chuckling). I don't think I have somehow convinced the child to be queer.

MARCIA: Would you like more time after we all check in to talk about this case?

JOSH/JESS: No I think I'll pass on that. Who's next?

GERDA: I can go. I am having difficulty adjusting to seeing my clients online. I find myself more distracted and I think they are more distracted as well. It's especially hard working with my younger kids online and I am not quite sure how to address that. I'd like some time to talk about that with other people who are working with children. Kiara, I think you're up.

KIARA: It's good to see everyone. Gerda, I can really connect with what you said about it being difficult to work online. I only see a few children and it is so challenging.

MARCIA: I agree. It's brutal. I have a few ideas I am happy to share with the group, and I would be happy to try to brainstorm together if we have some time today

KIARA: Gerda if you think that would be helpful, I would love to spend some time on that. Thanks for offering your ideas, Marcia. Aside from that, I guess things are going okay clinically. Personally, my younger son is having some challenges at preschool that have been on my mind. He's only four but it feels like the teacher expects him to have the emotion regulation of an adult. It's hard for me not to worry about how the teachers are responding to what I think is pretty developmentally normal behavior. Sometimes I struggle to block out those concerns when I am in a session, especially because I work with a lot of parents who frequently talk about their children.

(The group is quiet for a few moments.)

CARLA: OK, who wants to start. Marcia?

MARCIA: Sure. I need some ideas about how people are talking about and collecting payment. Right now, some people bring a check in, some use a credit card, but I have some who, for whatever reason, I have offered to send a bill to and they pay it that way. In particular, if I am seeing an adolescent, I will do this because their parents are often the ones paying. But then I end up having to spend some time doing the billing, and then chasing people down if they don't pay the bill in a timely manner. How do other people handle this?

JAY: Marcia, could I provide some feedback?

MARCIA: (tentatively) Sure.

JAY: (gently) It seems like this is related to some other boundary topics you have talked about before – like clients wanting to call or text at all hours and it being difficult to end sessions on time.

MARCIA: You must think I am a terrible clinician. Boundaries are counseling 101 and you don't think I have any!

JAY: I don't think you are a terrible clinician, Marcia. Boundaries are hard. But it does seem like this has come up a few times in different ways for you.

JOSH/JESS: I have a hard time with this too, Marcia. I find it uncomfortable to talk about payment because it makes me worry that the client will think that all I care about is being paid, rather than caring about them.

GERDA: Asking clients to pay for a service they have agreed to pay for is not showing that we don't care about them! We pay all kinds of other helpers – our doctors, dentists, and teachers without thinking that they don't care about us. Why is it any different paying for counseling?

MARCIA: Cognitively, I get what you are saying Gerda. But I still have a hard time with it.

JOSH/JESS: How do you talk about payment during the intake and informed consent process?

MARCIA: It's in all of my paperwork that payment is due at the time of service. And I let clients know during the intake process that I can take a credit card or check at the time of their session.

GERDA: Then you just have to do it! I don't quite get what the problem is.

JAY: Gerda, sometimes it's easier said than done.

In the first section, I reviewed broad considerations for providing Process Observations. In the following section, I will discuss specific topics that often merit feedback from the PO to the group. As you read through each of the topics in the following section, consider their application to the case study you read above.

Process Topics

There are a number of process topics the PO might provide feedback about, depending on their role, the purpose of the group, and what they observe. While the discussion below is not exhaustive, it is a good place to start in thinking about process themes or topics that might be helpful areas to provide feedback.

Group Development

The PO might provide feedback on where the group is developmentally. While other theorists have written about group development (e.g., Corey et al., 2017, Jacobs et al., 2016), Tuckman (1965) and Tuckman and Jensen (1977) have written perhaps the most frequently cited conceptualization of the developmental stages of a group. These stages include: Forming, Storming, Norming, Performing, and Adjourning. In the Forming stage, it would be typical to observe members having safe and polite conversation – I often describe this as "cocktail party conversation." Members might discuss surface-level concerns, but you will notice that generally, people are dipping their toe in the water. It would be unusual (and notable) to see a group member sharing deeply, or willingly engaging in conflict at this stage. Members will heavily rely on the leader for guidance, and you will likely see a leader who is very active and involved.

The next stage, Storming, is characterized by some level of conflict. In counseling groups, there is frequently conflict between those who attempt to start sharing and engaging in the group in deeper ways and those who remain quieter. There also can be tension around the purpose of the group and the expectations of what members are supposed to "do" while participating in the group during this stage. It is likely there will be some challenge or pushback directed towards the leader(s). For example, comments from members that the leader is not doing enough or not being helpful enough.

As groups move into the Norming stage, they begin to resolve some of the tension associated with the Storming stage. Conflict is worked through, members begin having a better sense of how to engage in the group, and there is appreciation for all members and their contributions to the group. You might notice that conversation is more geared towards the purpose of the group, and that there is a sense of routine or predictability in terms of process to the sessions.

While each stage of development is important, we often think about the Performing stage as the area where a lot of the work is completed. By this time, members have learned how to navigate conflict, they understand the group's modus operandi, and they have increased confidence in how to participate effectively in the group. As the group moves into Norming and Performing, the leader should be able to take a less active role, as the group becomes more competent at facilitating itself. Members will freely give feedback without prompting, and discussion or behavior that breaks implicit or explicit norms is often called out by other group members, rather than the leader.

Finally, the Adjourning stage completes the cycle. During this stage, members are wrapping up the work they completed, saying goodbye, and thinking about how to apply what they have learned in their lives moving forward. It is to be expected that there is some sense of sadness and loss, especially in a high functioning group. Members who have historically had difficult losses may have a particularly hard time with this ending stage.

Feedback about group development can be particularly helpful when group progress along these stages is not as expected. For example, if the group has met eight times and you still get the sense they are in the beginning (Forming) stage of development. Another example where noting the group's development can be helpful is if you have seen no conflict, transition, or Storming stage. While Jacobs et al. (2016) suggest that good leadership will help bypass a Storming stage, many other authors who write on group development indicate there is often a period of time where there is more conflict than usual, prior to the group moving into a solid working stage. As the PO, you might wonder about a group's tendency to avoid conflict if the group has met for a considerable period of time without ever experiencing some tension or conflict.

- Knowing what you know about group development, how would you characterize the developmental stage of the group in the vignette above?
- What factors contribute to how you have characterized the developmental stage of the group?

- Is the stage of group development something you would want to provide feedback about?
- If so, what would you say? If not, what would be the reason for not sharing what you notice?

Group Norms

Very broadly speaking, group norms are the sometimes spoken and very often unspoken rules of interaction in the group (Yalom & Leszcz, 2020). Sometimes the norms are related to procedure – like when the group starts and if there is a specific structure or format that is typically followed. Implicit norms are those that operate without being explicitly stated. Oftentimes, group members are not able to identify the implicit norms that exist in the group because they are the scaffolding within which the process occurs without ever being explicitly stated (Yalom & Leszcz, 2020).

The reason a PO pays attention to the group norms, is they can either be helpful in facilitating the group, or unhelpful. Norms, almost like group habits, develop over time. Because group members, and sometimes even group leaders, cannot "see" the norms at play, there can be unhelpful norms operating without the group or the leader being aware. For example, perhaps the first time there is any kind of conflict in the group, the leader essentially brushes the conflict under the rug. Or perhaps one or more members gets into the habit of rescuing another member anytime they are given feedback because it is clear the feedback is difficult for the member to hear. Over time, this dynamic can considerably impact how the group interacts.

- What would you identify as some of the norms in the group above, based on the brief conversation you see?
- If you were the PO in this group, would you provide feedback about the norms you observe?
- If so, what would you say? If not, what would be the reason for not sharing what you notice?

Conflict

Another process issue for the PO to attend to is conflict, either that which is spoken and engaged with by the group, or conflict that is clearly present but unaddressed in the group. When conflict is approached in the group, the PO might provide feedback on the way in which the conflict was navigated, and check in on anything that feels unresolved. When there is an undercurrent of conflict that is not addressed by the group, the PO would provide feedback about their observation that there appears to be some tension in the group that has not yet been addressed.

-ist Comments

A more specific example of conflict that deserves its own attention is anytime an "-ist" comment is made in the group – this could be a racist, sexist, ageist, heterosexist, ableist, microaggressive or macroaggressive comment. Ideally, the group leader would "hear" this type of comment and respond to it, and the job of the PO would be to explore from a process perspective how the comment and/or resulting group discussion impacted members as well as the group dynamic. However, it is also possible for the group leader to miss this type of statement, or fail to respond to it directly. In this situation, the PO can highlight the content and then examine how it impacted both individuals as well as the group process.

- As you consider the group above and the transcript you see, what do you notice about any conflict or tension that is present in the group and in particular, any conflict that is related to an "-ist" comment?

- If you notice any conflict or tension, does the group appear to engage with it or is it left unaddressed?
- What, if any, feedback would you provide to the group around this?

Interpersonal Processes

Particularly in growth, counseling, and therapy groups, observing how members of the group are relating to one another (including how they are relating to the leader) can be an important process issue for the PO to attend to. This can include noticing who is talking to one another, who seems to be "in" and who seems to be "out," the nonverbal reactions members have while others are speaking, tension between members (or between member(s) and leader), rescuing behavior between members, deferential behavior from members, and dominant behavior between members (Yalom & Leszcz, 2020). This list is not exhaustive, but gives some ideas about common relational themes the PO might observe.

- As you consider the group above and the transcript you see, how does the group seem to be relating to one another?
- Do any members stand out as being "out" of the group?
- Are there any members who seem to relate particularly well?
- Are there any interpersonal dynamics you see that might be impacting the development of a cohesive group?
- If you were the PO in this group, what, if any, feedback would you provide about how the group is relating to one another?

Energy of the Group

As the PO, you will see both periods of high energy, where the group is very engaged in the discussion, as well as lower energy, where the group does not seem to be as engaged. While the expectation is not that the group needs to always be discussing something with high energy, it can be helpful for the PO to notice when the energy is higher or lower, as well as when there is a change in the energy of the group. For example, perhaps the conversation is moving along with good energy, and then a group member makes a comment and all of a sudden, the conversation stalls. Or more broadly, maybe the last time the group met, the members were engaged in the conversation with high energy and at the current meeting, the leader takes the group back to the discussion and there is no longer much energy around it.

As you consider the group above and the transcript you see, is there any feedback that would be helpful to provide around points of high or low energy? If so, what would you say to the group?

Unfinished Business

A final area of note for the PO is any unfinished or unresolved business that is still lingering when the meeting or session has ended. There may be something unfinished because the group ran out of time, in which case, it can be helpful for the PO to provide feedback on this so that the group can remember to revisit the topic at the next meeting. But something can also be unresolved because the group moved on from the issue quickly, because group members did not engage with the issue, or because even though the group as a whole feels satisfied with the resolution of an issue, an individual member, or members, may not.

Although you do not get to see the entire session play out in the group transcript above, from what you see is there any feedback that would be helpful to provide around unfinished business? If so, what would you say to the group?

Conclusion

In conclusion, there are a number of core tenets to keep in mind when you are providing feedback as the PO in an effort to facilitate process development. The feedback should be connected to your role that has been established by the leader or group, and the feedback should be connected to the goals of the group. The PO enters the group with a certain amount of power already, and it is important for the PO to consider how their intersecting identities and the intersecting identities of the group members impact the power dynamic in the room. While it can be challenging at times, it is important to remember that you do not need to share every process you observe in your role – rather, only the processes that are related to your role and the goal of the group need to be shared. Feedback should be delivered in a nonevaluative way so that members are able to hear and digest it. Observations that you share with the group should be specific, with a focus on process concerns rather than a summary of content. Finally, after Process Observations have been shared, it is helpful to check in with members about their reactions to the feedback.

There are a number of different process topics that might be appropriate to provide feedback about. You might discuss where the group is developmentally or the helpful or unhelpful norms that guide interaction. When conflict or tension occurs, particularly when it appears to be present without being attended to or there are any type of "-ist" comments that are made, it is helpful for the PO to point this out and allow for processing. Particularly in a group where there is a focus on interpersonal dynamics, the PO might also provide feedback on how group members are relating to one another. Noting points of high and low energy is another area where the PO can provide helpful feedback. Finally, it is helpful for the PO to take note of any unfinished business that appears to be present. Business that is clearly unfinished is likely to be remembered by all. However, that which is more subtle, for example a member making a microaggressive statement that is not recognized by the group or leader is less likely to be returned to. Thus, the PO can be helpful in bringing this to the attention of members when it appears to be blocking the group's progress.

Overall, it is important to remember that although the role of the PO and the goal of the group will vary, the overarching goal of the PO is to support effective group development (Barnlund, 1955). The way in which you as the PO engage with the group, the frequency with which you provide feedback, and the topics you choose to highlight in your observations will all come back to this broad goal, regardless of your group.

References

Barnlund, D.C. (1955). The use of group observers. *Communication Education*, *4(1)*, 46–48.

Corey, M.S., Corey, G., & Corey, C. (2017). *Groups process and practice* (10th ed). Cengage.

Jacobs, E.E., Schimmel, C.J., Masson, R.L., & Harvill, R.L. (2016). *Group counseling strategies and skills* (8th ed). Cengage.

Tuckman, B.W. (1965). Developmental sequence in small groups. *Psychological Bulletin*, *63(6)*, 384–399.

Tuckman, B.W., & Jensen, M.A.C. (1977). Stages of small-group development revisited. *Group & Organizational Studies*, *2(4)*, 419–427.

Yalom, I., & Leszcz, M. (2020). *The theory and practice of group psychotherapy* (6th ed). Basic Books.

Chapter 6

Group Focal Conflict Theory

A Model for Guiding Process Observation in Group Work

Katy Schroeder, University of Iowa

Process Observer (PO) effectiveness involves conceptualizing key interpersonal themes that support or hinder a productive group environment. Group Focal Conflict Theory (GFCT; Whitman & Stock, 1958; Whitaker & Lieberman, 1964) lends itself well to helping POs conceptualize the ways in which group process unfolds, how group members face or avoid topics that raise anxiety, and determine what group leadership interventions will maximize group outcomes. In the simplest of terms, GFCT provides a roadmap for identifying interpersonal concerns that impact group development and individual change. The theory's guiding principles can aid POs with unpacking the complexities of group dynamics in such a way as to identify unique group dynamics, motivations, goals, and possible interventions. In this regard, GFCT provides a very useful framework for understanding the unique norms and culture of a group, and how group-member interactions generate specific issues, as well as resolutions to conflict.

GFCT is rooted in several influences including social psychology, psychodynamic theory, and systems theory (Berk, 2011). GFCT is an extension of work originating from Thomas French, an American psychoanalyst who developed nuclear conflict theory (French, 1952–1953). It was French who first coined the term "focal conflict" to describe the event-related expressions of peoples' core psychological conflicts stemming from early childhood and familial relationships, a phenomenon he described as the "nuclear conflict." GFCT took shape during the 1950s and 1960s through the collective efforts of Drs. Roy Whitman, Dorothy Stock Whitaker, Morton Lieberman, and Thomas French. Their formal work on GFCT began at the Veterans' Administration Research Hospital in Chicago, Illinois through the compilation of numerous observations on persons in psychotherapy groups (Berk, 2011).

As their research and clinical work progressed, members of the team developed central concepts and tested the theory while studying a variety of groups such as short-term residential therapy groups for veterans and long-term outpatient therapy groups for adolescents and adults (Berk, 2011). Initially, the research group aimed to determine if the concept of focal conflicts drove what could be observed in group members' interactions in sessions. Through subsequent systematic investigations, a theory for explaining how groups function emerged (Berk, 2011; Whitaker, 1982).

Key Assumptions and Terminology

GFCT is grounded in certain assumptions about group functioning (Whitaker, 1982, 1) groups of people develop unique norms and belief systems, as well as experience interpersonal concerns that sometimes resonate with one member, subsets of members within a group, or resonate with the group-as-a-whole; 2) interpersonal concerns may or may not be expressed explicitly but are

DOI: 10.4324/9781003281955-8

exposed through group interactions (e.g., verbal and non-verbal behaviors); 3) group interactions will reveal interpersonal themes, which often repeat over the course of a group experience until they are dealt with; 4) group interactions involve finding solutions to conflict and reducing collective anxiety to achieve equilibrium; and 5) groups that avoid interpersonal issues achieve equilibrium at the expense of interpersonal learning and growth.

Let's unpack these assumptions and dig into the GFCT terminology. First, GCPT assumes that when a group of people come together whether for support, therapy, or work, shared interpersonal concerns will naturally arise over the course of their group experiences. These concerns are unique to a group and must resonate with more than one person. What does or does not become an issue will vary according to the unique composition of personalities, backgrounds, and a group's purpose. Take for instance a newly formed work task group. If more than one member of the group has long-standing fears about giving and receiving constructive criticism, it is possible this will become a central issue for the group. Depending on how the group handles situations in which feedback exchange occurs, they could develop specific beliefs and norms about criticism such as, "Feedback should always be positive," or "Only the project lead can give team members feedback about their contributions."

This assumption emerged from French's earlier research on the intrapsychic development of individuals. These concepts are *disturbing motives*, *reactive motives*, and *focal conflicts*. In GFCT, disturbing motives signify a group's shared interpersonal wishes, such as the desire for closeness, or need to resolve conflicts (Kline, 2003). For example, when observing the early stages of a group, PO's may notice disturbing motives materialize when members navigate boundaries:

> Selma has been asked to provide process observation for a fellow school counselor in her district. Her colleague, Lynn, is facilitating a psychoeducational group on bullying for 6th graders. During the third group session, a member named Jamie arrives 10 minutes late for the second time in a row. As Jamie sits down, Selma notices the nonverbals of some other group members, such as grimacing faces, folded arms, glances at the clock, and glares directed at Jamie. Selma jots down some notes about this event and the behaviors she observes among the group members.

In this brief example, the non-verbal behaviors of group members suggest an emerging conflict and potential needs (e.g., disturbing motives to express feelings and resolve conflict).

Disturbing motives are opposed by reactive motives, which is a GFCT concept that can be described as people's internal fears, concerns, or perceived guilt about expressing their needs to others (Kline, 2003). Reactive motives are often centered around common interpersonal concerns such as fear of rejection, or feeling guilty for wanting support (Kline, 2003). These fears may manifest in overt or covert ways following a precipitating event. Let's return to 6th grade bullying group example to illustrate this concept:

> While Jamie settles into his seat, Lynn invites Selma to share a process observation with the group. Selma shares that she noticed when Jamie arrived today, some members looked visibly upset during his arrival. Nodding, Lynn follows up on Selma's process observation with a question to the group, "This could be a good time for us to talk about how the group felt when Jamie arrived late today. Would anyone like to share how they are feeling?".

Most group members nod their heads no, and a couple members share that they don't mind if Jamie shows up late. Other group members roll their eyes, but remain silent. Selma notes the verbal and non-verbal exchanges among group members might suggest some potential interpersonal fears (reactive motive) about self-disclosure of feelings in this group.

In this example, both disturbing and reactive motives are at play as the group navigates Jamie's late arrival to the session. Some members might want to share their feelings, but there also appears to be some tension around sharing those feelings. Significant moments of interpersonal tension (i.e., the convergence of a disturbing and reactive motive) constitutes the group's "focal conflict." You can think of a group focal conflict as the interaction between what group members would like to do or say (disturbing motives) in the here-and-now and what they believe will be the consequences of voicing their wishes to the group (reactive motives) (Kline, 2003). Jamie's late arrival is significant and represents a notable moment of interpersonal tension for the group. The incongruence between how members are acting, and what they are saying (or not saying), could be further explored to determine what fears they might harbor about confronting Jamie and sharing their feedback about how his late arrival impacted them. For example, some members might have relationships with Jamie outside the group and worry he will reject them. Other members might have previous experiences of someone else directing anger at them when they self-disclosed feelings, and therefore they have a strong fear of being retaliated against.

Importantly, group focal conflicts often center around universal issues in groups such as feedback exchange, conflict resolution, and emotion expression (Kline, 2003). It also is important to note that disturbing and reactive motives emerge from intrapsychic issues (i.e., occurring within the individual's mind) and are sometimes unconsciously triggered and played out by group members and/or group leaders. Members might even purposely hide wishes and concerns from others as a protective mechanism. Disturbing motives, reactive motives, and focal conflicts are concepts that represent the core confluence of intra-and-interpersonal experiences, and manifest through behavior and group interactions.

So how do we know when something has become a central issue for a group? The next two assumptions in GFCT suggest that we can see these concepts emerge by observing repetitive patterns in member-to-member interactions, as well as member-to-leader interactions, and group-as-a-whole interactions.

In the early stages of any newly formed counseling or psychotherapy group, it is typical for members to feel anxious about finding common ground with others or wonder how others will respond to them when they share their thoughts and feelings. This issue may resonate strongly with the group-as-a-whole; however, members may not voice their discomfort, or consciously recognize the source of their discomfort.

Take for instance an early session of a grief counseling group. Members may wonder how others will react to them if they share the struggles they experience while coping with a significant loss. This reflects a potential interpersonal concern centered around feeling accepted. Evidence of this focal conflict could surface through verbal exchanges (e.g., switching topics) and body language (e.g., looking away or fidgeting). One possible pattern of group interaction that could reveal the ongoing concern is that when the group leader brings up the topic of coping difficulties, several members avoid the discussion by talking instead about how *well* they are coping with loss. If the focal conflict also resonates with the group leader, there is potential they inadvertently collude with the group to avoid the topic as well. Here is where a PO could be valuable.

As time goes on, evidence of this focal conflict (acceptance/rejection) might show up in other ways such as the group identifying one member as the designated "patient" who needs their help, thereby avoiding a spotlight shone on their own coping difficulties. For this group, a unique theme around acceptance could impact the group's interpersonal dynamics, stages of development, and ultimately, each member's therapeutic outcomes. Therefore, it is imperative for a person providing Process Observation to look for these patterns in order to assist the group leader and/or the group members in identifying and finding resolutions to their focal conflicts.

How do we know if a group has successfully resolved a focal conflict? This question ties into the fourth and fifth assumptions of GFCT, and more key concepts from the model. The concept of *solutions* stems from Thomas French's work on how individuals navigate focal conflicts, which he described as personal solutions. This concept was later found to exist in group behavior as well. In the GFPT model, solutions represent how individuals and groups handle disturbing and reactive motives. The solutions agreed upon by a group (or even a subgroup) can be considered their attempts to eliminate (or directly address) fears that threaten to overwhelm group cohesion, while also satisfying wishes that resonate with some, or all the people in a group. These solutions are described as *restrictive* and *enabling solutions* (Kline, 2003).

Restrictive solutions have an immediate effect of lowering everyone's anxiety in the group by allowing an escape hatch of sorts for group members to avoid facing their fears (Kline, 2003). In GFCT, groups may believe that the restrictive solutions they are using are successful, but in fact, these solutions can stifle healthy group development. Let's go back to the example of the work task group. Group members are collectively anxious about the feedback process and wish to feel accepted as productive members of the group. If anxiety about feedback exchange reaches a point of feeling unmanageable, the group will seek a quick solution to lower tension, while still feeling validated in their respective roles (that wish to feel accepted). This restrictive solution could appear through specific behaviors of the group, such as members only giving positive feedback to each other. A solution like this provides short-term relief from rejection yet blocks members from gaining valuable information about themselves to improve their contributions to the group tasks. Ultimately, if restrictive solutions become a group norm, the group-as-a-whole may not achieve the outcomes they had set out to accomplish.

In contrast, enabling solutions require confrontation of fears (reactive motives) to satisfy wishes (disturbing motives). Enabling solutions temporarily raise anxiety in the group because members essentially agree to work through their fears and bring those fears out into the open (Kline, 2003). This type of solution manifests in group interactions, such as a work group discussing what constructive criticism means, concerns they have about feedback, and how the group will approach feedback exchange.

It can be downright uncomfortable and anxiety-provoking to share criticism about someone's work, but the rewards for group functioning are much higher if they can successfully enact enabling solutions around this issue. In my previous example of the grief counseling group, if the group leader sees that members are uncomfortable talking about coping difficulties, and the group agrees to talk about this openly, it enables them to explore feeling vulnerable with each other and discuss ways to make the group feel safe for everyone to share their struggles.

Another related term to consider is what GFCT refers to as *personal habitual solutions*. GFCT assumes that people bring to group their go-to solutions for handling interpersonal conflict or discomfort. These habitual personal solutions form in early childhood relationships and are more observable in groups proceeding a member's display of increased anxiety during the course of group interactions (Kline, 2003). For example, let's say members in the grief counseling group example have successfully navigated talking about coping difficulties, but as the final sessions of the group approach, a process observer notes that for some members, expressing feelings becomes more difficult around certain topics, such as saying goodbye. One member of the group is so anxious that when others try to express their feelings about the group ending, she attempts to steer the conversation back to coping difficulties. In this case, the group member is facing an interpersonal experience that feels overwhelming and she uses a habitual personal solution to protect herself from feeling intense emotions around the group coming to an end.

In regards to restrictive, enabling, and personal habitual solutions, PO's can play a key role in helping a group identify the solutions they are enacting to address focal conflicts. Let's return to the school counseling group again for an example:

> Selma has spent several more sessions providing process observation for the 6th grade psychoeducation group. She has noticed that the group tends to use restrictive solutions (e.g., silence or going off topic) when discussions steers toward sharing feelings. She shares this process observation with the group leader, Lynn, after the 5th group session. Lynn utilizes this information in the next session to try out modeling an enabling solution for the group through here-and-now self-disclosures of her own feelings.

Solutions connect with another assumption of group focal conflict theory that suggests groups will work to keep collective anxiety low. In the case of the grief counseling group example provided earlier in this chapter, the group-as-a-whole might reduce anxiety by avoiding discussions about coping difficulties. In essence, they are attempting to maintain equilibrium and interpersonal connection, which is another central concept of GFCT.

Similar to general systems theory, GFCT conceptualizes small groups of people as dynamic systems, always striving to maintain homeostasis; however, GFCT focuses more specifically on patterns of interpersonal communication in the context of conflict and anxiety within groups (Kline, 2003). A group can maintain equilibrium by avoiding challenging issues. If a group chooses not to work through an issue causing interpersonal stress, the issue will come out sideways, so to speak, until it is directly addressed. Another important related concept here is *solutional conflicts*. Solutional conflicts may occur when there is disagreement among members about how to resolve feelings of anxiety generated by a focal conflict. Some people may choose to verbally express their fears and therefore put forward enabling solutions, while others engage in denial or avoidance, which are restrictive solutions. Solutional conflicts will upset the balance a bit, as the group strives to maintain cohesion.

Group process observation (GPO), conceptualized through GFCT, can serve a critical function for groups through identification of solutions and solutional conflicts occurring at various stages of group development. In the school counseling group, the PO, Selma, initially identified reactive motives that most likely led to restrictive solutions she could see (i.e., group member silence, lack of eye contact). She could continue to track the types of solutions the group enacts and utilize this information to conceptualize potential sources of ongoing anxiety for the group. For instance, she could look for signs the group has made a compromise to share feelings and then follow the group process for any shift back to restrictive solutions for one or more group members. Often the reappearance of restrictive solutions indicates that a particular focal conflict resonates more strongly for one or more group members, and could signal that members have hit the upper limit of what they can tolerate emotionally. This is important for POs to recognize, especially in cases when the leader or the group strive to enact enabling solutions to move the group forward, but instead overwhelm a person's capacities to cope (Kline, 2003).

Structuring Process Observation through an GFCT Lens

Let's turn now to working through a practical example with a hypothetical case vignette. In this vignette Andie, Allie, Peter, Laurie, and Brook are participating in an outpatient substance-use counseling group, led by Miguel, an experienced facilitator.

- Andie has been in recovery for six months, and struggles with setting interpersonal boundaries. Her boundaries tend to be more diffuse, and she often overshares before getting to know people.

- Allie has been in recovery for two years. Allie has struggled in the past to voice her feelings and needs for fear of being rejected, and she has been working hard to show up authentically with others.
- Peter has been in recovery for eight months. He can become emotionally overwhelmed and dysregulated due to significant interpersonal trauma from his past. He tends to feel the most overwhelmed when he senses conflict with others and falls back on avoidance to protect himself.
- Laurie has also been in recovery for a year. Like Peter she is working on staying present in relationships and coping effectively with interpersonal conflict. When she senses discord, she tends to deflect during a conversation, though she is not always aware, in the moment, that she is doing this.
- Brook has been in recovery for a year, and they are working on interrupting a pattern of "going along along with the crowd" to maintain relationships. Brook is very empathetic and attuned to others; however, sometimes this means they end up rescuing or colluding unconsciously with people who are afraid to face feelings of emotional discomfort.

Miguel, the group's leader, begins the fifth session of a substance use counseling group with a series of warm-up go-arounds. In the final go-around, Miguel asks the group members to share how they are currently feeling about working with each other in this group experience.

ANDIE: I feel like we've developed a lot of trust in this group over the last couple of weeks. I feel really comfortable sharing my struggles with sobriety.

ALLIE: [Shifts several times in her seat] This is hard for me to say because I don't want to offend anyone; everyone here is awesome! But I disagree a bit with what Andie just said. I'm not ready to share everything with this group yet.

MIGUEL: [Looks around the group] Would anyone like to respond to what Andie or Allie just shared?

PETER: [Remains silent, looks down at his shoes and starts tapping his left foot.]

LAURIE: This discussion reminds me that I'm becoming more and more worried about a friend of mine. I don't trust her as much ever since she shared something personal that I told her in confidence. I've had a hard time telling her how I feel about this. I am so mad at her. Could I process this with the group for a few minutes?

BROOK: That's sad to hear, Laurie. There's nothing worse than a friend betraying your trust.

PETER AND ANDIE: [nod their heads in agreement and shift their attention to Laurie.]

MIGUEL: It seems as if the group is feeling concerned for Laurie and wanting to offer her support. Laurie, can you tell us a bit more about the situation with your friend?

Questions to Consider in the PO Role

1. Who participated in a restrictive solution?

   a. Why was it restrictive?
   b. What were the potential needs and fears surrounding this solution?

2. Who participated in an enabling solution?

   c. Why was it enabling?

3. Write out some process observations you might share with Miguel or the group:

   d. Examples to the group leader: I noticed that you asked the group to respond to Andie and Allie, rather than first reflecting their comments. When there was discomfort, you seemed to give the group permission to move away from the topic. Could you share what you were noticing and responding to?

e. Example to the group: I noticed that Andie shared something important to her about trusting others in the group, and Allie had different feelings about self-disclosing to the group. The group decided to shift from the here-and-now to discussing an issue Laurie has outside the group. What do you all think about the conversation moving away from Andie and Allie so quickly?

Discussion

In order for this group to move forward, a PO might assist the group by helping them recognize enabling solutions that would allow group members to resolve a disturbing motive and face reactive motives. Allie's disclosure represented an enabling solution; however, it also appeared to intensify discomfort among members, resulting in the appearance of a restrictive solution enacted by the group to avoid discussing the disagreement that just occurred. Even the group leader appears to have colluded with the members by allowing the focus to shift to Laurie's relationship issue outside of the group.

In this case example, Allie appears to express a disturbing motive as a wish to share that she disagrees with Andie. We can infer from other group members' reactions that they may harbor fear or discomfort about the consequences of weighing-in on the disagreement. There could be myriad reasons for heightened anxiety at this moment. Peter, Laurie, and Brook all have interpersonal struggles around conflict, and when anxious, they might fall back on personal habitual solutions to cope and stay engaged in the group process. These reactions could reflect reactive motives such as fear of rejection or of being criticized by others. For example, after Allie shares her feelings, Peter's nonverbals and silence suggests he is not comfortable speaking up and might want to avoid involvement, while Laurie could be equally uncomfortable when she brings up an issue she is experiencing outside the group.

It is possible that a focal conflict has emerged regarding members' expressing disagreement and what will happen if they were to do so. This focal conflict has created a certain amount of anxiety among members as expressed through various reactions to Allie's statement about trust. Trust versus mistrust could also be a central issue that generates a focal conflict for the group. Beyond discomfort about disagreement, it is possible the group is too anxious to discuss their level of trust with each other, and Laurie's solution is to bring the issue up covertly by talking about a relationship outside of the group.

In order to develop a holistic picture of this group and how they handle disagreements, what other questions might a PO keep in mind? Some questions to consider: Have issues pertaining to trust and navigating disagreements come up in their interactions in the past? Are there any unwritten rules the group may have developed about what to do when a disagreement happens? Have there been other disagreements? How did members handle them? What did the disagreements center around? Were some disagreements easily addressed? If so, why might the stakes have been lower? In other words, what types of disagreements tend to trigger restrictive solutions? If there are never disagreements, what is that about?

Similar questions could be posed regarding the level of trust among members in the group. It is possible other disturbing and reactive motives are at play for this group, such as a need to express feelings about trust and fears about being able to handle how others respond to expression of emotion. In regards to Miguel, a PO might ask if he intentionally allowed the focus to shift to Laurie in order to keep the level of anxiety in the group tolerable, or was the shift stemming from leadership issues he needs to explore in consultation, such as countertransference. It is possible that the emerging focal conflict resonates with the group leader as well, and this would be important for a PO to explore further.

The ultimate objective of conceptualizing group interactions and development through GFCT is to help members develop interpersonal effectiveness and positive self-perceptions in their relationship with others (Kline, 2003). Process Observation can be particularly helpful for identifying and interpreting the sources of interpersonal tension in a group, while also supporting group leaders in recognizing what solutions could be negotiated and enacted within a group to support change. There are myriad ways a PO might use GFCT to assess, observe, and interpret group dynamics and stages of development.

GFCT in Different Types of Groups

Depending on the purpose and goals of a group, such as with counseling or psychotherapy groups, Process Observation might involve deeper exploration of interpersonal communication within a group, or in psychoeducation and tasks groups, GFCT could be a means to provide brief assessments of roadblocks a group might be experiencing. Importantly, GFCT involves understanding how the intrapsychic influences the interpersonal dynamics of a group. In this regard, POs must take care to adjust their input based upon the type of group.

Champe and Rubel (2012) proposed the application of GFCT to psychoeducational groups, as this type of group creates unique leadership challenges related to balancing content with process. For example, a group leader's failure to address group dynamics or member reactions to the psychoeducational content can impact the quality of the learning environment. Psychoeducation learning activities may produce a certain amount of member anxiety, which is necessary for learning engagement. However, too much anxiety can decrease engagement and subsequent knowledge acquisition.

Thus, Process Observation can be utilized to identify specific concerns, assess the level of discomfort in a group, and generate effective, enabling solutions. Viewing psychoeducational groups through an GFCT lens also can be particularly useful for establishing safe and responsive learning environments using group process to engage members' feedback exchange and allowing space for group members to share their reactions to the content in personally meaningful ways (Champe & Rubel, 2012; Kline, 2003).

In a work task group, intrapsychic issues such as fear of criticism might well be at play. However, the PO should take care to not focus on the personal in such a way that members are asked to think about there-and-then experiences rooted to fears. It would be more functional to the task group to frame interventions to highlight solutional conflicts happening in the here-and-now, and then scaling the level of comfort the group has with making changes to how they give and receive feedback.

Key interpersonal concerns members may experience in this type of group involve group perceptions of members' task-related competencies, role clarity and boundaries, leadership and decision-making, and overall group effectiveness (Baker, 2001; Thomas-Hunt & Phillips, 2004). Members may experience salient fears including concerns about asserting themselves in the group related to their areas of expertise or worry that their ideas will be criticized by members of the group. These types of interpersonal tensions can interfere directly with group members' satisfaction and their task performance (De Dreu & Weingart, 2003). For example, pre-conceived gender expectations related to areas of task expertise may elicit anxiety, and thus go unexamined and unaddressed, leading to negative impacts on group cohesion, morale, and goal accomplishment (Thomas-Hunt & Phillips, 2004). In an organizational environment, POs can use GFCT to identify the interpersonal issues that might be connected to less productivity in a task group and bring these concerns to the forefront for resolution.

Given that some amount of fear, anxiety, or discomfort is universally experienced by people participating in different types of groups, POs can use GFCT to identify sources of interpersonal tension that could hinder group development. To do so, POs can frame their observations through a GFCT lens by considering verbal and non-verbal communication, as well as contextual cues in the group environment. When engaged in GPO through the lens of GFCT, Whitaker (1982) points out that a good starting point is to focus on the solutions a group is using and the related themes that seem to weave through all the group interactions. To determine what type of solutions are being enacted in a group, some examples of questions POs might ask themselves during observation are:

- What topics does the group appear to avoid, or spend less time discussing?
- What topics does a group spend quite a bit of time on, or revisit often?
- How often do irrelevant discussions occur, and how long do these discussions last?
- What happens when a disagreement occurs? What is said or not said?
- What happens when someone in the group expresses their emotions?
- Does everyone arrive on time? Does anyone leave early?
- Who attends every session and who misses sessions?
- How does the group react to a late arrival or when someone misses a session?
- Who occupies which roles in a group and when, if ever, do roles shift?

Stock Whitaker (1989) suggests looking for other cues as well, such as body language, pacing, silence, tone of voice, member interruptions, and sudden shifts in topic. It is also important to track how individual group members participate in the events of each session. For example, when a specific topic is broached, who becomes distraught, who challenges, and who cooperates with the established norms of the group (Stock Whitaker, 1989)? Once potential solutions are identified, POs can ask themselves the following question to identify potential disturbing and reactive motives: What needs, or fears, might be connected to these solutions?

Conclusions

Group Focal Conflict Theory provides POs with a structured framework for assessing a group's level of interpersonal effectiveness, with a focus on patterns of interaction that could raise anxiety and impede the group's overall development. GFCT is an effective conceptualization tool for Process Observation when specific interpersonal issues resonate with a group thereby impacting the group's development. POs can utilize key concepts from GFCT to identify the motives behind behaviors, recognize themes leading to focal conflicts, and assess a group's use of enabling and restrictive solutions. For further reading on GFCT, readers might find W. B. Kline's (2003) *Interactive group counseling and therapy*, to be an especially helpful resource for a more in-depth exploration of GFCT terminology and interactive group interventions through a GFCT lens. Following is a worksheet for utilizing FCT with GPO.

Worksheet 1

Group Focal Conflict Identification

PO: ______________________________ **Date:** ______________________________

Group Session Notes:

Time	*Content/Focus*	*Communication and Behaviors (verbal and non-verbal)*	*Disturbing Motives*	*Reactive Motives*	*Examples of Solutions: Enabling or Restrictive*

Observations of Group Interactive Processes

- What topics and/or group interactions appear to raise or lower anxiety?
- What themes/patterns of interaction occur in this group?
- When and how do group members express emotions?
- How does the group leader(s) intervene when group interactions become unproductive (e.g., a disturbing motive is not being addressed)?
- What impact does the group leader(s) interventions have on the group? Do the interventions increase members' use of enabling solutions or restrictive solutions?

References

Baker, D. F. (2001). The development of collective efficacy in small task groups. *Small Group Research, 32(4)*, 451–474.

Berk, T. J. (2011). The group focal conflict theory revisited. www.lulu.com.

Champe, J., & Rubel, D. J. (2012). Application of focal conflict theory to psychoeducational groups: Implications for process, content, and leadership. *The Journal for Specialists in Group Work, 37(1)*, 71–90.

De Dreu, C. K., & Weingart, L. R. (2003). Task versus relationship conflict, team performance, and team member satisfaction: a meta-analysis. *Journal of applied Psychology, 88(4)*, 741.

French, T. M. (1952–1953). *The integration of behavior* (Vols. *1* &*2*). Chicago: University of Press.

Kline, W. B. (2003). *Interactive group counseling and therapy*. Merrill Prentice Hall: Upper Saddle River, NJ.

Stock Whitaker, D. (1989). Group focal conflict theory: Description, illustration and evaluation. *Group, 13(3)*, 225–251.

Thomas-Hunt, M. C., & Phillips, K. W. (2004). When what you know is not enough: Expertise and gender dynamics in task groups. *Personality and Social Psychology Bulletin, 30(12)*, 1585–1598.

Whitaker, D. S. (1982). A nuclear conflict and group focal conflict model for integrating individual and group-level phenomena in psychotherapy groups. In *The Individual and the Group* (pp. 321–338). Springer, Boston, MA.

Whitaker, D. S., & Lieberman, M. A. (1964). *Psychotherapy through the group process*. Atherton Press.

Whitman, R. M., & Stock, D. (1958). The group focal conflict. *Psychiatry, 21(3)*, 269–276.

Chapter 7

Process Observation for Diversity, Equity, and Inclusion

Devika Dibya Choudhuri, Eastern Michigan University

Christopher J. McCarthy, University of Texas at Austin

Introduction to DEI Issues in Group Process Observation

Most helping professionals are now trained to be culturally competent and work with sensitivity to the impact of social identities on interpersonal work and group dynamics. However, a group leader can be culturally competent and yet still unaware of diversity concerns in their group. A Process Observer (PO) can be uniquely positioned to see patterns across time and members that can reveal beliefs and norms that are antithetical to true equity. In standing outside the system, the PO can have an easier vantage point to see systemic repetitions and interrupt more effectively. This may be particularly true when the group leader(s) are themselves members of marginalized populations: group members not sharing a marginalized identity might dismiss comments from the leaders as being due to over-identification with their marginalized identity, not what is happening in the group. On the other hand, the observational perspective of a PO, regardless of their social identities, is more difficult to disregard.

Even though all of the other chapters in this book acknowledge the importance of equity and inclusion, the topic merits a specific focus on the unique opportunities and challenges that PO's have in culturally responsive group work.

Dimensions of Identity

The major social identities that we focus on for the purposes of this discussion include race and ethnicity, culture, gender, class, sexual orientation, (dis)ability, religion or spirituality, age, and language. However, there are many more that acquire differential salience in a member's life depending on context, content, or experience (see Figure 7.1). These multidimensional aspects of identity express that how one experiences one's world is based on a constant interaction between the self, others, and environment (Amini, 2020). As you can imagine, that is the core of group work, and therefore deeply relevant to the work of group Process Observation (GPO).

All of the salient identities such as race/ethnicity, gender, and age are integral aspects of group dynamics. Essentially, as assembled human beings, no group can possibly be neutral or free of the influence of these identities, since there are no generic human beings who do not possess these identities. Even in posed stock pictures, the group of people laughing, discussing, arguing, or texting have ascribed races, genders, ages, visible disabilities, and so on. These identities, designed to delineate relative categories of social worth, operate interpersonally. In other words, an individual human alone on Mars in a spacesuit may well be generic because the markers of race, gender, class, sexuality, or religion are irrelevant, since there is no one else with whom

DOI: 10.4324/9781003281955-9

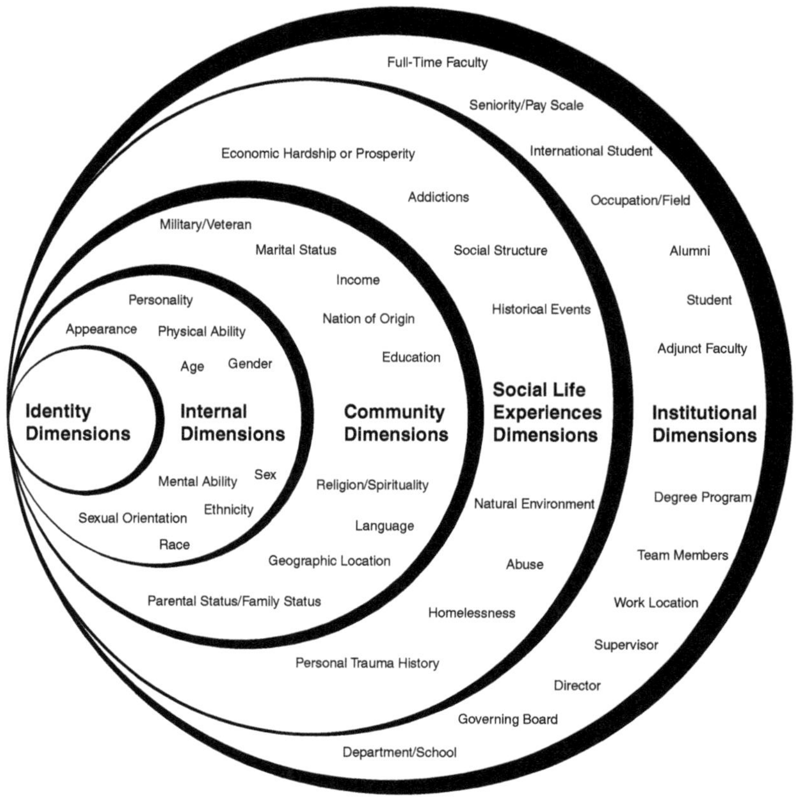

This model of a Diversity Wheel was proposed by Loden (1996), and particularly for educational settings (North Central University).
Londen, M. (1996). *Implementing Diversity, Burr Ridge*, IL: Mc-Graw Hill Publishing

Figure 7.1 Diversity Model

to interact. With other humans however, all those identities come into play in interaction with each other (Romero, 2018). As the adage goes, if in individual counseling people tell you their problems, in group work, they show you. This is as true for racism, sexism, classism, ableism, homophobia, antisemitism, ageism, or ethnocentrism; all of which eventually emerge within the group process (see Table 7.1).

When these aspects of social identities interact in a group setting, power differentials associated with each identity become salient in the social microcosm of the group. We are socialized to view some aspects of identity as normative and privileged, leaving other identities as marginalized. So, while a young woman and an older man in the group both have a gender identity, the young woman could experience herself as having less power and authority to make her point in a group. During a discussion she may become silent after the older man interrupts her to tell a story about his own experience, whereas the older man may have no such compunction (see Figure 7.2). Even more pernicious for the group, those with dominant identity statuses may be unaware of power and privilege because it is so normative for them, while those on the margins in the subordinate status are well aware of such dynamics. Such differences in experience and socialization associated with identity can result in some members feeling marginalized in the group, that they do not matter as much as others.

Table 7.1 Social identities in interaction

	Race/ Ethnicity	*Gender*	*Age*	*Sexual Orientation*	*Religion/ Faith*
Race/ Ethnicity		*Josh/Jess and Jay are often empathic with each other for a sense of shared trans/nb POC identity that they feel the others don't experience.*		*Kiara and Mike connected more deeply because both identified as straight Black Christians. Other group members speculated if Mike and Kiara might have dated but the two have not disclosed that, though they do go to the same Church.*	
Gender			*Marcia and Carla are beginning to experience perimenopausal symptoms and laugh with each other about the heat flashes.*		*Mike and Dan often went out after the group for coffee and would say between themselves that now they could be "toxically masculine"*
Sexual Orientation		*Marcia and Gerda are careful to leave their relationship out of the group, but often conflict at home can express itself in the group.*		*Josh/Jess, Marcia, Gerda, and Jay have often socialized outside the group at LGBTQ events.*	
Religion/ Faith	*Jay has often felt isolated in the group, as a Hindu and South Asian. He feels that he will always be exotically foreign in a way that even Gerda is not.*				*Kiara, Dan, and Mike all connected in a sub-group because the program they came from identified as a Christian school, congruent to their beliefs.*

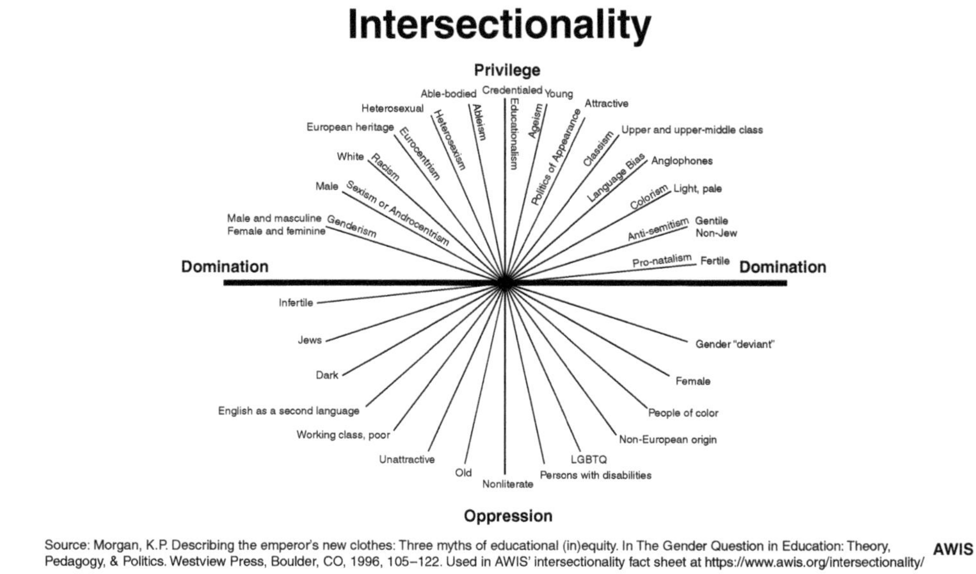

Figure 7.2 Intersectional aspects of identity together with power

Cultural and Diversity Competence

While group leaders, and by extension, POs, should be culturally competent, often this discussion has been focused less on power differentials and more on group leaders who are from the dominant cultural groups understanding, accurately interpreting, and being responsive to members who are not from their cultural group. These discussions rarely take into account the intersectional aspects of social identities, framing it as issues of cultural homogeneity and heterogeneity. Of course such an understanding implies for example, that a group of older Asian American women will respond similarly, taking no account of lived experience as well as sexuality, disability, religion, immigration generation, that may create large differences in member interaction. The leader's contextual understanding of the differences in presentation and interaction amongst members that are due to diverse cultural norms is helpful. However a PO could have a much better lens on how the leaders' expectations and preferences for member appearance, communication, behaviors and perceptions influence their understanding and response to members.

A related aspect of group cultural competence is members' perception of the leader in terms of competence, credibility, and trustworthiness. Again, a PO is more likely to notice when members interrupt, ignore, or otherwise downplay a leader's authority due to their age and speech impediment, while also noticing when the leader does the same to certain members, leading to such members feeling less valued or heard (Brown, 2018).

Unexplored issues around implicit bias (Stevens & Abernethy, 2018) amongst members and leaders can negatively impact the interpersonal group environment, functioning, and outcomes. It is particularly salient to the work of a PO, since so much implicit bias occurs on a subconscious level where there is little awareness or conscious intent. A PO however, can, through field observation over a period of time, pick up on the subtle patterns of deference or marginalization to diverse members. Brown (2018) pointed out that aspects that are often indicative of the influences of implicit bias that the PO can attend to include:

1) Verbal participation – observing who speaks spontaneously, who volunteers, who is invited to speak and who is ignored or interrupted, and who speaks to whom and is listened to by whom.
2) Influence and power – observing who is deferred to, whether there are social identity groups that are deferred to over others such as men over women, or older over younger. Whose opinions about scheduling or times carry weight, as well as group time given to listen attentively is often telling, as is the use or non-use of titles and forms of address.
3) Decision making – group decisions may at times conflict with individual member values and how is the conflict handled or even noticed.
4) Task functions and responsibilities – Both cultural values as well as biased expectations can shape how member task performance is viewed. Does the group start on time even knowing there are members who are habitually late? Does the group go over even knowing that some members have to drive far or have child care responsibilities?
5) Expression of feelings – While much of expression of affect is culturally based, groups often implicitly require that members self-disclose feelings. Such disclosure often requires a willingness to be vulnerable without a history of having been wounded for doing so. Members from cultures where emotional privacy is important and one is expected to mask feelings, may appear closed off or resistant to the group process. On the other hand, there are members who may overshare and drown the group in relating feelings and diverse groups often struggle with balancing both styles.

Mattering and Marginalization

Identities are connected to the idea of mattering. Articulated by Schlossberg (1989), mattering is the sensation that people have when they feel that others are engaged with them and value their input. The components of mattering include: 1) Attention, which refers to being noticed by others; 2) Importance, where you perceive that your feelings, thoughts, and actions are significant to others; 3) Dependence, which is believing that your contribution is valued and necessary and that others equally depend on you; and, 4) Ego-extension, the belief that others will be empathic with your successes and failures (Corbiere & Amundson, 2007). In groups, when members experience mattering, trust, safety, and cohesiveness are all heightened, which in turn increases the effectiveness of the group in meeting member goals and objectives. Marginalization, on the other hand, is the sense of not fitting in or not being appreciated for one's presence and input, a social exclusion both implicit and explicit that serves as barriers to access, participation, and resources. Over the long term, marginalization can lead to almost permanent feelings of lack of belonging, disconnection, and ultimately alienation (Schlossberg, 1989). Mattering and marginalization are both factors that POs can notice through patterns of interaction among members – whether some members are systematically denied the invitations to participation that others are given, and what aspects of identity may be associated with this denial.

Group work is clearly impacted by the subtle dynamics around identity and how members react, respond, and interact around interpersonal contexts of oppression and privilege. We will next describe microaggressions as another form of discrimination experienced by those with marginalized identities.

Microaggressions

Sue (2010) defined microaggressions as "the everyday slights, indignities, put downs and insults that…those who are marginalized experience in their day-to-day interactions with people"

(p. xvi). These subtle verbal and nonverbal slights are based on social defined identity group membership. First articulated by Harvard psychiatrist Chester Pierce about the dismissiveness he saw inflicted on Black Americans (Sue, 2010), the concept and examples have burgeoned to all aspects of marginalization, including gender, sexuality, class, disability, and religion (Wong et al., 2014). Microaggressions can be delineated into three types, all showing up in subtle ways in group work. These are:

1) Microinsults consist of demeaning messages that repeat or rely on stereotypes about a group. For example, a 4th generation Japanese American teenager in the group is complimented on how well they speak English, rather than on what they said.
2) Microinvalidations are communications that dismiss or negate the lived experience of members of marginalized groups. For example, when an older White man in the group tells an older Black woman that all she has to do is "play the race-card" to get what she wants, after she speaks about being underpaid.
3) Microassaults can involve derogatory name-calling or put downs that rely on oppressive stereotypes. For example, a Latina member being told by a heterosexual cisman, "Hey, I can cure you of being a lesbian if you give me the chance!"

Microaggressions are particularly useful for POs to attend to, because their subtlety makes them more difficult to notice and respond to from within the group. Some of these factors include difficulty interpreting the interaction as a microaggression because it is often unintentional and comes from another peer; wondering if it is worth confronting in the group; taking responsibility for having to confront it as a member who may feel less powerful; determining how to confront and invest energy; and finally responding to the microaggression. Targets of microaggressions may often underestimate the negative impact on mattering and the burdensome cumulative effect of microaggressions, while a PO might more readily notice a member subtly pushed out over a series of what appear to be random incidents and remarks (Nadal, 2013).

The PO can give careful attention to not just the occurrence of microaggressions but more importantly how they are noted, responded to, and the subsequent impact on participation, relations and interactions. These may include:

1) Lowered feelings of trust and safety amongst certain members, which is then picked up on and responded in the group as if they are personality traits of guardedness and withholding.
2) Frequent receivers of microaggressions can monitor themselves to avoid receiving more microaggressions, reducing their ability to be genuine and spontaneous.
3) Receivers can become isolated and scapegoated because of their reactions, and treated like they are the "identified patient." Eventually, they can explode or leave the group that then feels let down.
4) Members who have not directly received microaggressions can still feel the tension without necessarily being able to identify the source of the discomfort. They too may withdraw trust because they are uncertain and eventually drift away.

Those who experience microaggressions face a dilemma – confronting the microaggressor directly often has repercussions, because it can be dismissed as rude, complaining or hypersensitive, while not addressing it can create added stress as the targeted person. Brown (2018) speaks to the receiver's Double Bind when microaggressions are challenged directly by the receiver. A well-meaning micoaggressor may often extend an apology and emphasize the unintentionality of the offense. At this point, the receiver may have to either minimize the hurt received and accept the apology, or refuse and then be in the position of hurting the sender of the microaggression who feels shamed, misunderstood, and wounded. These apologies, while sincere, often have no real understanding of the depth of the wound and are imposed on the receiver. This leads to the receiver being hurt again and having to then take care of the aggressor. When bystanders or onlookers intervene, it is generally more validating for the target, who then experiences support. Having others intervene can also make it more likely the perpetrator will acknowledge the microaggression more fully, since it is harder to dismiss the reactions of more than one person.

Sue et al. (2019) point out that such "microinterventions" can make the invisible discrimination visible, foster learning for the perpetrator and others, and enlists support and greater group cohesiveness. Microaffirmations, microvalidations, and microinterventions all seek to congruently address the insults, invalidations and assaults received by members of marginalized populations. When a PO can share patterns they have noticed with the group, it lessens individual defensiveness and can be tackled as a group process.

Case Discussion for DEI in Process

In this part of the chapter we will be using the following vignette of a group to identify and discuss dynamics around Diversity, Equity, and Inclusion (DEI). You may notice that simply by adding in details about the identities of these participants, these elements are much more highlighted and visible, as are potential interpersonal interactions.

A peer supervision group of counselors has been meeting for several months, on a biweekly basis, for a two-hour time block on Saturday mornings. While the group started as eight people, it has recently had two original members drop away. Most of the members knew of each other either by practicing in a similar agency, graduating from the same program, or having done their supervision for licensure under the same supervisor. They developed the group through word of mouth, as an egalitarian peer supervision space to consult with each other about their clinical concerns, ethical dilemmas, and professional issues. The current membership consists of:

- *Marcia, a 42-year-old Irish-American Buddhist lesbian cisfemale who has been practicing for three years.*
- *Kiara, a 37-year-old African American Christian heterosexual ciswoman, who has been practicing for nine years.*
- *Josh/Jess, a 29-year-old biracial (Black/White) non-binary pansexual Agnostic, who received their full license last year.*
- *Gerda, a 35-year-old German lesbian ciswoman who identifies as a White Wiccan social worker and was introduced to the group because she has been in a relationship with Marcia.*
- *Jay, a 39-year-old South Asian Hindu transman, practicing for 11 years in total, but one year post transition and considers himself asexual.*
- *Carla, a 40-year-old Italian-American non-observant Catholic heterosexual ciswoman, who has been practicing the longest at 14 years.*
- *Mike, a 41-year-old Black, heterosexual Christian cisman, practicing for 6 years.*

- *Dan, a 46-year-old French Canadian origin White heterosexual Christian cisman, who had graduated from the same program as Kiara and Mike 4 years ago.*

Recently, Mike and Dan dropped out. Both identified as heterosexual Christian cismen in their early 40s, one Black and one White. Both had different reasons but were increasingly distant before they left, which was after a series of heated discussions on diversity, equity, and identity issues. Since these members left, the group is finding itself adrift, with meetings where members seem reluctant to bring cases or discuss professional or personal struggles with clients. Gerda and Marcia both fear that the group is now "playing it safe" to protect the group. Someone suggests getting some assistance, and someone else suggests a Process Observer. The group asks Layla, an Arab American heterosexual ciswoman of 50-something, who Jay, Josh/Jess, and Marcia know as a former professor. Layla considers the issues present before deciding.

Selection of PO

As addressed in Chapter 4, selecting a PO is often done on the basis of some familiarity with the person, respect for their groupwork competence, and availability. Here, however, the group has been more thoughtful, choosing Layla as someone who has those aforementioned attributes, but also appears to be likely to work with the group in an objective position since she is primarily a counselor educator. She is less likely to "take over" than a fellow practitioner, and more likely to view the group with respect for its purpose, longevity, acceptance of the leaderless style, along with an expertise in clinical group supervision rather than in practice. In addition, having known some of the members as former students, and being familiar with practitioner perspectives, may give her an advantage in joining the group without immersion. Having gotten details of the group addressed in the checklist provided in Chapter 4, and been fully informed about the concerns for social identities and their relevance to the group process, Dr. Layla believes she has the necessary DEI competence to work with the group due to her experience in teaching the social justice and multicultural counseling courses at her institution.

Self-Audit

In the necessary self-audit to determine the ethical dimensions of how her values, beliefs, and attitudes might impact the Process Observation, as referenced in Chapter 3, Layla considers how this may impact her engagement. Layla is comfortable with reflecting on her Arab-American identity and considers its implications intersectionally with those of the group. While she is heterosexual and cis like several members of the group, she also believes that she has a knowledge of, sensitivity with, and respect for the sexual and gender expansive identities in the group, as evidenced by Jay, Josh/Jess, and Marcia seeking her services. In some ways, she feels her third-generation Lebanese-American identity might be an asset in the group process, as other BIPOC members might feel potentially more comfortable, while the White members might give her process comments more attention. On the other hand, while she considers herself a woman of color and visibly looks it, in the legal understanding (U.S. Census Bureau, 2020) she is considered White. While she has a DEI statement that she knows will be reassuring to the members, she also determines that this must be a part of the opening conversation with the group explicitly, given their concerns about safety and offense. She is also keenly aware that the differential clinical and life experiences of the group members will determine differential levels of safety and confidence.

Subgrouping may have been a part of the reason Mike and Dan left the group. She hopes that she will have permission from the group to reach out to those members and have a conversation with them about their reasons for leaving. One of the impacts of DEI work in groups is that while on the one hand, social identities always have an ongoing influence in group dynamics, on the other, hypersensitivity such as White fragility (DiAngelo, 2018) can mean that some folks explain all interactions from BIPOC folks solely through their racial/cultural identities.

She determines that she has the professional disclosure and informed consent documentation, and that her first meeting with the group will include a thorough discussion of confidentiality and its exceptions given that the group consists of active practitioners with clients. She decides that she will ask the group if they would be willing to give her the standing of a mental health supervisory consultant to provide her the protection of legal standing for privileged communication.

Finally, in thinking about the engagement, Layla intentionally decides that while it is a leaderless group, she will charge them a reasonable collective fee for her presence as PO for three sessions. Her decision is based on the understanding that the members collectively pay for the space they use and the logistics of the group format, and while they might have differential incomes, all have an income and charge their own clients. She reflects on the socioeconomic issues and wants to refute the notion that mental health work is purer and more compassionate when unpaid. The protocol of fees, she decides, will have the group taking the PO's role more professionally since, as Master's level counselors, they were not formally trained in it nor have they been practiced in clinical group supervision.

Initial Contract

Layla sets up a time to have a special meeting with the group, that is not their usual biweekly meeting, to underline the singular nature of the meeting. At the meeting, she introduces herself, shares her professional disclosure, and begins to work through some of the expectations and objectives that members want her to meet. The group decides that they would prefer that Layla attend the meetings and be in the room rather than observe through a two-way mirror or watch a recording of the session. At one point, Kiara jokes nervously, "I'll feel perfectly safe 'cause I'm pretty sure you're not a terrorist." Layla at this point, chooses to smile and shake her head, knowing that her tightly wrapped headscarf has caught Kiara's attention. Layla notices the microaggression of equating Arabs with terrorists, but also notices that Marcia, Josh/Jess, and Carla all have nonverbal reactions where they glance at each other and barely seem to hold back a roll of their eyes in exasperation. On Layla asking permission to speak with Dan and Mike, Kiara leans forward and says that she misses them and would love to have them rejoin the group. "If you can make them feel welcome again, it would be so great. I mean they're friends and we all graduated from the same program–so like, we just process in the same way, you know."

Layla finally asks if the group will set aside 15 minutes at the end of every group meeting where she can do a process debrief, sharing her immediate impressions of the session. She also says that at the end of the three observed sessions, the group can choose to meet for a fourth special meeting to debrief in far more detail, address strategies and decide if they are done with the engagement, or wish for more Process Observation. Each member of the group signs the contract Layla provides laying out the terms of the arrangement.

Preliminary Exploration

Before proceeding with the Process Observation, Layla contacts both Dan and Mike through a phone call using the information Kiara shared, and arranges a meeting with both men. When she does meet with them at a coffee shop they suggest, she finds that they seem a bit shocked, and she senses their discomfort with her headscarf. She decides to start by telling them about her arrangement with the group, and introduces herself jokingly as someone who has three jobs as a Counseling Professor, a wife and mother. They laugh sympathetically, and Dan says that he has a family too with two young children, and Mike bemoans that he can never find the right woman to marry. They relax after that and start talking about their experience in the group. Layla notes that they are more relaxed when they have "placed" her in an acceptable set of womanly roles.

Both Mike and Dan say that the group seemed to become so "woke" that talking about clients became impossible when you had to work so hard just to describe them. With bitterness, Dan says, "I just wanted to know how to help this kid with ADHD, and I get a lecture on whether he might be coming out! Why can't he just be a kid and not be thinking about sex but his math grade?" Layla took a moment, then responded, "You're telling me you didn't think about sex at his age?"

Mike laughs and points a finger at Dan, saying,

> She got you there! Yeah, we did, but it was about girls which was normal. None of this crazy stuff, and I don't mean that the sex stuff is crazy, but why does it have to be everywhere and in everything with kids having pronouns!

Dan shakes his head, then looks at Layla seriously and says,

> I miss the group, but I'm not going to go someplace where I have to feel bad about myself every time. I go to Church, I try to do good, I help a lot of people, and I don't want to have to feel guilty about this woke stuff.

Mike agrees, and then says, "And it's not like there wasn't racism, but it wasn't really addressed and if White women want to cry about sexism, I'm out of patience." Layla thanked them for their honesty and feedback and ended the conversation.

Process Observation

For the next three meetings of the group, Layla attended the group meetings and observed their process. She noticed at the first such meeting, members would often look at her glancingly to check on her reactions, and Carla and Marcia would often preface their discussion of clients with an introductory note to Layla, such as "I know you won't know this, so it's is a client I've talked about before who presents as…." She also noticed that Josh/Jess and Jay, both former students of hers, would address trans issues in their clinical comments, with a smile towards her as if her presence gave support.

Layla observed that the group members would discuss clients without identifying them as to their race/ethnicity, sexual orientation or class background unless that was the origin of the presenting problem, but often identified clients by generic age and gender, such "Remember that young teenager I mentioned before, she started bingeing again and mom called…"; "My old guy who has that porn addiction…"; "That young Black dude mandated to see me by the court missed another appointment and I'm going to report him to his probation officer!"

Giving careful attention to patterns across sessions, Layla observed that members tended to be self-congratulatory when they had a session where there was no conflict or where members were largely supportive and appreciative of clinical work. These were considered successful sessions. When members might comment that a cognitive behavioral or solution focused or alternative theory might be useful, the comments tended to be accepted without much resistance. When a member raised a disagreement with a clinical intervention that led to heightened tension, usually it tended to be around some aspect of client identity that the clinician had not considered as a competing explanation for symptoms. For instance, when Josh/Jess suggested to Kiara that her young, Black, mandated client might be missing sessions because with his license removed for a drug charge and inability to get to work, the public transportation system was very erratic and a long commute, Kiara became defensive and responded, "Well, it's his responsibility to make the sessions if he wants his license back. And we are on the bus line at least; what do you want me to do about it – Uber him to sessions?"

While Layla gave Process Observations at the end of every group and people often commented on how interesting it was to see themselves through this lens, there seemed little impetus to change group norms or for the group to think about different alternative processes. Thus Layla urged them to make time for a special meeting after three sessions where she could do a full report and debrief. In addition, she asked and received permission from the group to invite Dan and Mike to that meeting. Both said they would come, but only Mike showed up.

Process Observation Debrief

Layla welcomed the group and appreciated their efforts to strive to make the experience even better, and valued that enough to pay for it. "It is," she told them, "One of the reasons why I wanted to work with you and have this meeting so that you are more likely to create changes to justify and make the most of this report." She then used a handout to assist them to follow along, as she shared major themes she had noticed in the group process. These included clinical consultation norms; harmony and agreement norms; conflict norms; and DEI norms. For this chapter, we will only focus on the DEI norms Layla covered.

Layla began by describing some of the interactions she had observed around DEI, including focusing on ways that members took it for granted that others would know where their perspective came from. She said,

> Your familiarity and knowledge of one another is quite remarkable and a testament to the work you have done to make yourselves known to each other. It allows you to speak from your perspective without having to laboriously identify it each time, because you believe and trust that others know and remember. On the other hand, with different group members who have joined at different times, some of the knowledge is more historical as opposed to directly experienced. It can mean that you may assume knowledge of yourself that isn't always there, and when met with ignorance, assume it is ill-intentioned forgetting rather than not knowing. So microinvalidations can occur and be unaddressed.

The group discussed these points and decided that it might be helpful to have each person reintroduce themselves from time to time and update each other on their life circumstances.

She also addressed an issue the group had never explicitly discussed but had often been a source of tension. "You have not spoken about your belief systems though you may have named them," she remarked, "and for many of you this is a strong element of who you are." Layla recognized this because she noticed how often members looked at her head covering and wondered about her religion, but never felt able to explicitly ask. She raised that issue, saying,

> I am sure you have wondered if as an Arab-American with a head scarf, I am Muslim. But I am more curious about why it was difficult to ask me. I believe that discomfort about exploring religious and spiritual beliefs directly is one of the sources of tension in this group.

Kiara responded to that saying, "I don't understand. I love the Lord and I'm not ashamed of it." Jay jumped in and said, " I know what Dr. L is talking about. Like you all know I'm Hindu and Gerda is Wiccan, but you don't ever ask us about it." Mike asked, "Well, why do I need to in this group? No offense," he said to Layla, "but why should I care what your religion is?" This exchange goes to the heart of mattering (Schlossberg, 1989), in that several folks felt that identities deeply salient to themselves were not of importance in the group.

The conversation continued with Layla pointing out that issues of religion and spirituality came up often enough with clients and that developing competence with different faith traditions might be clinically helpful. However, Jay pointed out,

> So maybe you listen to me because then you can learn something to use for your next Hindu client, not because you care about my comfort or well being. But when it's your holidays, I have to know about it because it's shoved down my throat. Isn't that what oppression is; not having a choice?

Jay's palpable pain held the group quiet and after a long moment, Kiara said, "I'm so sorry. I'm so sorry that I didn't treat you with respect or care. I feel so ashamed." Layla said gently,

> I appreciate that. Being a Black woman in this society can be an everyday struggle, and if you gain hope from your Church, it's easy to overlook how that might also be difficult for others who don't have that. You don't have to lose your joy in your Lord or give that up to make room for different perspectives.

Finally, Layla brought up the purpose of the group in the examination of DEI themes. She acknowledged that the focus on support, peer consultation and supervision were essential. As she pointed out, the group valued Marcia's expertise with play therapy, Carla's rapport with teenagers, Mike's knowledge about addictions, or the insight Josh/Jess had with sexuality and foster issues. However, when someone raised an issue about class, gender, or religion, or sexual orientation, the recipient often became defensive. By not being able to openly address DEI issues the group put much of its resources to assist each other in storage. Using the example of the young Black man who might be missing sessions because of access and income, she pointed out that the reactive nature of the discussion and its abrupt ending was unfortunate to a fuller understanding of the client. The race, class, and gender implications of this client being in the justice system never received the opportunity to be explored, potentially making the clinician's work more successful and effective.

In the end, the group thanked Layla for her efforts, and asked her if they could do some work and then perhaps invite her back after several months to provide a periodic check in on their process. She accepted, congratulated them and left after saying her farewells. Getting into her car, she unties her headscarf and takes it off to reveal her bald head, sighing in relief as she does so at the cool air. She is glad that the group did not end up asking her about being Muslim, since she had not wanted to distract them with her cancer diagnosis, but it came in very useful regardless to explore the issue of religion.

Conclusion

As can be seen from the above case discussion, the presence of DEI issues in groups are inescapable. One of the challenges for POs is to decide which elements to focus on since otherwise it can be quite distracting. A rule of thumb is that those aspects that appear to cause tension, are distracted from, or raise resistance or deflection are worthy of note, simply because the group is working so hard not to notice them. Often groups will argue that they don't want the group to get distracted by DEI issues from the "real" purpose of the group. However these are ultimately integral to the authenticity, safety, and meaningfulness of the group for each of its members. Refusing to deal with these issues is akin to carrying around a heavy bag full of resources as a weight and a burden, rather than using the resources to explore in greater depth and richness because the full range of human experience is now available. POs who do not notice and address these issues do their groups a profound disservice.

References

Amini, A. (2020). Social identity: A composite concept in social science research. *Journal of Social Science and Humanities Research, 8(3)*, 26–32.

Brown, N. W. (2018). *Psychoeducational groups: Process and practice.* Taylor & Francis.

Corbiere, M., & Amundson, N. E. (2007). Perceptions of the way of mattering by people with mental illness. *The Career Development Quarterly, 56*, 141–149.

DiAngelo, R. (2018). *White Fragility: Why it's so hard for White persons to talk about racism.* Beacon.

Nadal, K. L. (2013). *Processes of Dealing with Microaggressions.* Washington: American Psychological Association, pp. 152–173.

Romero, M. (2018). *Introducing Intersectionality.* Polity Press.

Schlossberg, N. K. (1989). Marginality and mattering: Key issues in building community. *New Directions for Student Services, 48*.

Stevens, F. L. & Abernethy, A. D. (2018) Neuroscience and racism: The power of groups for overcoming implicit bias. *International Journal of Group Psychotherapy, 68(4)*, 561–584, DOI: 10.1080/00207284.2017.1315583.

Sue, D. W. (2010). *Microaggressions in Everyday Life: Race, Gender, and Sexual Orientation.* Hoboken: John Wiley & Sons.

Sue, D. W., Alsaidi, S., Awad, M. N., Glaeser, E., Calle, C. Z. and Mendez, N. (2019). Disarming racial microaggressions: Microintervention strategies for targets, White allies, and bystanders. *American Psychologist, 74(1)*, 128–142.

Wong, G., Derthick, A., David, E. J. R., Saw, A., and Okazaki, S. (2014). The what, the why, and the how: A review of racial microaggressions research in psychology. *Race and Social Problems, 6*, 181–200.

U.S. Census (2020). About the topic of Race: Within Race. Retrieved from https://www.census.gov/topics/population/race/about.html September 29, 2022.

Sample Statement of Diversity, Inclusivity, Respect, and Social Justice

Every member in this group is valued. You enrich us all with your intersecting identities of race and ethnicity, culture, gender, religion, class, national origin, sexual and affectional orientation, ability, age, background, political affiliation, or any other identification. In this group, you have the right to determine your own identity. You have the right to be called by whatever name you wish and for that name to be pronounced correctly. You have the right to be referred to by whatever pronoun you identify. You have the right to adjust identifications at any point. It is important that you matter and belong as a member of this group, and if that is obstructed, the group as well as you are impoverished.

As the Process Observer, It is my intent to be culturally respectful and address current realities of the society we live in. Your suggestions are encouraged and appreciated. If there are aspects to my engagement that you experience as barriers to your inclusion, please contact me privately since there is no reprisal. If you feel uncomfortable connecting with me, please contact the group facilitator to discuss this.

I want to acknowledge that regardless of one's own identities (such as disability or socioeconomic status, age, or religion), individuals can be at various points along the cultural competence continuum in awareness, knowledge, and skills. While every member can share their own experiences, no member is ever presumed to speak as a representative of a particular identity or be expected to either educate or protect others from themselves.

Bibliography of DEI Work that May Be Helpful

Hays, P. A. (2016). *Addressing Cultural Complexities in Practice: Assessment, Diagnosis, and Therapy* (3rd Ed.). Washington, D.C.: American Psychological Association.
Kendi, I. X. (2019). *How to be an Antiracist* (1st Ed.). New York: One World.
Lambers, F. (2021). *Diversity in Clinical Practice. A Practical & Shame-Free Guide to Reducing Cultural Offenses & Repairing Cross-Cultural Relationships*. PESI Publishing Inc. Available at Amazon.
Menakem, R. (2017). *My Grandmother's Hands: Racialized Trauma and the Pathway to Mending our Hearts and Bodies*. Central Recovery Press.
Saad, L. F. (2020). *Me and White Supremacy: How to Recognize your Privilege, Combat Racism and Change the World*. Quercus. E-Book.
Boyd-Franklin, N. (2006). *Black Families in Therapy: Understanding the African American Experience*. Guilford.
Harvey, J. (2019). *Raising White Kids*. Abingdon.
Jun, H. (2018). *Social Justice, Multicultural Counseling, and Practice-beyond a Conventional Approach* (2nd. ed). Springer.
Jordan, Judith V. (2018). *Relational Cultural Therapy* (2nd Ed.). Alexandria, VA: APA.
Lipsky, L. van D. (2009). *Trauma Stewardship: An Everyday Guide to Caring for Self while Caring for Others*. Bernett-Kochler Publishing.
Loden, M. (1996). *Implementing Diversity*. Burr Ridge, IL: McGraw Hill Publishing.
Chugh, D. (2018). *The Person You Mean to Be: How Good People Fight Bias*. New York: HarperCollins.
DeGruy, J. (2017). *Post Traumatic Slave Syndrome: America's Legacy of Enduring Injury and Healing*. Author.
Di'Angelo, R. (2018). *White Fragility: Why it's so Hard for White Persons to Talk About Racism*. Beacon.
McGoldrick, M., Giordano, J. & Pearce, J. K. (Eds.) (2005). *Ethnicity & Family Therapy* (3rd Ed). New York: Guilford Press.
Rastogi, M. & Wieling, W. (2012). *Voices of Color: First Person Accounts of Ethnic Minority therapists*. Thousand Oaks: Sage.
Sue, D. W. & Spanierman, L. B. (2020). *Microaggressions in Everyday Life* (2nd Ed.). Wiley.
Sue, D. W. & Sue, D. (2016). *Counseling the Culturally Diverse* (7th Ed). Wiley & Sons.
Tatum, B. D. (2017). *Why Are All the Black Kids Sitting Together in the Cafeterias: And Other Conversations About Race*. 20th Anniversary Edition. Basic Books.
Walker, R. (2020). *The Unapologetic Guide to Black Mental Health: Navigate an Unequal System, Learn Tools for Emotional Wellness and Get the Help you Deserve*. New Harbinger.
Wilkerson, I. (2010). *The Warmth of Other Suns: The Epic Story of America's Great Migration*. Randall.
Wilkerson, I. (2020). *Caste: The Origins of our Discontents*. New York: Random House.

Websites of Interest

Asian Mental Health Project: To support Asian Americans to receive the mental health they need.
https://www.youtube.com/watch?v=1KKd5djWB34: Race, Health, and COVID-19 Panel discussion hosted by the Asian Mental Health Project and COVID-19 Group Therapy (5/20)

Dr. Jennifer Mullen hosts Decolonizing Therapy

Dr. Joy: Therapy for Black Girls podcast and blog

LatinX Therapy: Created by Adriana Alejandre, LMFT, this is a bilingual podcast and directory that relates to the Latinx community.

Brown Girl Therapy by Sahaj Kohli: Newsletter and Instagram

Queer Trans People of Color Mental Health on Facebook

We Are Native: A comprehensive health resource for Native Youth by Native Youth

Inclusive Therapist Directory: The directory includes a wealth of providers to reaffirm that "all identities in all bodies deserve equal access to quality, culturally responsive care." They achieve that by featuring therapists who are ready to work with patients at each of their possible intersections.

National Queer and Trans Therapist of Color Network: healing justice organization committed to transforming mental health for queer and trans people of color (QTPoC).

National American Indian and Alaska Native Mental Health Technology Transfer Center Network: They work with organizations and treatment practitioners to provide mental health services to American Indian and Alaska Native individuals, families, and tribal and urban Native communities to strengthen their capacity to deliver quality care.

Part III

Settings for Process Observation

Chapter 8

Utilizing Process Observation in Group Counseling and Group Psychotherapy

Maria T. Riva, PhD, University of Denver

This chapter describes the definition, utilization, and advantages of a group process observation (GPO) within sessions of group counseling and psychotherapy. For clarity, group therapy, psychotherapy, counseling, group treatment, and group work will be used interchangeably in this chapter. The focus will be on the complex group processes and group dynamics that occur in counseling and therapy groups rather than the more structured content that transpires in task and psychoeducational groups (see Chapters 9 and 10 in this book).

Some authors distinguish between group counseling and group psychotherapy. For example, Corey et al. (2018) define group counseling as having a "focus on interpersonal process and problem-solving strategies that stress conscious thoughts, feeling, and behaviors" (p. 9). The context here is usually that counseling groups deal with less severe problems. These authors define psychotherapy groups as those that "remediate psychological problems and interpersonal problems of living" with "group members who are often having acute or chronic mental or emotional problems that are evident by marked distress, impairment of functioning, or both" (p. 10). Here the focus might be unconscious material, long-standing, and deep-seated problems. Given the overlap in these two definitions, and the reality of what actually happens in these groups, this chapter will not distinguish between them.

Yet, counseling and psychotherapy groups are different from psychoeducational groups that Corey et al. (2018, p. 7) describe as those that "focus on developing members' cognitive, affective, and behavioral skills through a structured set of procedures within and across group meetings with the goal to provide members with targeted education" such as new parent training or assertiveness skills. Psychoeducational groups often are brief, structured, include didactic material, and use less group processing than group counseling and psychotherapy (see Chapter 9 for a discussion of Process Observation in psychoeducational groups).

Counseling and psychotherapy groups are complex, multidimensional, and frequently address intrapsychic and interpersonal dimensions. For these reasons, becoming adroit at recognizing and responding to group dynamics highlights how the use of Process Observation can be advantageous (Hogan et al., 2006). First, GPO can be instrumental in training new group leaders who observe, comment on, and receive supervision or mentoring on these multilevel group dynamics. Second, Process Observation also can include experienced group counseling and psychotherapy facilitators that provide discerning feedback to the group leader(s) to improve group functioning.

Although the role of training will be addressed in the initial portion of this chapter, the larger emphasis will be on the inclusion of an expert group facilitator as a Process Observer (PO). In both prongs, a person observes the group who is not a member of the group. Sometimes the observer sits in the room with the group but outside of the group circle, or behind a one-way mirror. It is important that the group members are informed and understand the purpose of the

DOI: 10.4324/9781003281955-11

observer process, requiring the group leader to be clear about the purpose and able to relate that purpose clearly to group members and the PO.

This chapter is one of the first to take an extensive look at GPO for counseling and psychotherapy groups. The literature is sparse with many unaddressed areas and different views about the observing process. Some of the areas that have not been defined include who is the observer, what is being observed, was there any training, what method does the observer use to deliver feedback to the leaders, what is the goal for the Process Observer and the group, and will the observer use a standardized form to structure the comments, to name just a few.

Certainly, besides group work, there are other uses for GPO such as those used in staff and board meetings or in school classrooms (Fazio-Griffith & Curry, 2008) to ensure that the process does not stall and the goal of the group continues to move forward. These nonclinical aspects of using a PO are beyond the focus of this chapter, although many of the concepts and strategies described generalize to other types of groups as well (please see Chapter 11 for Process Observations in nonclinical settings). This chapter will focus specifically on clinical groups that are therapeutic in nature and integrate counseling/psychotherapy as a main feature in the group processes.

Over 20 years ago, Gans et al. (2002) provided an excellent article on demonstration groups where members observe the group process that simulates therapy. Although this is different than GPO in an actual therapy group, many similarities exist. For example, these authors stated that group members must be thoroughly informed about the reason for the observer prior to the inclusion of this person and that the same standards apply for observers with regards to professionalism, confidentiality and ethical conduct as the group leader. Much like the leader, group POs are privy to intimate details of the lives of group members and without the Process Observer adhering to strict confidentiality and professionalism, group members are likely to be harmed.

Using Process Observation as a Way to Train Group Leaders

Yalom and Leszcz (2020), like Weiss and Rutan (2016), suggested that novice group leaders glean a tremendous benefit from watching a group facilitator at work. This type of process observing is an opportunity to provide training for the observer who is likely to facilitate a counseling group in the future. The role of a Process Observer can be a benefit to new group leaders who are able to view the dynamics of a group unfolding in real time especially when watching rather than responding is their primary task. Weiss and Rutan also pointed to the benefits of GPO by learning to tolerate the intense affect of counseling group members and "their own reactions, emotional and countertransference tendencies" (2016, p. 253) and to appreciate how to work in the here and now (Yalom & Leszcz, 2020).

Most avenues of training do not delve deeply enough into the intricacies of facilitating a group with the complex dynamics that occur in counseling/psychotherapy groups or allow group leaders-in-training to observe actual groups. The advantage of observation of an actual group is seeing these dynamics in action and noting the leader's responses to them and then the ensuing responses by members and leaders. The model of using GPO with actual groups could require having a group observer vigilantly observing and documenting their observations and process insights, (and questions for the leader) and then after the group is completed they could meet with the group leader to discuss their impressions and debrief the experience. Process Observation can be used as a prerequisite training to leading a group and folded into a group counseling course. The role of PO for an early group leader has the potential to decrease anxiety, increase confidence, and provide some comfort in the process of giving and receiving feedback from the leader.

It is a fair question to ask whether GPO enhances the learning process of novice group leaders, although it seems intuitive that under the appropriate circumstances this method should result in substantial gains for the early group leader-in-training. Unfortunately, criteria for conducting skillful POs and learning opportunities have not been studied. Several areas that seem necessary for success are: 1) for the novice group therapist to be aware of what the observation expectations are, 2) Be encouraged to comment on their observations and have those comments valued by the group leader even if they miss the mark, and 3) receive supervision on their comments and on the group process experience.

There are several ways to incorporate Process Observation in the training of novice group leaders. First, it can (and maybe more strongly "should") be integrated into a group course where students have the opportunity to learn directly from watching a live group, possibly behind a one-way mirror. Another feasible option is to have videotapes of actual groups that allow comments after stopping the tape at different sections of a session. Both of these methods include actual and not artificial groups. Although no research has compared student learning using actual vs simulated groups, it is likely that viewing the dynamics that occur in actual group counseling and psychotherapy sessions will be more congruent with the group experience that students-in-training will have once they graduate.

For any GPO method, the observer would need to have some understanding of group dynamics and group ethics prior to beginning any observation. This is even more true if incorporating a student in an actual group as it is unfolding. This preparation can be built into group counseling, ethics, and professional practice courses. This may be aided by watching videos of group work, reading group theory and research, and through role-plays, practicing the role of the group leader that includes the often complicated mosaic of group dynamics. Coursework is the predominant practice that often includes an experiential group as part of the class. Unfortunately, the number of group psychotherapy courses taken in graduate school has decreased, particularly in doctoral programs. Other methods of training group leaders often are leading or co-leading groups in field sites, and trainings provided by organizations such as the *Association for Specialists in Group Work* (ASGW) and the *American Group Psychotherapy Association* (AGPA).

Unfortunately, there is a lack of empirical information on best practices on training group leaders. A vital domain would be for observers to understand the key areas to direct their attention. The observer needs to understand group structure (e.g., norms, goals, expectations, etc.) and the purpose of the group and specified outcomes. For group counseling and psychotherapy, areas such as cohesion, conflict, quality of the alliance, ruptures, and feedback might be specific targets for observation. One strategy would be for observers-in-training to use a standardized or structured observation method to help center their observations around the critical aspects of the group dynamics.

While observing the group dynamics, group leaders-in-training generally make written observations that are then discussed with the group leader, typically after the completion of the group session. Many of the components of Process Observation are flexible depending on the type of group, length, goal, and so on. Yalom and Leszcz (2020) stated "the postmeeting discussion is an absolute necessity in training and there is no better time for the group leaders/teachers to meet with the student observers than immediately after the meeting" (p. 643).

It goes without saying that the group leader needs to encourage comments without judgment or defensiveness towards the PO who is providing self-disclosure of their perceptions. Yalom and Leszcz (2020) noted that self-disclosures should not be met with criticism. The goal is to provide opportunities for future group leaders to intently observe, identify, and articulate the process components that are occurring in the group.

In summary, GPO can be an excellent supplementary component in the training of early or future group leaders. If included in all or many of the group sessions, prospective group facilitators can observe the responses of group members and group leaders in actual counseling and therapy groups across time. The dynamics in psychotherapy groups often move quickly, are intense, and stray off topic. POs can begin to identify these elements, notice how the group leader reacts and responds to them, and understand the essence of group dynamics and group leadership on a deeper level. (Please see Chapter 12 for additional information about PO in clinical training.)

Process Observation to Increase Leader and Group Effectiveness in Counseling Groups

A second objective for using GPO is to increase the effectiveness of group counseling and psychotherapy by having a person with group expertise witness the dynamics and comment on them to the leader in real time, after the group session has ended, or while watching a videotape of the group meeting. One strength of GPO is similar to a real-time consultation for the group leader. In-session comments may breakup the flow of the group, yet brief interjections from the expert Process Observer such as "you may want to redirect the group to the here and now," "there seems to be a lot of eye rolling," "the group is circling this topic," or (to the leader) "your comment seemed to confuse several members" could immediately address a dynamic that is causing the group to stall.

Waiting until after the group session has ended may be a preferred strategy when needing a longer discussion between the group leader and the PO. For example, the observer might notice the potential for favoritism of a member by the leader, or that the leader is not waiting long enough for group members to respond to process comments from the leader such as "What does the group think?" or observing that the leader seems to be irritated at the lack of progress being made by the group. At either time-point, the group leader will need to be open, nondefensive, curious, and willing to consider the feedback given by the observer. If occurring within the group meeting, how the leader receives and integrates the process comments could serve as a model for group members to receive feedback.

One of the most important variables in group psychotherapy is cohesion. Forsyth (2021) stated that "the concept of cohesion is central to understanding group and group processes, and recent research has yielded substantial advances in understanding the nature, the sources, and the consequences of this key group-level process" (p. 213). In highlighting a number of possible benefits of incorporating observers as raters of therapeutic process, Luong et al. (2022) noted that "observers may be better placed to capture difficulties within therapy relationships" (p. 101). These authors conducted a study to assess the correlation between group member and observer ratings on cohesion and found that while "both client and observer-rated group cohesion independently predicted treatment outcomes" (p. 101), client and observer rating of cohesion were unrelated to each other, suggesting that the two groups appeared to be assessing different aspects of cohesion and that both may be beneficial (p. 109). In addition, a recent study by Dolgan et al. (2020) found that group leaders and group members did not agree on the level of cohesion in their groups with leaders underestimating the view of group members. The likely variance in member–leader perspectives for many different variables appears to be one potential benefit for an unbiased Process Observer to assess the agreement/disagreement between group facilitators and group members on important elements.

Another potential vital group dynamic for a PO's attention could be looking at ruptures and repairs in group psychotherapy. Although ruptures and repairs have been studied in individual psychotherapy, there has been little attention paid to the impact in group psychotherapy (Marmarosh, 2021). "Identifying alliance ruptures and repairing them during treatment is linked to greater treatment success" (Eubanks et al., 2018). Marmarosh (2021) stated that "the level of experience, empathy, personality, and attachment style of the leader will likely influence the leader's capacity to identify ruptures and strategies for repair" (p. 1). GPO can also help as the group expert is a less biased observer, a step removed from group membership. The alliance between the group leader and group members is a fundamental element in whether there will be positive outcomes in group counseling and group psychotherapy. Most research concerning the alliance between the group members and the group leader has relied on responses from the group members or the group leader. Ardito and Rabellino (2011) pointed to an increasing call among group researchers who study process-outcome variables to include neutral independent observers to assess relationships in group therapy. Although the methods of observation, including the specific dynamics of focus are undefined, it does seem prudent to attend to those elements that are most critical and ones related to positive group outcomes.

Racial microaggressions are common in group counseling and psychotherapy. Sue et al. (2007) defined racial microaggressions as "brief and commonplace daily verbal, behavioral, or environmental indignities, whether intentional or unintentional, that communicate hostile, derogatory, or negative racial slights and insults toward people of color" (p.271). Sue et al. (2007) stated that they are often subtle, automatic and the perpetrator is often unaware of their damaging communication. Since microaggressions are often indirect, subtle, and instantaneous, the group leader can easily be caught off guard by a comment or a nonverbal gesture, or miss the interaction entirely. The PO also can notice when the microaggression comes from the group leader such as misgendering a group member after being corrected several times, expecting a group member to represent their culture by teaching other group members what is it like to be from that cultural group, or making statements that minimize their hurtful comments by saying "I am not racist" or "that was a joke."

In a recent study that looked at microaggressions in group supervision, more than half of the microaggressions reported by the supervisees were generated by the group leader (Kaufman & Riva, 2022). Similarly, these authors found that most of the microaggressions went unaddressed.

Ruptures are not resolved effortlessly or quickly although some authors see the repair process as therapeutic in providing examples of how conflicts can be resolved or at least addressed differently than those that occurred in members' childhood. This is similar to the Yalom and Leszcz (2020) description of the therapeutic factor of the recapitulation of the primary family experience. In a recent case study by Miles et al. (2021), the authors used the *Rupture Resolution Rating System (3RS)* to code ruptures and repairs. They found that ruptures in group counseling and psychotherapy were mostly the withdrawal type, while one fourth of them were the confrontational type with most of the repairs imitated by the group leader. This type of coding system may benefit POs when needing to provide specific, concrete, and behavioral examples to the group leader.

POs can play an essential role in the rupture and repair process as they unfold in actual group counseling and psychotherapy sessions. Skilled Process Observers can identify the complex and multilayered dynamics that result in a rupture that are at times difficult for the group leader to see all of the components that can occur in a group, especially if several members of a group are involved in the rupture. At the time of the rupture, it might be enough for a PO to say, "it seems like something just happened that caused several group members to respond with strong feelings."

There are many other impacts in group dynamics where a PO may assist in helping the group move forward. Some concern verbal attacks on a group member or the leader, multiple absences by a member, members who talk about others in the group on social media, group members who monopolize the group time, etc. are all ripe for intervention from an unbiased observer. One common difficulty in group psychotherapy is silence in the group by a single member or multiple members. The vignette that follows demonstrates how an experienced group leader who is assigned to the role of Process Observer can intervene when group members are quiet and the reason for the silence is unknown.

Vignette

A psychotherapy group is meeting for the 17th session of a 20-week psychotherapy group. An experienced group facilitator, Angela, was asked by the group leader to provide comments to this group given that the leader stated that "the group feels stuck and the members continue to be dependent on me." The group leader also wants to make sure to provide a beneficial termination to the group members, many of them having felt abandoned by a parent. Angela is sitting approximately ten feet outside of the group to clearly demarcate that she is not a group member. She has been in every group since the 10th week when the group leader was concerned about the few number of sessions left and the "lack of progress." At that time the group members were prepared for the inclusion of a PO to help the leader provide the members with the best care possible.

The goal of the psychotherapy group is to help members improve their relationships in general, as group members have had difficulty with trusting others which has generalized to the leader and the other members. Angela notes that the leader is providing accurate and helpful process comments such as "The group today seem really low energy and I wonder what is happening." After the comment, there is a long pause from the group members when one person states "I am really exhausted and do not feel like talking today." Several of the eight group members state that they "totally agree" with the exhausted member. One member says, "maybe we can end early today as we are not getting anything done," and another member states, "but I paid a lot of money to be at this group." Other members remain quiet.

Angela is observing and noting that the group members seem rather uncomfortable and looking down, fidgeting with their hands, and remaining silent. She also notices that the group leader is grimacing and states "Help me understand what you are all thinking about right now" to which the member restates that they are tired and they do not want to work today. Angela has written down several observations such as the group seems to have gotten quiet, especially when the group leader stated that there were only three more sessions left after this one, and Angela remembered that in the last session several members provided very personal information about trauma they experienced in their childhood. Angela wonders if this group needs to talk about their fears and other intense feelings they may be having about termination, but are held back by thinking that it is too late for the group to do any more work since there are only three more sessions left.

Angela also is aware that the group leader may also be having strong feelings about termination, which could be causing the leader to have ambivalent feelings. Termination can be as hard for group leaders as it is for group members "since powerful experiences are often shared and strong relationships are built during group" (Riva & Smith, 2018, p. 245). Angela decides to make a short comment to the group leader, saying "It seems like people may be having lots of feeling about ending the group." "It seems like a good idea to discuss endings." The leader considers the feedback from Angela and states, "yes, that is a good idea. Let's take today's session to talk about your feelings about ending the group."

The group members continue to be quiet, yet the leader is confident that the silence has strong meaning about termination, abandonment, trusting the leader, and fear they will no longer have the group as support. The group does begin to share their anger, sadness, and fear about the ending of the group. Angela meets with the group leader after the group to underscore the leader's effective processing and to talk about plans the leader has contemplated for the next three sessions. Angela comes to the last three sessions. She writes comments down during each of the sessions and shares them with the leader after each session has ended. At times group leaders may think they are not getting enough done if they spend four sessions discussing termination. Angela reminds the group leader that the final stage of the group "can offer the members an experience with a healthy ending to a relationship which will be therapeutically important because of their past experiences with problematic loss and abandonment" (Riva & Smith, 2018, p. 246).

The group leader and Angela discuss some of the potential consideration in the termination process. For example, Smith et al. (2007) stated that "group leaders need to acknowledge, and even predict that some members may find it easier to leave group before the scheduled ending" (p. 68). Some group members may request additional sessions feeling disappointed that group was too short, that the group sessions did not address all of their concerns, that they had just begun to address their problems, or the group is abandoning them. The group leader and Angela also discuss safety plans for the members after group has ended.

Some Reflections on the Vignette

This GPO was beneficial because the leader had a positive relationship with the observer and was able to react to brief comments to move the group forward. The observation process occurred over several weeks allowing the group members to become more comfortable with the observer. The observer made short and impactful comments rather than longer instructions that would have distracted from the group process, inserted the PO into the group, and possibly confused the group members as to who was the "group leader." The PO's suggestions were neutral and not critical. Although not addressed in this vignette, a short evaluation of the group could be included and with a question that asks about the benefit of the Process Observation.

Conclusion

This chapter reviewed how Process Observation could be used in both training and in providing comments to group leaders during or after an actual group to help create a successful group that does not get bogged down in the many potential quagmires that can occur in group counseling and psychotherapy. Very little has been written about process observation for counseling and psychotherapy groups, which are groups that are complex, multidimensional, and rely heavily on group process. POs seem like an excellent choice for these types of groups.

This chapter also discussed group leaders-in-training who will benefit from observation and the opportunity to check out their perceptions with a group leader similar to supervision. Since so much of group work consists of awareness, knowledge, and skills, Process Observation can serve as an apprenticeship model to learn how to be aware of group dynamics in the moment, develop knowledge interpreting these observations, and acquire facilitation skills of these dynamics by watching experienced group leaders. The complexity of psychotherapy and counseling groups are experienced first-hand by this method, without the consequences of inexperienced group leaders being thrust into a leadership role underprepared.

POs have a unique role in group psychotherapy which could be described as consultation in-the-moment for those groups led by an experienced group leader who may need a person who is not enmeshed in the group to help with clarity. It is often said that group leadership is a dynamic and continuous process as new learning can take place in every group that is led. For this, Process Observation seems prime, yet group leaders will need to be open to feedback and curious about how their leadership is seen by another experienced leader. This is an element of vulnerability and an aspect of being willing to submit themselves and their skills for examination, which can be difficult though necessary. Ultimately, increasing the use of Process Observation in group psychotherapy and counseling could lead to more substantial training and better group outcomes.

References

Ardito, R.B., & Rabellino, D. (2011) Therapeutic alliance and outcome of psychotherapy: History excursus measurement, and prospect for research. *Frontiers in Psychology*, *2*, 270.

Corey, M.S., Corey, G., & Corey, C. (2018). *Groups: Process and Practice* (10th ed.). Boston, MA: Cengate.

Dolgin, R., Riva, M.T., & Owen, J. (2020). Clinical congruence of cohesion in group psychotherapy. *Professional Psychology: Research and Practice*, *51*(6), 598–605.

Eubanks, C.F., Muran, J.C., & Safran, J.D. (2018). Alliance rupture repair: A meta-analysis. *Psychotherapy*, *55*(4), 508. https://doi.org/10.1037/pst0000185

Fazio-Griffith, L. & Curry, J.R. (2008). Professional school counselors as process observers in the classroom: Collaboration with classroom teachers. *Journal of School Counseling*, *6*(20).

Forsyth, D.R. (2021). Recent advances in the study of group cohesion. *Group Dynamics: Theory, Research, and Practice*, *25*(3), 13–228.

Gans, J., Rutan, J., & Lape, E. (2002). The demonstration group. A tool for observing group process and leadership style. *International Journal of Group Psychotherapy*, *52*, 233–252.

Hogan, C., Harris, R.S., & Cassidy, J.M. (2006). The impact of process observers on interpersonal group therapy. *Journal of College Student Psychotherapy*, *21*, 21–32.

Kaufman, G., & Riva, M.T. (2022). *The Impact of Microaggressions on Group Supervision Dynamics*, Poster presented at the American Psychological Association Conference, Minneapolis, MN.

Luong, H.K., Drummond, S.P.A., & Norton, P.L. (2022). Can you see what I see? A comparison of client and observer perspectives of the alliance and group cohesion in CBT, *Cognitive Behaviour Therapy*, *51*(2), 100–113.

Marmarosh, C. (2021). Rupture and repairs in group psychotherapy, Introduction to the Special Issue. *Group Dynamics: Theory, Research, and Practice*, *25*(1), 1–12.

Miles, J.R., Anders, C., Kivlighan, D.M. III, & Platt, A.A.B. (2021). Cultural ruptures: Addressing microaggressions in group theory. *Group Dynamics: Theory, Research, and Practice*, *25*(1), 74–88.

Riva, M.T., & Smith, R.D. (2018). Termination in group therapy: The neglected stage. In D. Viers (Ed.) *The Group Therapist's Notebook* (2nd ed., pp. 245–253). New York, NY: Routledge.

Smith, R.D., Riva, M.T., & Rings, J.A (2007). Activities for termination. In D. Viers (Ed.) *The group therapist's notebook: Homework, handouts, and activities for use in psychotherapy* (pp. 67–74). New York, NY: Routledge.

Sue, D.W., Capodilupo, C.M., Torino, G.C., Bucceri, J.M., Holder, A.M.B., Nadal, K.L., & Esquilin, M. (2007). Racial microaggressions in everyday life: Implications for clinical practice, *American Psychologist*, *62*(4), 271–286. DOI:10.1037/0003–066X.62.4.271.

Weiss, A.C., & Rutan, S.J. (2016). The benefits of group therapy observation for therapists-in-training. *International Journal of Group Psychotherapy*, *66*(2), 246–260.

Yalom, I.D., & Leszcz, M. (2020). *The theory and practice of group psychotherapy* (6th ed.). Basic Books.

Chapter 9

Process Observation in Psychoeducation Groups

Theresa A. Coogan, Ph.D., Raleigh, NC

Chris Godwin, Ph.D., Campbell University

Sam Steen, Ph.D., George Mason University

Process Observation in Psychoeducation Groups

Process Observers (POs) of psychoeducation groups can play an important role for leaders by helping the leader focus on the topic of the group as well as on the dynamics and interactions of the group as a whole. POs are in a position to observe group dynamics to assess all factors while they are unfolding, and offer feedback for the group leader and group members' consideration. Psychoeducation groups by design involve explicit opportunities for intra- and interpersonal reflection. Expanding beyond the scope common within task groups, psychoeducation groups invite a deeper level of introspection and guided reflection through member dialogue. Task groups center on a specific task or purpose for the group, which may result in more concrete outcomes. The outcome(s) of psychoeducation groups may be harder to see concretely as the growth and development that occurs, beginning as early as the first session informs the thoughts, feelings, or behaviors of each individual member and the entire group throughout every phase of the psychoeducation group process. Both groups intentionally recognize and understand how aspects of each member in the group inform and influence the overall group dynamics. These aspects affect group productivity and effectiveness. A PO of a psychoeducation group is primed to observe, monitor, and address the naturally changing dimensions of dynamics, behaviors, and personalities as topics of the group are discussed, naturally creating changes observed in member-to-member interactions and communication styles.

POs offer clarity to a group or group leader by understanding that "processing" is described as spending time discussing thoughts, feelings, and ideas that result from different experiences unfolding in a group session. These thoughts, feelings, and ideas might go unaddressed or unnoticed without a PO who is intentionally monitoring these pieces throughout a group. They have the potential to influence the group dynamics and group experiences in adaptive or maladaptive ways. Mindful of the myriad of information, dynamics, and cues occuring every second in a group, even the most seasoned group leaders can miss processing opportunities. A group leader with a PO can leverage the PO's neutral perspective to identify situations and opportunities in every group session from the beginning to the end. The PO can also facilitate processing the reflections, awareness, and insights for the group and its members by highlighting what is occurring or has occurred within a group experience.

Processing as a tool is also useful for group leaders outside of the "live" group experience. Group leaders use processing to examine and reflect on the group at various stages of development. A PO can aid a group leader with this effort as well by offering perspectives and insights grounded in both learning and reflecting whereas the leader may have a narrower focus on the stated goals and objectives of the psychoeducation group. Remember, the role any person has in a situation or a group will shape and influence how they view, understand, and interpret

DOI: 10.4324/9781003281955-12

information and experiences while they remain in that role. This is not a value judgment, rather, a contextual perspective to be mindful of as we consider a key aspect of processing experiences for ourselves and with others. For example, the leader may be driven by a motivation to see the goals of the group accomplished regardless of the expense to interpersonal dynamics or rapport. A leader may be mandated to lead a group that has goals or objectives that conflict or challenge their own point of view that they may not yet have reached a level of awareness about or resolution, and thus, by leading the group they are exerting their personal influence on a group or its outcomes. The PO is a tool and supportive resource to assist both a group leader and the group as a whole by facilitating processes, monitoring and observing the interactions of members and leaders, and identifying and tracking complexities associated with dynamic group experiences. Process Observations enhance the work that is occurring in session by offering insight on patterns in others and the various interactions more easily than the leaders or members may be able to. Additionally, Process Observations can energize and give useful information affecting intra- or interpersonal awareness and growth to those involved.

Learning and Growing in Psychoeducation Groups

Psychoeducation groups provide a platform for members to actively and dynamically engage in a myriad of developmentally appropriate strategies that highlight and challenge the adaptive growth of interpersonal and intrapersonal awareness. Coogan and Steen (2022) posit "most psychoeducation groups provide continual opportunities for individual members, as well as the group as a unit, to learn, reflect, and make meaning from their experiences in the group" (p. 21). In other words, the group environment and interactive dynamics innate to group work helps the members explore the topic at hand and provide at least one plan to guide next action steps in a way that is unlikely to be experienced or gleaned from an individual or solo effort.

During the psychoeducation group experience, the group offers tools and skills necessary for members to be able to navigate a similar situation in the future. While the experiences that have occurred in the past are not to be discounted, acknowledging how it is that those experiences lead to the immediate present for each member of the group, how they are all in the present group together, is essential. This is often referred to as focusing the group and members in the "here-and-now." Group leaders strive to maintain this through the facilitation of the group and POs are in an essential role to observe the ebbs and flows of the focus of the group and individual members. POs may also see patterns emerge from the group or members around specific topics and when focus might shift to the past, present, or future. Often, the shift in focus and time-orientation is a subtle or unconscious shift for a member or the group. POs in their role can effectively "pause" the group to reassess and consider all elements influencing and affecting the group's progress and dynamics. A major question is how can we focus and enhance the present experience while appreciating and learning from our past, and informing our future in healthy and adaptive ways? Psychoeducation groups will equip members with skills of reflection, introspection, and interpersonal communication to help answer this question. POs can prompt these questions through observations of the group dynamics and efficiencies observed.

Generally, there can be different levels of processing that can occur including exploring the patterns such as frequency and length of salient interactions, choices members make about whom to interact with, and triggers that could emerge from various member and leader interactions (Trotzer, 1979). A PO within a psychoeducation group can offer important feedback that consistently sheds light on themes that may hinder or fuel successful outcomes.

Basic steps suggested by scholars as a useful framework within a session or throughout the life of a group include, but are not limited to, defining the PO's role, giving and receiving feedback, and offering and soliciting reflections on goals (Johnson & Johnson, 2017). Within a psychoeducation group, many of the same steps will also be useful to guiding the process and experience.

Psychoeducation groups may find it helpful to give extra attention to concrete behaviors and interactions between and among group members when giving and receiving feedback as well as conducting unobtrusive observations. Recall our earlier discussion highlighting a feature of psychoeducation groups as being a forum to practice developmentally appropriate strategies around interpersonal and intrapersonal growth and awareness. Focusing on feedback based on observed concrete behaviors and specific interactions help to facilitate insights and awareness linked to process and/or content as a part of a group process. Additionally, when a PO delivers the feedback, they are modeling how to give feedback to a member or the group, which invites each member to learn and grow. Respecting how every exchange in a group, especially a psychoeducation group, is an opportunity and invitation to explore the process or content exchanged between and among members is a central element of a PO's role in these groups especially.

Let's explore how a PO can zero in on these specific aspects of members and the group to support their contributions to a psychoeducation group process.

Identifying Empathy Among Members in Psychoeducation Groups

A very well recognized contributor to the field of counseling and psychotherapy is Dr. Carl Rogers. He pioneered person-centered therapy in the 1940s that focused on individual counseling and psychotherapy as the delivery mode. In the 1970s, Dr. Rogers expanded to intentionally engage group process and group psychotherapy demonstrating the flexibility and versatility of his foundational constructs grounding the person-centered therapy approach. At the core, there are three key constructs to guide the person-centered therapy work. These constructs are **empathy**, **unconditional positive regard**, and **congruence**. For decades, these fundamentals have been used in individual and group counseling and adapted to explore and seek to understand perspectives from almost any situation imaginable. Dr. Rogers explained how a constructive change outcome is influenced by high levels of empathy, unconditional positive regard, and congruence (Rogers, 1957).

The practical application definition of person-centered therapy key constructs:

Empathy: An intentional choice made by the counselor/therapist to seek to understand, hear, and perceive from the client's perspective without taking on ownership, changing, fixing, or otherwise adding their own subjective judgment. Rogers (1957) described how the counselor/therapist seeks to "sense the client's anger, fear, or confusion as if it were your own, yet without your own anger, fear, or confusion getting bound up in it" (p. 99). Put into action, Rogers offered a quote from a client who described in their own words how powerful and effective a counselor/therapist's empathy can be to the therapeutic process. "Every now and again, with me in a tangle of thought and feeling, screwed up in a web of mutually divergent lines of movement, with impulses from different parts of me, and me feeling the feeling of its being all too much and suchlike—then whomp, just like a sunbeam thrusting its way through cloudbanks and tangles of foliage to spread a circle of light on a tangle of forest paths, came some comment from you. [It was] clarity, even disentanglement, an additional twist to the picture, a putting in place. Then the consequence—the sense of moving on, the relaxation. These were sunbeams" (Rogers, 1957, p. 99).

Unconditional Positive Regard: Is a judgment and value-free space in the relationship between the client and the counselor/therapist given by the counselor/therapist. There are no conditions of acceptance, meaning, *if* you say, do, feel —, *then* I will accept, like, respect, appreciate, etc. you. The foundation of this construct is caring for another soul at the basic level of being a fellow human. It recognizes that the only person who can and will ever truly know and understand a full story of another's situation, life, context is that person living it. It accepts the role of the counselor/therapist is not to take ownership of the situation the client is experiencing as that will not support or guide the client to constructive change. Rather, the counselor/therapist can create the space and relationship where the client is able to embrace a value-neutral space to explore, consider, and decide their growth and change path for themselves. Rogers (1957) described "experiencing a warm acceptance of each aspect of the client's experience as being a part of that client" (p. 98). Rogers (1957) offers the following examples of statements a counselor/therapist who practices this construct might say when asked about a client: "…I feel no revulsion at anything the client says; I feel neither approval nor disapproval of the client and his statements—simply acceptance; I feel warmly toward the client toward his weaknesses and problems as well as his potentialities; I am not inclined to pass. judgment on what the client tells me; and/or, I like the client" (p. 98).

Congruence: There is alignment between what the Client perceives and the reality of the actual situation or event. Rogers (1957) noted, "When the individual has no awareness of such incongruence in himself, then he is merely vulnerable to the possibility of anxiety and disorganization" (p. 97). Similarly, there is an expectation of the Counselor/Therapist's intentional efforts to be fully engaged and aligned with the client as an essential element to create, build, and maintain a healthy and productive working relationship. As Rogers (1957) described, for constructive personality change to occur, one of the key requirements is that "two persons are in psychological contact… or integrated in the relationship" (p. 96). The counselor/therapist accomplishes this by being present and aware of their thoughts and feelings "live in the moment" in honest genuine reflection.

Consider the specific construct of empathy as one example. **Empathy** can be defined as the deeper comprehension of another person(s) subjective experiences (Meier & Davis, 2019). A common misconception of empathy is that it is agreement with another person, or intentional efforts to relate or share in the exact experiences along with the person(s). These actions may be well intended and perhaps provide a temporary sense of support to a person(s) in crisis, unfortunately, they do not invite the self-reflection, self-awareness, and ultimate growth and development that can be an outcome of empathy. Further, it is important to note that one's experience of giving or receiving empathy may very well not match another, especially along the continuum of cultural identity. For example, East Asian and Western cultural influences on empathy differ when comparing personal distress and empathic concern in adolescents (Chung, et al., 2010)

Exploring and attending to the construct of empathy has direct relevance for psychoeducation groups as well as POs. POs are able to share observations and feedback about examples of empathy that occurred in a group "live" or were demonstrated through the comments offered by a member about an external situation they may have experienced. The awareness and acceptance of empathic behaviors towards oneself and others can have a larger impact on the group dynamics. It can also empower other members in the group to explore feelings and see opportunities for growth versus advice-giving and ruminating by retelling a story with no true active reflection to guide meaningful change occurring. What's more, practicing empathetic behaviors and interactions with others in a psychoeducation group provides an invaluable safe space for learning that has tremendous implications for socializing interpersonal skills outside of the group.

There is a common saying in counseling and therapy groups: "what is said in the group stays in group; what is learned in group leaves group." Learning empathy towards self and others and practicing these skills to be aware of how to think, feel, and behave with intentional empathy towards self and others will inform relationships and dynamics of any individuals' life outside of the group. POs are encouraged to intentionally and mindfully model empathetic skills and interpersonal interactions by continuously focusing on feelings as they provide feedback or comments to a member or the group. By focusing on feelings observed, the receiver(s) is invited to consider the information through that lens, which maintains a focus on a deeper exploration of the feelings and subjective experiences by the person(s). POs offer clarity to a group or group leader by understanding that "processing" is described as spending time discussing thoughts, feelings, and ideas that result from different experiences unfolding in a group session. Within a psychoeducation group, the PO's role allows them to observe, monitor, and address the naturally changing dimensions of dynamics, behaviors, and personalities as the natural flow of the group occurs discussing various topics. The PO understands a natural product of the group experience is the opportunity for and the occurrence of changes observed in member-to-member interactions and communication styles along with overall growth of the group as a unit.

Case Study

Let's look at a scenario of what a PO might say in a group to invite awareness and the practice of empathy.

Casey, a 31-year old Caucasian heterosexual female, is a group leader of a psychoeducation group for a fast-growing information technology company that is focused on how to establish, maintain, and retain healthy, active, and energetic employees. Casey is going to lead a six session group with eight new employees in middle-management level positions who will have some administrative responsibilities aligned with the company's continued aggressive growth objectives. Casey is not a licensed or trained counselor, and sees an opportunity to collaborate with a trained counselor when preparing and leading these groups. Casey connects with a local counseling service that provides consultation to companies and businesses in a way that blends organizational psychology with group and individual counseling. Alleigh, a 42-year old biracial heterosexual female, is a licensed clinical mental health counselor with experience in group counseling and organizational psychology with the local counseling service and takes on the role of the PO collaborating with Casey.

In their second session, Casey starts the group with a prompt inviting a reflection and recap on the topics discussed and takeaway points of learning from the first session. This includes how these new employees had been settling into their new roles at the company. Quickly, the group's energy shifts from calm and happy to anxious. This growing anxious energy specifically focuses on comments and experiences the members have had that illustrate how it is common for most people to be overwhelmed when transitioning into a new position. The pressures of task completions, not yet having a rhythm to completing their work, acknowledging a lot of processes, practices, and people have not yet been identified were all quickly themes members were expressing. While there was a sense of normalizing and validating that the members were all having shared experiences and they were not alone in the transitional phase, the group dynamics were forming a competitive arena among the members. The energy and comments shared by one member almost seem to feed on each other where a "one-upping" of the previous member sharing was being observed by the PO. The PO was noticing how each member appeared to be trying to convince the group (and perhaps themselves) that the reason why they were able and expected to be overwhelmed was because of how extraordinarily busy each individual was. It appeared a sense of "if i'm not overwhelmed and busy, i'm not doing it right" was forming in the group as an unspoken theme that was becoming counterproductive to the goals Casey had set for the group and this specific session.

In their preparations before the sessions started, Alleigh asked Casey what non-verbal indication they would like to use between themselves if Casey needed or wanted Alleigh to offer a Process Observation. The goal here was to provide a space for Casey, as the group leader, to choose when to engage the PO while knowing that support was always available to access in a non-disruptive way to what might be happening in the moment of the group. They agreed that it would be a physical gesture where Casey would put her right hand on her right knee and hold it there as the physical sign for Alleigh to step in at that moment or a moment appropriate as soon as possible to offer a Process Observation and help guide the group back to Casey to continue leading.

To ensure the physical space contributed to group success, the group was set up in the room in a circle that had an opening space at one end equivalent to the distance of space that another seat might fill if there was another chair in the circle. Alleigh's chair and table area would be outside of the group's physical circle but close enough to be able to observe, thus emphasizing the relationship of the PO to the group as a whole. Alleigh benefits from the additional open space for viewing the group and Casey would sit on the opposite side of the circle facing Alleigh. This way, Alleigh always has an unobstructed and clear line of sight to Casey.

Alleigh, seeing Casey's hand on her knee, cleared her throat first and then spoke up raising her voice loud enough to be able to grab the attention of the other members who were fully engaged in the task-oriented conversation at this point. This brief, yet important, shift in who was speaking and the change in tone as well as volume was sufficient to pause the energy flow that had been building momentum up to that point. As a PO, Alleigh was able to offer observations to the group about how the energy and engagement of the group had shifted from the first weeks' session and took a quick and steep incline in this session right now in the here-and-now to begin this group. In addition to a general observation about the group dynamics, Alleigh offered a concrete comment to the group

> *As the group shifted the topic of conversation into the budget review, and specifically began discussing the requirement to cut costs by 20% by the end of the quarter, I sensed increases in anxiety about the present and future. I wonder how this observation resonates with each member and if you might share with each other more about how transitioning into a new role in a fast-paced environment is affecting you all now. I suspect there may be more shared feelings and experiences in the group between and amongst you.*

Casey as the group leader was able to connect to that observation comment and redirect the group by offering,

I wonder if we can identify and focus our conversation in this group on the specific feelings, thoughts, or behavior elements that are meaningful to each of us as we recognize that starting a new position is hard work! Lets first break into dyads and share in pairs for five minutes, and then come back to the group with a sense of what you want to share.

With Casey demonstrating engagement in the leader role, Alleigh as the PO can apply silence at this point and shift into observing how members received the feedback and the outcomes of the invitations offered to refocus the conversation in the group. In many situations, members might begin a conversation about this feedback among the group sharing feelings and reactions from their personal subjective experiences based on the here-and-now. In this situation, the group leader offered a concrete invitation to guide this type of reflective conversation based on the goals of the group. Given the unease the group had already expressed, the breaking into pairs allows the members to share safely, and then risk larger sharing with greater authenticity. As is helpful to the group leader, the PO can assist with facilitating the conversation as needed. In this example, both the PO and group leader collaborated on shifting the group energy by engaging the group in a non-judgmental and fully accepting way, acknowledging feelings observed based on comments and interpersonal exchanges between and among members. They modeled empathy. The invitation offered by the group leader, Casey, to redirect the conversation invites the members to reflect and dialogue with each other to practice empathy skills. We also observed how the goals of the group were highlighted while normalizing statements were made reminding everyone how change and transition can be a complex process for every person. It might be that Casey might use self disclosure of how difficult she experienced her transition to be, so that the leader is perceived as allowing vulnerability.We see how the role of the PO was to inform the group process, offer a relevant and timely observation, and set the group leader up to smoothly continue the dialogue in their role as leader. Either in the group or in a one-on-one debrief after group with the leader, the PO can offer more insights and observations as to how the dynamics of the group may have been affected after the feedback was shared.

Communication Styles Among Members Observed in Psychoeducation Groups

As we have seen, psychoeducation groups have the opportunity to become rich with complexities as each member increases awareness, understanding, and growth about themselves and their interactions with others as a natural course in any psychoeducation group process. One of the foundational ways group leaders and POs can help illuminate these complexities as well as successful developments are by observing and offering constructive feedback regarding communication styles. This includes how members speak about and to themselves as well as how they speak about and with other members in the group. Often in groups, the behaviors and interpersonal relationship dynamics observed mirror other relationships the person has with one or more people in their lives separate and distinct from the psychoeducation group experience. Thus, group leaders and POs intentionally focusing on communication styles as a concrete way of observing intra- and interpersonal dynamics in the group has the potential for impacting the members in and out of the group. As we continue, we are mindful that most of the information presented is through the lens of western cultural standards and norms and lacks explicit discussions on the impact of race, gender, class, gender expression, spirituality, and so forth concerning communication in particular. We encourage the reader to expand on this information as they see fit using their own intersections of identities to make meaning.

Table 9.1 Categories of Communication Style

PASSIVE • Low openness of communication with others • High consideration of others • Emotionally dishonest and indirect • "I lose, You win" • Self-denying and blaming.	**ASSERTIVE** • High openness of communication with others • High consideration of others • Appropriately honest and direct • "I win, You win" • Self-enhancing, self-confident, and empathetic to emotions of all involved.
PASSIVE-AGGRESSIVE • Low openness of communication with others • Low consideration of others • Emotionally dishonest and indirect • "I lose, You lose" • Self-denying at first; self-enhancing later at the expense of others.	**AGGRESSIVE** • High openness of communication with others • Low consideration of others • Inappropriately honest and direct • "I win, You lose" • Controlling and attacking or blaming, and self-enhancing at the expense of others.

The most common foundation of determining communication style across industries uses a four-dimensional square with the quadrants reflecting *passive*, *aggressive*, *passive-aggressive*, and *assertive* (see Table 9.1). Contextual and situational factors may also be influencing a communication style that a person employs. As discussed earlier, only the individual will know their full context and situation. This is an excellent opportunity for group leaders and POs to model and encourage the skill practice of Carl Rogers' three key constructs of empathy, unconditional positive regard, and help to point out observations of congruence and incongruence as constructive feedback to the member exploring a situation.

For example, a member may utilize assertive communication in most aspects of their life, including at work and in social situations. This style is observed by clear and confident messaging (delivering and receiving), a sense of higher self-esteem, active listening, and observable efforts to clearly communicate their thoughts and feelings. As such, the assertive communication style is often regarded as the most effective communication style in groups. It is possible, however, that a person may exhibit this style in some situations, but perhaps the dynamics within their family at home is drastically different and, in that environment, they shift to a passive communication style. The passive style is often referred to as a "people pleaser" and can be recognized by a person avoiding conflicts, being agreeable with others to avoid conflicts, submissive in communication messaging (delivering and receiving) and behaviors, and the person can find it difficult to express their thoughts or feelings clearly or accurately. If one or more members in that group dynamic are aggressive or passive-aggressive, this may exacerbate and inhibit a passive communicator from choosing to engage in a change process. The *passive-aggressive* communicator can be the hardest to identify as often the overt presentation appears amenable and collaborative, yet, this communicator is actually fueled by covert resentment, anger, and other destructive emotions and feelings that have not been resolved or perhaps identified by the person. These communicators can be identified by observing what they say (content) as well as how they communicate (process). Often, gossiping, minimizing or dismissive comments are made, and subtle efforts to fracture progress, relationships, or stall growth are the results of their comments. In contrast, the *aggressive* communicator can be hostile and at times threatening. These communicators may observe the goal of communication as a competition illustrated by needing to "be right," being the last person to speak, or overshadowing other comments shared. Aggressive communicators' messages are often lost because of the profound negative delivery of their message(s) that can raise defenses in others in the group. POs are encouraged to watch for this communication style especially as it can hinder progress in groups, and it can be a tremendous opportunity for all members of the group to learn and grow; a unique aspect invited in psychoeducation groups.

It is possible that a person employing *aggressive communication* believes they are advocating for their point. In this way, the person may not be aware of how their communication style is blocking and hindering the group's progress or others hearing their message. This communicator may have valid and accurate points that might have the potential for major impact; however, the style of communication being used is distracting from this.

POs can offer feedback to the member as well as the group as a whole. POs can guide explorations of how we communicate with each other as a way to support each member and the group. One strategy for a PO and a group leader to consider is including a check-in about the observed communication styles as a part of the on-going conversation during a debriefing or planning session before and/or after a session. This can also be a key discussion point when setting expectations before a group begins for a PO to discuss with a group leader. It is strongly encouraged that this conversation takes place when a possible collaborative partnership is being considered between a group leader and PO. After all, these two roles will rely heavily on active and healthy communication and must be clear on the expectations they each have as to how communication will be shared to set each role up for success in their partnership. This is a smaller-scale example of the critical importance of communication styles that will be visible between and among members of the group.

Let's take a look at how this might come to life in a clinical mental health setting and strategies for a PO to support success.

Clinical Mental Health Vignette

In the clinical mental health setting vignette, we meet Mat, a volunteer who has participated in several self-help support groups throughout his life. Mat wants to create and lead a group to serve his religious community membership focused on career skills, interviewing, and job searching. Mat is not a trained or licensed mental health provider, but he has always had an intrinsic passion for helping others. Mat identified this community need through conversations within the religious community. Mat learned how several people, including some close friends, have been laid off or lost their jobs due to company downsizing. As a majority of the community members are adults in their forties or older, several are uncertain how they will make ends meet and how to engage in the world of work, noting the labor market and workforce appear very different from when they entered. Concern and self-doubt around useful skills to compete in a current workforce are dominating the community narrative. Mat has gone through career changes personally, with success and learning from the challenges and obstacles he has experienced. He feels he can relate and understand the community, and wants to help. Recognizing the limits of his skills and training planning and leading a support group, Mat reaches out to a local counseling center for assistance. A seasoned group facilitator, Aria, volunteers to serve as a process observer for this group. The plan is to meet for an hour and a half bi-weekly over a three-month period.

Support groups and related self-help groups can be psychoeducational when the group is designed to blend learning and growth with intrapersonal development enhanced by intentional reflection and awareness. In this vignette, Mat takes initiative that stands to benefit themself and the group. Selecting the right PO to guide and support Mat is also an important element to setting the stage for success not only for Mat, but for the group and its members. As we learned in Chapter 1, there are several factors to be mindful of when selecting a PO. Let's apply the four considerations when choosing a PO that Mat explored as he began conversations with Aria:

(1) **The Purpose of the Group.** In his conversation with Aria, Mat shared his vision for the group and how he identified this as a need in the community. The key question Mat was answering for Aria was, "What is your group trying to accomplish for its members, and how is it designed to reach those goals?" To explain, Mat included information about the community, the specific members he would target for inclusion, approximate size of the group and frequency of meetings along with other logistical considerations such as where they would meet, if there were any language, physical, intellectual, or emotional challenges anticipated they could plan pathways of support for in advance, and ultimately, what are the goals that Mat has envisioned. What will the outcome be at the end that leads Mat to say "Yes! This was successful!"? In this conversation, Aria and Mat discussed ways to be concrete and objective with goals and purpose of the group to aid in the overall evaluation of the group as well as planning for success. With this foundation clarified, it positioned them well to continue to discuss the next point.
(2) **The Expected Role and Function of the PO.** Aria is able to share with Mat what she has heard him state as his goals and how she expects to be able to advance these goals for the group. She describes strategies for intentional involvement that she has taken in other groups as a group leader and PO to facilitate a conversation with Mat about expectations, roles, and clarify how this PO role can best support Mat as the group leader. Discussions about the evolution of the group and the parallel dynamic role of a PO set the stage for this partnership opportunity that they are about to embark on. Additional details about the pre-planning related to logistics, group structure, membership numbers, or pre-screening for goodness of fit can also be areas where a seasoned PO might offer ideas to a group leader. The key here is that the PO is not attempting to control the group leader, or impress a leader with skills and knowledge. Each group is unique and it is important to leave space for a group to organically evolve.
(3) **The Competencies the PO will need in Order to be Effective in their Role.** The conversation from the first point will identify what specific competencies may be needed by the PO. This may be subject-matter expertise or specific training area to ensure the overall safety and wellness of members. In this instance, Mat and Aria may discuss competencies related to the religious community and how this lens may inform the group objectives or goals. It is not required that Aria be trained as a faith-based counselor, or that Aria is a member of this religious community, or even that Aria is a member of any religious community to be a competent and effective PO for Mat. It is important, however, that Mat and Aria engage in the conversation to help clarify the expectations and how that will influence their partnership in advance of the group starting.
(4) **The Type of Relationship that will be Necessary between the PO, Leaders, and Group Members.** You'll recall from Chapter 1, this element is important to consider in the context of the responses noted for points 1, 2, and 3 above. Aria and Mat are reminded as noted in Chapter 1 of this book "the relationship between you as the leader and the PO needs to be made as explicit as possible" (p. 000). As an intentional part of the conversation generated from these questions, Mat and Aria should be well equipped with information to come to consensus on important aspects of their collaborative relationship.

This vignette also illustrates the role of a group leader need not be someone who has formal training or a license in mental health counseling or a related licensed-eligible clinically trained specialization. Many support groups can be created and facilitated by individuals with a variety of training backgrounds, knowledge basis, and differing clinical skills but who share an intrinsic passion and motivation to help others. Especially in these cases, POs who are trained formally in group counseling and ideally licensed for clinical counseling practice invite these group leaders to expand the potential reach and effect of their efforts.

The group leaders centralize their efforts on designing and facilitating the content of each session and the group, while the PO can play an integral role to focus on the process. In these situations, it might be helpful for the group leader to semi-structure process observation check-ins as a direct part of the group. Physical setup of a group in these situations recommends the PO to be across from the group leader in a direct line of sight. This helps with continual non-verbal communication between the two roles, even though the PO is not a co-leader of the group. When in an online group environment, having the group leader and PO ensure their video remains on, even if members are provided an option to turn off their video can be a helpful strategy (Coogan & Steen, 2022). Similarly, group leader and POs may find it helpful to set up their own chat dialogue box independent of the group in an online environment, which may be possible within a video conferencing app (Coogan & Steen, 2022). For example, in Microsoft Teams, a separate chat can be created between the PO and group leader if they are both enabled in the licensing subscription to do so. In Zoom, chatting with a direct member versus "everyone" is an option to select in the chat function. It is important to note here the goal of having a chat function is to use it only when needed, mitigating the environment the group is located in (online vs in person). It is not to serve as a detailed record of the meeting, nor is a private chat between the PO and group leader meant to be a forum for personal opinions. They should not be saved nor should sessions be recorded, essentially mirroring similar practices to what would be commonly expected for an in-person group.

Possible challenges and opportunities in the group a PO may encounter could be related to culture, privileges, and other social and intrapersonal norms, traits, and characteristics. POs and group leaders will need to consider how these features of the group profile may have direct and implicit impacts on their respective roles.

Uniqueness and Challenges in Psychoeducation Groups

As we consider the role of a PO, we can see how this unique perspective adds tremendous value to counseling and therapy groups. With the significant variety of ways psychoeducation groups can be designed and the vast number of topics they can address, it can be a challenge to identify what exact contribution and focus of a PO will be the most helpful. Within groups, there may be times when explicit comments and feedback based on observations of the process are essential to help the group or members work through impasse or reach new levels of insight. Other times, comments and feedback about the content could be more helpful and impactful. When we consider **content** in groups, we are focused on *what* is being said; when we consider the process in groups, we are focused on *how* the message/content is received and the impact observed between and among members.

Especially within psychoeducation groups, POs are challenged every moment to be asking these questions – which is more helpful: process or content comments? Recognizing how fast groups move from a process perspective and appreciating that observations about content and process dynamics are continually occurring at the same time, whew, it can be overwhelming for a PO! Which is more helpful for the group at that moment? For example, is it more helpful for a PO to offer content feedback to a group by sharing, "I noticed that as the group talked about the upcoming charity event, the leader seemed to talk more about concerns and possible challenges that need to be addressed, yet, members' comments and ideas appeared to focus on other aspects of the event...." Or, might it be more helpful to offer feedback based on observed group process by sharing, "...there appeared to be a significant rise in energy, enthusiasm, and overall excitement as the group began talking about the upcoming conference event versus the other topics that the group has been discussing tonight up to this point. The group really seems to come together quickly and with positive energy when brainstorming and future planning topics are the focus of discussion."

The setting of a psychoeducation group may also have a direct effect on how a PO engages with the group, if at all. Consider a school setting as a primary example. Depending upon the topic and who the group leader is, there are likely psychoeducation groups being facilitated at all grade levels (kindergarten through senior year of high school) by school counselors as a part of standard training of a professional school counselor (American School Counselors Association [ASCA]). However, these are not the only styles and formats of psychoeducation groups often facilitated in a school, and due to limited personnel and limited resources, often, classroom teachers or other staff who have not had any formal training in counseling or group work are facilitating lessons that mirror the tenants of a psychoeducation group based on the outcomes and design. A classroom with 25–30 students could be the audience of a psychoeducation group for example. At the high school level, it may be as large as an entire grade level. For example, a common event for high schools is a "financial aid night" inviting parents and their children who are considering post-secondary planning to attend. In these events, the major tenets of psychoeducation groups are the foundation of the event and program. These events may exceed 100 attendees! How a PO is presented to the group, or the charge given to the person who will hold that role may need to shift based on the format, delivery goals, and attendance of the group planned. In fact, in cases like these, there may be more than one PO. Considering post-global COVID-19 pandemic times, virtual meetings are now a normal way of communicating and doing business. The role of a PO as noted above in a virtual setting may also look different than how the role may engage in a traditional face-to-face environment see Chapter 15 for more information.

Group leaders are encouraged to consider what the need and expectations are of a PO role as an intentional aspect of the planning and design process with their group. Group leaders can be creative in how they want to plan and structure their group sessions based on the identified need and expectations. They may also identify different needs and expectations based on the delivery format of the group or specific group sessions being in-person versus online, for example. These pre-planning considerations are strongly recommended to be shared and discussed with a PO before the first group meeting. This helps to ensure both the group leader and PO have a shared understanding of the group needs and expectations. It also helps the PO to gauge and prepare for how to best support the group leader if they know what they are working towards. If a PO is a supportive resource to the group leader (and the group by extension), knowing the ideal end goal and objectives positions that person to be as helpful as they are able.

Aspects to inform pre-planning for the group leader might consider the following:

1. aspects of their racial and cultural backgrounds and the impact this has on their leadership style,
2. overall goals for the group that could be facilitated,
3. specific areas of growth particularly around leadership skills,

4. ideas for the group's schedule, and
5. potential session structure and format.

Group leaders may choose to write out responses to share with the PO, or they may use these aspects as a guide for a verbal conversation. Group leaders and POs can use this opportunity not only to address these important pre-planning aspects but, also to clarify and test giving and receiving feedback. As previously discussed, this specific communication exchange of listening and providing feedback is essential to the group leader and PO relationship. Should there be clarifications or suggestions regarding how feedback is offered to best support either party, this is a great time to identify this need and discuss further. The time spent providing feedback allows conversations about whether or not to work together in the future.

After discussions have concluded, group leaders may wish to use some of the points discussed in their first group session with the members to describe and discuss the groups' expectations and goals. Group leaders may choose to be creative with this effort. For example, if the group is planned to be an online group, a group leader could create a short video or advertisement discussing the aspects, expectations, and needs for the group.

Recommendations to Consider for Next Steps

The opportunities for psychoeducation groups are endless and applicable in a variety of settings including schools, businesses, residential facilities, and more are likely already engaging in a variety of psychoeducation group work through continuing education and professional development training. Are these being delivered in a true group format? Perhaps due to limited funding, resources, or persons trained to facilitate in a dynamic psychoeducation group way, these educational and interpersonal growth and development opportunities are being self-directed, computer-based training, or another format available to a company or school. We invite and encourage you to consider how you can begin with a current training or professional development opportunity and enhance it by applying and integrating some of the psychoeducation group concepts we introduced and discussed in this chapter? If you are running groups, are there opportunities for you to collaborate and invite a PO into the experience as a way to enhance? Are there community partnerships that can be forged with local individuals who are trained in group counseling that are available to consult and be contracted to serve as a PO?

Conclusion

With an overall goal of learning and growth, psychoeducation groups are adaptable to a variety of environments and industries with almost any individual. As such, psychoeducation groups can be helpful delivery frameworks to meet strategic goals and objectives within education, hospitals, human resources, corporate or private businesses, and much more. Often called "professional training" in other industries, psychoeducation groups can be any size, focus on a variety of topics, and balance content learning along with intra- and interpersonal growth. A PO may be a participant or member, or they can be external to the group used as a resource and support for the leader and the group. With smaller-sized groups (typically fewer than 12) and developmentally appropriate levels, it may be helpful to invite a rotating PO role among the group members. This invitation may positively affect and increase accountability and engagement in the process simply by offering a shift in the members' awareness, focus, and perspective in the group.

References

Chung, W., Chan, S., & Cassels, T. G. (2010). The role of culture in affective empathy: Cultural and bicultural differences. *Journal of Cognition and Culture, 10(3–4)*, 309–326.

Coogan, T. & Steen, S. (2022). *Group counseling leadership skills for school counselors*. San Diego, CA: Cognella, Inc.

Johnson, D. W. & Johnson, R. T. (2017) The use of cooperative procedures in teacher education and professional development. *Journal of Education for Teaching*, *43(3)*, 284–295. DOI: 10.1080/02607476.2017.1328023.

Meier, S. T. & Davis, S. R. (2019). *The elements of counseling* (8th ed). Long Grove, IL: Waveland Press, Inc.

Rogers, C. R. (1957). The necessary and sufficient conditions of therapeutic personality change. *Journal of Consulting Psychology*, *21(2)*, 95–103.

Trotzer, J. P. (1979). Developmental tasks in group counseling: The basis for structure. *The Journal for Specialists in Group Work*, *4(4)*, 177–185. DOI: 10.1080/15496295.1979.11728580.

Chapter 10

Process Observation in Task Groups

Theresa A. Coogan, Ph.D., Raleigh, NC

Chris Godwin, PhD., Campbell University

Sam Steen, Ph.D., George Mason University

What is the last project you volunteered to help complete? If you have children, have you ever served on the Parent Teachers Association (PTA) at their school? Perhaps you are on a committee at work planning team events or meetings to achieve organizational vision, mission and goals grounded in fostering a collegial community for the employees. Perhaps you have led recurring department meetings within your college or university or clinical team meetings with members of a community health agency. These are some examples of task groups!

These are utilized frequently although not always recognized as being a formal group. Task groups have unique features that distinguish them from other common types of groups such as psychoeducational, counseling/growth, or therapy groups. Key elements observed in effective task groups include interpersonal dynamics, communication, and connection among and between the members of the group modeled and facilitated by the leader. Independent of a pre-defined endeavor or set of business that task groups often have pre-identified prior to the group beginning their work, these key elements are central to the effectiveness of the group to meet the objectives and the relational experiences that occur.

Task groups rely on several elements working in unison. If your experience is as a member, a leader, or a Process Observer (PO), all perspectives can provide a symphony of elements to the effectiveness of a task group for both the concrete objectives as well as the experience of the members. Typically, this pre-defined *task* or set of tasks influences the theme or outcome of what the group is striving for or expected to produce.

The PO's role contributing to the task group experience has impacts on both the task group leader and the members informing content and process experiences. Task group goals and objectives are often very concrete; including design an event or a product, conduct a business meeting, or complete a consultation. The PO will bring experience as a task group member as well as experience as a task group leader. They are often in a unique position to enhance the impact of the task group leader, balancing a role as an objective colleague who has led these groups along with supporting the task group leader to grow and engage all their strengths related to this group. The PO offers the leader feedback in a similar manner to how we understand a supervisor/supervisee role in individual clinical counseling. Even the most seasoned counseling practitioners benefit from engaging in a meaningful supervisory experience with another practicing counselor. For example, the supervisor offers a new perspective and plays a sounding board role. The supervisor can help create a safe space for the supervisee to explore the content and process of the clinical practice. As we apply this understanding to that of a PO and a task group leader, we can clearly see the transferable and related applications.

DOI: 10.4324/9781003281955-13

Reflective Questions

Consider the prompts below as you reflect on your past experiences with task groups. As you consider each prompt, we invite intentional awareness to the role that you primarily held as you explore each memory and experience. Were you a member, leader, or PO in each memory and how did that role specifically inform your response to the prompt?

- Are there specific themes or topics that you remember which increased your engagement and contributions to task groups?
- How effective and productive do you tend to find task groups?
- What styles of communication do you observe most often in task groups? What style of communication do you most often bring to task groups?
- As you consider other individuals who are members in the task group(s), what behavior observations and patterns (overt and covert) are you aware of as you consider how members of the group tend to contribute, interact, and appear to experience the group?
- What behavioral observations and patterns are you most often contributing and experiencing in task groups?
- Have you experienced or observed a specific leadership style to be more effective when leading specific task groups? What do you think were contributing factors that led you to experience these groups as effective and successful? Which of these factors do you feel proficient in now as a group leader and which might be areas for continued development?
- What factors as a group leader have helped you to be effective and successful as a group leader in your experience?
- How do you typically receive feedback and/or engage in a supervisory relationship?

During this reflection, you may have recalled some experiences in task groups that you could see were efficient, productive, and seemed to "go well." Perhaps this was identified in experiences where you were a member as well as other experiences where you were a leader. Perhaps you spotted overlapping patterns or factors in both perspectives that may be central to yielding efficient and productive task group results.

Conversely, you may have recalled some experiences that may not have accomplished the task, but the journey to get to that end result may have felt more draining, disappointing, or deflating as an overall experience. In other words, the energy required to accomplish the task at hand was notably different. In these experiences, to what extent was the task the factor, versus the group leadership, versus group members interactions, or the process the group experienced from start to finish?

Understanding and Identifying Group Process

POs, group leaders, and group members are all active participants in a task group. As such, each role has an essential part to play to contribute to the group dynamics. When one (or more) of the participants in a task group appear disengaged or are disinterested (regardless if participation was required or voluntary), the energy in the group and the dynamics between and among group members and/or the leader may be affected despite the outcome of the stated goals and objectives. This consideration of these fluid dynamics of the group as a whole along with its individual participants is referred to as group process (Hackman & Morris, 1979).

In task groups, group process is defined as "the 'how' of the group; often informed by inter- and intrapersonal dynamics" (Coogan & Steen, 2022, p. 24). When a group is making progress, that reflects an important part of the group process. When a group appears to be at an impasse, that also reflects an important part of the group process. Remember, group process explores the "how" of a group and its functions (Tuckman & Jensen, 1977). *How* members interact and engage; *how* the energy of the group ebbs and flows as a natural process; *how* the group evolves and grows as a function of the objectives they were brought together to accomplish. *What* the group concretely does (also referred to as "group content") is also important. The number of group meetings scheduled, the time of day they are scheduled and their duration, the specific agenda items for meetings, or concrete tasks/deliverables identified are all "group content" that inform the effectiveness and dynamics of a task group. Even if all of the content elements are set up for success, a task group can struggle or fail to meet its identified goals if the *process* is not adequately addressed. This is where a PO can be an essential asset to a task group and the groups' leader. The PO monitors the *group process* and engages with the group leader and at times members, in a collaborative relationship offering on-going feedback about the group process throughout the duration of the task group. As a group leader, having this additional perspective and support can enhance the leader's focus on the content and task group objectives as well knowing that if they miss or overlook an important process element, the PO will communicate that with them.

POs and task group leaders are reminded this relationship is collaborative support. Perspectives and feedback about the process are offered and shared by the PO for a task group leaders' consideration. Ultimately, the task group leader considers and decides how or if they will act on the feedback offered. Group leaders and POs are encouraged to discuss expectations for communication, feedback, and other details for each group prior to the group starting whenever possible to ensure transparency before a group begins. While a seemingly obvious practical suggestion for best-practice, this detail can be overlooked at times noting many task groups are quickly formed and begin out of an immediate need to address an issue. Prevention planning is encouraged whenever possible.

Intensely focusing on a predetermined goal, outcome, or purpose can distract even the most seasoned group leader from observing in "real-time" significant influence of group process on the overall experience. With experience and practice as a group leader and a PO, we can all hone these skills to contribute to our effectiveness with each group we are a part of. Remember, in counseling (even with task groups), we embrace the concept that everyone has room for growth and development. We all bring strengths to a group, and we can all learn from the group. This can be a powerful outcome of any group! With the support of a PO, as mentioned throughout this book, the group leaders and members may become more conscious and actively aware of the influence of group processes.

How to Recognize a Task Group

As noted at the beginning of this chapter, it is often the case that task groups are unrecognized as a "group." Instead, task groups are more often recognized and labeled as a "standing meeting" or perhaps as a "committee." For instance, how often have you gone to work and attended a standing business or department meeting and heard your supervisor or department chair begin the meeting by acknowledging that the folks at this table are all members of an important task group charged to address the needs of relevant stakeholders? This is usually not the typical introduction.

Some hallmarks of how a task group begins includes a review or discussion about goals and objectives overall or specific to that meeting; clarification of members' roles; and, a review of how the dynamics of the members will impact and inform the overall efficiency and productivity of the group. Now consider recent committee meetings or standing meetings you have been a part of. Did the person leading those meetings begin or infuse these elements into your meeting? Perhaps they did but it was woven into the entire meeting. Perhaps it was not addressed and assumed to be common knowledge. From your perspective as a member of that group, how was the group impacted by the explicit discussion of the group process?

Leaders who desire to offer robust task groups could provide key elements at the beginning of the meeting, and perhaps at the start of subsequent meetings as this information is helpful to the members (Coogan & Steen, 2022). As you consider the following suggestions, think of a task group you are currently leading or plan to lead soon. In addition to the following key elements, what other elements come to mind? Expand upon this list tailoring it to your task group needs:

- What are the major outcomes or end-goal(s) of this task group? How will you know concretely this task group successfully completed the task(s)?
- What are the primary and secondary objectives of this task group? Especially when there are recurring meetings planned, how do these objectives break down further to inform each individual task group session or meeting?
- How will each member be set up for success to clearly understand their role in this group and the contribution their role is expected to have throughout the process?
- How will you, as the leader, monitor the productivity and efficiency of the group based on the intra- and interpersonal dynamics observed? What are the benchmarks or milestones you are watching for as the group progresses and the task(s) are accomplished?
- How will confidentiality be discussed and addressed as sensitive material emerges?
- How will race, ethnicity, and cultural backgrounds broadly speaking of the leaders and members foster a creative atmosphere while also balancing known and anticipated risks associated with the task(s) at hand?

Many people attend meetings with different goals and purposes on a regular basis as a normal responsibility of their job duties. That said, not all group leaders clearly state the purpose or desired outcomes of each meeting or the larger goal of the group who are meeting. Most members or leaders will be able to tell you if they felt the meeting went well or not as soon as it is concluded. In this way, people are attending and responding to a question of perceived effectiveness of a group meeting based on the dynamics of the group even if they are unaware this is what is happening.

Now more than ever, an increasing social norm of the world of work appears to include "meeting overload." In some cases, this is directly related to the COVID-19 that is still pressing upon us as we write this chapter in 2022. In fact, folks may feel like they are attending a meeting out of a requirement or obligation or because their calendar told them they need to be somewhere. This sense of mandated attendance (versus voluntary attendance) can have an impact on a member or a leader's experiences as well as that of the others in the group.

Moreover, with many of these meetings being offered virtually, it can be difficult to make a clear distinction between work life and family balance. Several workers experienced this throughout the global pandemic as kitchen tables, living rooms, and bedrooms in one's home became the creative office space, sometimes also shared with the children's make-shift classroom. We can identify some elements that may have helped build interpersonal relationships from this mandated adaptation we all experienced such as learning more about the members of a person's family or having a glimpse at their personal space at home on a video conference call. As you reflect on your personal experiences, who did you get to know more about as a direct result of engaging with the person on video conferencing through the pandemic? Consider why a pandemic may have been needed to learn more about that person and how knowing more about who the person is helped shape and guide your interpersonal relationship. You see, these details are informing the process of your working relationship with another person. Perhaps you learned more about the person that you never knew you had in common and that has opened exciting new areas of shared interest between you. Perhaps you learned more about the person's communication or organization skills that may or may not be a good match for you. No matter what, by getting to know more about the person, you learn and grow. Context and dynamics are part of what a PO can assist with to promote and support the group striving towards efficiency and effective outcomes.

As stated earlier, a primary job of a PO is to monitor and track a group's interactions and offer suggestions and feedback to improve its effectiveness. We will provide examples throughout this chapter to illustrate the ideas and recommendations offered. We also encourage and invite you to consider an upcoming task group for you that you can have in mind to apply ideas and concepts to in advance. Keep in mind, one of the overarching tenets of a PO's role is to provide an objective "outsider" view and feedback, which includes monitoring and tracking the dynamics and interactions throughout each session and the whole group.

A Closer Look at Task Groups

Essential tenets of task groups include a specific goal(s), that may be prescribed before the group has the first meeting (e.g., complete project X) or it could be a group that needs to set its goal(s) (e.g., committees or boards). Task groups may have significant variation in the frequency, duration, and length of meetings from one meeting necessary to standing meetings that are on a schedule (e.g., monthly team meetings for one hour). Task groups may have closed membership or open membership that may also be on a varied frequency (e.g., a person serves on this committee for a three-year term) where appointment may be voluntary, mandated, or an elected position. Typically, with task groups, the majority of the meeting time of the group is dedicated to the content and focus of the work or goals that the task group was created to address. With the work content or product outcome driving the focus of the group, there are positive impacts and influences that information from Process Observations regarding the group process can have on the task group.

Task groups will have similar roles (member, leader) as other group types and will also establish a set of group norms and group rules. It is possible these important aspects to group function and group dynamics are established unknowingly by the group based on individual assumptions and social norms that might already exist in the organization or by the preferences of the group leader. To set a task group up for success, it is recommended to engage the entire group in an open, transparent conversation about these aspects that will inform how the group functions, completes its work effectively, and engages in the interpersonal dynamics that is group work.

Process Observers in Task Groups

A PO can help to prepare a group leader and/or assist in the facilitation of task group conversations and meetings. The extent of direct engagement during the actual task group meeting can vary based on the leader's preference or the goals of the group. This flexibility in the PO's role supports the PO to serve a wide variety of needs and goals of a group process. For example, a PO may recommend activities or assessments to the leader or members to use in group meetings that can align with the group to increase effectiveness of the task accomplishment and productivity. Alternatively, the PO may recommend activities or assessments to the leader to support their development and effectiveness as a group leader, such as increasing awareness of their personal leadership style and discuss individually with the leader how they may observe influences on their work in the group. The PO may also interject (spontaneously or at semi-structured points of a meeting based on a pre-set agenda) process comments that provide observations of the group's behavior inviting awareness, learning, and ultimately group effectiveness. These efforts are not therapy and not about diagnosis; rather, they invite, guide, and aid in the exploration and self-awareness of the roles held by the leader and members through the context of the group they are a part of.

Group process observation (GPO) in a task group may be happening unofficially at many of your meetings now. In fact, you have likely engaged in a variation of Process Observation in your career. Examples might include having a new hire who is shadowing you or a mentoring program plan to involve junior employees in meetings where they are present for the meeting to observe, listen, and learn, but might not be an active member at the table. If we think about it, we are all engaging in a version of GPO when we start a new job (paid or volunteer). We watch how other members of the company or organization interact. We pay closer attention to the supervisor(s) and the organizational structure or hierarchy to learn and become more aware of leadership styles, expectations, and what the social norms are that are rewarded, treated with indifference, and discouraged. In some organizations, the members may have direct awareness of these norms and unspoken rules of interpersonal behaviors. One of the most useful and productive ways a PO can be an essential support to a group leader or facilitator is by using the following actions as a guide:

Educating the group leader or the entire group around the constructs of communication, including verbal and non-verbal behavior, specifically through the lens of task group efficiency and productivity,

Observing as soon as possible join the group and begin taking notes, setting up norms for when this information will be discussed,

Offering feedback about communication styles used and those that were avoided,

Examining verbal and non-verbal communication and body language,

Reflecting on information and details discussed, and

Identifying aspects to improve *how* they communicate and seek to understand *why* they communicate the way they do.

These pieces directly and indirectly influence the dynamics of the group through the verbal and non-verbal communication. Communication is even more essential in task groups noting that by nature of this type of group, they may only have one meeting.

A common pitfall in communication, for leaders especially but also for some members, can be referred to as "The Curse of Knowledge." In task groups, it is easy for members and leaders to be hyper focused on the product or outcome and overlook the communication and group dynamics. This might cause leaders or members to make assumptions about the knowledge base of the topic being discussed among the group. Translated into fast-paced and possibly short-duration meetings, assumptions can easily be made about the knowledge that base members have. This may then negatively impact the understanding of the work to be accomplished by an identified goal. One strategy to counteract this includes the help of the PO to aid a leader by monitoring and observing the communication style including the rate of speech, tone, voice, and other key non-verbal communication and messages. POs are encouraged to share their role and overarching goals with the group. The following extract provides an example of how a group leader and PO might introduce a PO's role to a group as a part of the introduction session.

GROUP LEADER: I'd like to welcome our process observer Lineal to the table. They will describe their role in our task group and provide important details that will be useful for us to understand how to benefit from being observed. Lineal, please begin.

PROCESS OBSERVER: Thanks a bunch. It is really straightforward in terms of the way I will go about the process of observing your meetings. What will be less clear initially, is the motivation behind me doing so, as I am an outsider and not necessarily a primary stakeholder in any of this. However, I do desire to be competent in my interactions with you all and I am hopeful that what I bring to the table will add value to the experience and the outcome. Therefore, I do have a stake in desiring you all to accomplish your outcomes. What questions do you have for me?

As you reflect on this example above, what stands out to you? What assumptions can we make about the collaboration established between the group leader and PO before this first session took place? In other words, what preparation work can we assume the group leader and PO have already accomplished before this current session? What specifically should the PO share about their "role"? At this point, could you describe the behaviors that a PO will use?

Importance of Communication in Task Groups

Verbal and nonverbal behavior are commonly considered two distinct forms of communication informing and influencing how messages are delivered and received. We acknowledge both, more often, work in tandem even though verbal communication can be misunderstood as the primary or sole form of communication. Less often, we acknowledge the impact of various cultural factors that influence both forms of communication. While this can be less clear, it is important to seek for understanding amongst all involved in the group process.

Bonaccio et al. (2016) explained how nonverbal behaviors can repeat, substitute, accent, or contradict verbal messages. In a sense, the complexity level rises more considering verbal and nonverbal communication as the receiver(s) must continuously be assessing the extent of alignment of the verbal message received with the (conscious or unconscious) continuous verbal communication. Hence, intentional awareness to understand the content of a message as well as how it is being delivered and received are all critical elements to the broader communication exchange between two or more individuals. Again, cultural factors must be duly noted. As we consider the roles involved in a task group, we can see the role of the PO can be an essential role with a primary charge that focuses on the immediate here-and-now awareness of the content and process of communication between and among all members and the leader(s).

Hall et al. (2019) described communication as a series of encoding and decoding messages verbally/orally delivered and through perceptions and inferences of behavioral and nonverbal communication. We can see this clearly illustrated in task groups when we consider how group leaders verbally explain any key element of the task to the group, such as the specific deliverables or outcomes that the group is expected to produce. Now consider how the nonverbal elements may alter the perceptions, inferences, and how the message is ultimately decoded by members of the group.

In one scenario, perhaps the nonverbal communication occurring simultaneously while the group leader describes a key element of the group is verbally delivered with a soft and disengaged voice, tone in the speech style, and/or a slow rate and cadence of speech. Conversely, perhaps the group leader's nonverbal communication is higher pitched, or scattered in clarity or speech, and it might be at a rate that is very fast almost as if to rush through the conversation. As we consider the perspective of the receivers, the group members, perhaps eye rolls or other behaviors that might illustrate resistance or disagreement happen unconsciously by the group leader while describing the key elements. Or members have expressions of confusion or distraction that they may or may not be aware that they are making. Take this same scenario and imagine the people involved on a spectrum of identities. The scenario becomes more complex and there are a myriad of possibilities.

These scenarios consider a verbal and nonverbal communication exchange between a group leader and group members. The communication is happening simultaneously and is flowing moment-to-moment with new information. All possibilities present an opportunity to create a complex messaging situation within the group. A key suggestion to proactively minimize the complex messaging situations is the engagement of a PO role. The PO is in a prime position to observe and offer feedback to the leader and group in this case to influence the group dynamics and overall productivity of the group. In this scenario, a PO would notice the disconnected and mixed messaging between the group leaders verbal and nonverbal communication to the group as well as observing how each member appears to be responding, observing the sense of energy among the group as one whole unit, and noticing how members engage with the leader during this messaging. The PO can share these observations with the group leader in an individual session they may have scheduled for before or after sessions (similar to regularly scheduled supervision sessions, although the intention for these sessions have different goals than supervision sessions), or during a meeting more "in real time" if an appropriate opportunity presents itself.

When discussing tasks or needs pertaining to the goals of the group, leaders are encouraged to use concrete and simplified messages. POs are in a helpful role to offer feedback to a group leader. This effort is not about talking down to the members or having a lack of confidence in the leaders' skills or abilities. Rather, the effort seeks to minimize the risk of miscommunication between and among leaders and members. Additionally, one cannot assume that all members involved will always understand the languages spoken as they are intended in these scenarios especially as our society becomes more global.

This effort not only works well for traditional face-to-face group formats, but it also has translated exceptionally well to a virtual environment specifically when working with teams that are diverse in language as fluency levels and cultural differences may influence the receipt of the intended message being communicated. Each culture will have its own versions of sarcasm, idioms, and jargon and this language, if not understood by all members could limit the communication. Another example of a benefit is attending to different geographic locations of members resulting in time zone differences when people are all on the call. We all have different times of the day when we feel sharper and more attuned to our work. It is important to keep in mind when there are members of a group in different time zones how this may influence perceived energy and engagement levels. Different energy levels and attention capabilities understood by pure physiological functions may influence the team meeting dynamics in different ways.

Strategies for Process Observers to Support Groups

The following offers practical suggestions for POs to consider in collaboration with group leaders to support their respective roles and the overall function of the group. Groups often invite a level of creativity and freedom to meet a group "where they are." POs are encouraged to access their creativity and flexible thinking, adapting strategies and approaches to meet the needs of the group and group leader(s) with whom they are collaborating. Every group will be unique. The strategies below are easily adapted to fit the specific focus of any task group and aid a PO in their efforts.

Strategy #1: Meeting Mojo

POs can be instrumental to supporting the overall group effectiveness and progress by monitoring and tracking the **"Meeting Mojo."** This term captures and rates the energy of the group as a whole. As we consider the "meeting mojo" we acknowledge the ebb and flow as a natural process throughout each individual meeting as well as the broader duration of all meetings over the course of time. Observable factors a PO may notice include:

1. Tone,
2. Intonation,
3. Frequency of verbal communication,
4. Patterns of nonverbal communication,
5. The group rhythm and cadence around specific topics or themes discussed, and
6. The overall energy level.

A PO can offer feedback to the group around observations that have enhanced the dynamics and effectiveness to consider maintaining or increasing those specific efforts, and observations that have appeared to contribute to a stall or even inviting impasse for the group to consider how to address and overcome the barriers. Feedback could be offered in a quick nonverbal, illustrative way using a street light analogy where "green" means a high level of group mojo; "yellow" means the mojo is inconsistent; and "red" means it is not observed consistently or needs to be addressed before task work continues (see Figure 10.1).

A benefit to this type of approach that uses a graphic illustration to describe a perception or observation of the immediate group process is that it does so in a way accountable to the entire group as one unit. Rather than calling out a specific member of the group to begin the conversation, it acknowledges the group as a whole being at a specific energy or dynamic place. Before a conversation about *what* has occurred even begins, the entire group is reminded that they are one unit. Often, this small yet impactful intentional effort can mitigate natural defensive coping strategies that many individuals have. POs and group leaders are then in a strong starting place to invite a thoughtful and productive conversation to inform the group dynamics and effectiveness. Another helpful visual illustration may be a bar chart with a sliding marker to indicate where the group energy level is using a "high" and "low" scale. An abacus can also be repurposed and

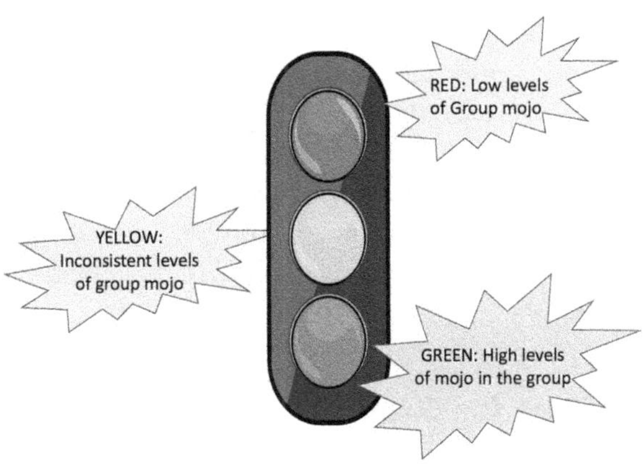

Figure 10.1 Group Mojo
Source:

creatively reimagined for this goal. Tactile and visual illustrations add value to actively and intentionally engaging in a process. It is also a non-threatening way of gleaning insights from each individual member before group dialogue begins.

Depending on the type of task group, frequency of meetings, and interpersonal norms between and among members, group leaders may wish to empower the members to call for a "meeting mojo check-in" at any point during a task group meeting as an interactive way to bring here-and-now awareness of the meeting dynamics into focus for the group as a whole. This practice can invite members to take ownership, accountability, and responsibility for the group dynamics. Group Leaders are invited to discuss and explore all options with the PO that might be a good fit. This pre-discussion also helps clarify the goals of the PO and what type of feedback will be most helpful to the leader and the group.

A challenge for POs around *Meeting Mojo* is often observed when the PO becomes "stuck." This type of impasse may mean the PO does not have the freedom to provide constructive feedback to the group or the group leader. Or, perhaps the PO does not have the authority to interrupt a group when they observe ineffective or maladaptive dynamics to mitigate them from happening or having more severe impacts.

It is important to remember that tensions are expected as a natural and normal part of group processes. In many instances, positive opportunities can grow from tensions. Just as tensions are a normal part of the process, so too are the expectations of member and group awareness, effort, and a willingness to engage constructively in a growth and change process. This can be easier said than done for many members or group leaders. The PO must negotiate the level of influence that the group leaders/members desire for them to have. This could be a flexible scale or one that is set with strict boundaries to ensure respect is maintained throughout the process. Ultimately, the group leader will typically guide the boundaries for the PO.

Strategy #2: The Bystander Effect

A second way the PO can be helpful to the overall group is by observing and monitoring for signs of **"The Bystander Effect."** This term is used in other contexts as well with a similar application and operating definition in task groups. This idea can occur when one or more members are less likely to take responsibility, take action, or engage (verbally or nonverbally) when there is clearly observed energy from one or more others doing so. This idea can also be linked with "diffusion of responsibility" and depending upon the engagement, with "bullying," "monopolization," and "power struggles." If a bystander effect is being observed in a task group, it is possible that barriers for productivity, performance, and overall group efficiency may be erected. This is more likely when it is not recognized or it is avoided by the group leader. In addition to thoughtfully sharing observations about engagement and communication patterns, POs may assist group leaders to counteract this by offering reminders of key behavioral tasks a leader can take. For example, as a part of the goals and task of the group, when a leader assigns specific tasks and responsibility to members ensuring everyone is involved in the group, the opportunity for the bystander effect diminishes.

Process Observer Tips for Group Leaders

Group leaders are encouraged to consider the following tips when assigning tasks to the group members. POs can alert the group leaders that these components will provide a structure for feedback as to how these areas were observed in delivery and receiving the messages.

Tip #1: leaders are encouraged to use simple and direct language that tells people who's responsible for getting something done and what they are expected to accomplish. Leaders need to already know what the end product or outcome is that they are expecting so this can be communicated to the individual or small group charged with the completion of the task. *How* it is accomplished is not the goal for the leader. When possible, breaking the task to a level where the person can answer a "yes" or "no" question of if the task was accomplished is best.

Tip #2: leaders are encouraged to first ask for volunteers for a task. When members volunteer, the ownership of completing and engaging the task actively tends to increase.

Tip #3: leaders are encouraged to assign responsibility of a task to one (1) specific individual and not a group of people. Assigning a task to a small group actually creates a bystander effect, and we're trying to reduce and eliminate this from occurring. When a smaller group is required to complete a task, leaders can identify one point person on behalf of the group or ask for a volunteer to serve as a point person. This also enhances overall communication strategies as leaders can communicate for status updates with one point person rather than multiple people while the task is in flight.

Preparation and Planning for Task Groups

There are several planning and preparation steps a PO can advise a group leader to consider and execute prior to each group meeting to support the overall dynamics and effectiveness of the task group. The PO can offer observations about the engagement levels and dynamics of each segment in a group meeting to assist the leader with preparation efforts. Here are some suggestions of actions a group leader and a PO can take prior to a task group meeting:

- **Prepare an agenda for that meeting.** The content of the agenda will be driven by the group leader, and the PO can offer suggestions for how to order and structure tasks considering process flow and the changing group dynamics. For example, a task group may need to spend time in a meeting reviewing a schedule of events for an upcoming conference and the group leader needs to have that on the meeting agenda. The PO may suggest the point in the meeting that might best support the productive and effective review of the agenda based on their understanding and observation of when this group engages best at complex, detailed thinking that requires fluid adaptability and creative team solution-solving. Notice even the POs use of the term "solution-solving" instead of "problem-solving" can inform the strength-based perspective of the group leader and reframe what might seem or feel like a daunting task to an achievable task. POs can support leaders and model how words chosen can intentionally inform group dynamics. The group leader may choose to re-word items on the agenda seeking suggestions from the PO to utilize strength-based language on the meeting agenda. Ideally, the agenda will be shared at least 48 hours in advance. As a result, the first time the members review the agenda, they are not with the group for immediate processing. Using intentional language can set the tone for the meeting even before everyone comes together in the same room. Similarly, having a consistent and predictable format/layout of the agenda can also be a small effort with a big impact on the group dynamics. Agendas do not need to be detailed or long. Capture the high-level topics that are planned for discussion and work in that meeting. This not only helps the leader but also helps focus the members on their comments, questions, or concerns around each topic.
- **Capture Notes or Minutes of the Meeting.** Not all meetings need to abide strictly by Robert's Rules of Order, but some form of notes summarizing the discussions and actions

determined are what we want to capture. It is the leader's responsibility to plan for this. They may delegate the note-taking task to a specific party who may be a member of the group or joining the group for that sole purpose. The role may also rotate between members with each meeting so all parties share the responsibility. The leader may find it helpful to glean insights from the PO to understand the roles of the members when considering what approach is best to plan to capture notes. What approach will yield accurate notes of the meeting that occurred while simultaneously ensuring all members remain actively engaged to contribute to the overall group's effectiveness? Is an external person with the sole person to take notes a useful approach for that group? Is a rotating responsibility approach where members take turns taking notes best? The PO can offer a leader insights about how the interpersonal and intrapersonal contributions of each member are informing the overall group dynamics and effectiveness. When capturing notes, it is recommended to focus in on three key aspects during each meeting: (1) the anticipated barriers or challenges expected to encounter in the future; (2) current issues or challenges; and, (3) action items that represent the immediate next-step tasks to be taken.

- **Assign owners and deadlines to actions**. Before the meeting concludes, the leader is encouraged to ensure that all actions identified have at least one "owner" assigned. Depending upon the task, the leader may choose to assign to a specific person or a small group, or may ask for a volunteer. If a small group is established, it is critical that one person be identified at this moment as the point person. Even in small groups, if there is not a pre-identified point person, the chances increase that work may not be accomplished as members may assume others in the group are doing work. Clearly specified expectations are helpful to uphold accountability and increase meaningfulness. A PO can offer feedback to the entire group "live" in the moment, if desired, that speaks to observations when these action steps are delegated and discussed. This may invite a rich conversation about process and maximize opportunities for members to engage their unique strengths as well as seek opportunities for development and growth through the group process. The PO is also in a unique position to offer the leader specific feedback during their one-to-one sessions as to how their communication style and messages were observed by the members. Feedback on communication style and leadership style can help leaders fine tune their skills while the group is in motion minimizing inefficiencies of the broader group process.

Possible Hurdles in Tasks Groups

Preparation and planning sets groups, leaders, and POs up for success out of the gate. And, it is possible there still may be challenges the task group encounters that might manifest themselves. Two key aspects to watch for are **conflict** and **resistance**. These may seem the same on the surface, but with closer examination from a process-oriented perspective, we can see how the impact has the potential for significant differences based on the type of group and group goals. All will be explored with specific attention to impact and effect within a task group.

Conflicts

Conflicts are often thought of in mainstream society as negative, abrasive, confrontational, and with any level of difficult or damaging impact. When searched in the online APA dictionary of psychology as the key term, conflict is defined as, "the occurrence of mutually antagonistic or opposing forces, including events, behaviors, desires, attitudes, and emotions" (APA, 2022).

Most attempt to avoid conflict given all these negative perceptions and connotations. However, in group work and from a process-oriented lens, conflicts are essential experiences within a group between and among members that influences the dynamics and overall group experiences. Conflicts can be different perspectives and opinions shared on a topic being discussed. It can be represented by a thought, question, or comment offered by one or more members that was perceived or received by at least one other member as offensive, disparaging, or insensitive. Microaggressions and macroaggressions, which are discussed more below, are also examples of catalysts that might occur in a group that creates conflict. This is not to minimize the experience nor imply the experience will always be negative either. Conflict can also occur when accolades are publicly provided to one or more members and perhaps other people or sub-groups are not included. While a positive comment was offered in the group, the experience or perception created a sense of tension and divided differences among members within the group that was not directly addressed. In a group setting, processing conflicts provides unique and specific opportunities for exploring intrapersonal and interpersonal responses and reactions to an event(s). The opportunity for learning and growth is endless when processing of conflicts occurs.

A possible challenge for POs is how and when to interject to invite and facilitate the processing of a conflict. The PO is encouraged to discuss (before the group has their first meeting) the process and procedure preferred to use when a conflict occurs. Often, the group leader will be responsible for addressing conflict as they observe it happening, and the sooner the better. Sometimes, the group leader is a part of the conflict, doesn't see it occurring, or perhaps may not know what to do or say, so they remain quiet hoping it will resolve naturally without intervention. A PO who has discussed in advance a plan with a group leader is less likely to be met with *resistance* or another type of blocking behavior inhibiting or shutting down the PO from addressing the issue(s) that occurred, or the residual effect occurring in the group as a result. If a PO is blocked from addressing a conflict in a group meeting, they are encouraged to speak privately with the leader after the group individually as a way of both processing the experience themselves as well as capitalizing on the recency of the experience to clarify and identify clear plans for next steps. It is recommended the beginning of the next meeting begins by addressing the conflict experience at the next session.

When searched in the online APA dictionary of psychology as the key term, resistance can be defined as, "generally, any action in opposition to, defying, or withstanding something or someone" (APA, 2022). We may observe resistance as creating or adding to conflict. We may also observe resistance in people as disengaging or challenging the norms, actions, or even status quo. Like conflict, resistance does not automatically assume it is negative, although mainstream use of the term often is in a negative context. Resistance is also what a PO may create to help illustrate, for a group, a pattern of behaviors that is occurring, which may be affecting the dynamics or the efficiency of the group. Resistance may also be what a member experiences as a part of a group process or in response to another member's actions or reactions.

Based on this understanding, let's explore possible challenges a PO may encounter and strategies to address them in the group by considering the scenario below. We will also identify and discuss challenges the PO may encounter within their unique role while working to bring light to the group about the challenges observed by the group.

Challenging Behaviors Scenario

A possibility of any group is when there are one or more members who use judgmental, oppressive, or otherwise disparaging comments and behaviors. These members may also be in roles of power or seniority in an organizational chart. These members may have other privileges or status to separate them from others in the group or the company, or they may have poor inter and intrapersonal skills. Examples of these types of behaviors in the group may be illustrated as talking over people, cutting people off, using discouraging language towards and about others. How the group responds after the comment(s) is made, the content and process of the communicator delivering the comment as well as the content and process of the receiver(s) of the direct comment, and the bystanders in the group who were not a part of the direct exchange but actively witnessed the comment may still be affected in similar or different ways than the direct communicators.

Sue et al. (2019) called upon us all when they stated "given the immense harm inflicted on individuals and groups of color via prejudice and discrimination, it becomes imperative for our nation to begin the process of disrupting, dismantling, and disarming the constant onslaught of micro- and macroaggressions" (p. 128).

It is not uncommon for a group as a whole and possibly the receiver of the comment to react with a strong moment of silence. It is difficult to challenge oppressive, power, and privileged language in many groups, which may result in many members feeling their only safe response is to be silent, try to become invisible, or another self-preservation and self-protection reaction to minimize the person and their voice (Sue et al., 2019). There are several defense mechanisms a person can draw out when they feel uncomfortable. One that is not uncommon in these types of scenarios, but often is maladaptive to the situation is humor. Typically, in these scenarios when humor is used, it redirects, deflects, and/or diffuses by minimizing the impact of the comment(s) made. In turn, this minimizes what a person may be experiencing or perceiving as rising conflict and tension in the group or among member(s). "In many cases, bias and discrimination go unchallenged because the behaviors and words are disguised in ways that provide cover for their expression and/or the belief that they are harmless and insignificant" (Sue et al., 2019, p. 128).

For example, let's say we're in a large board meeting of 20+ members, where approximately half are senior leaders, and most of those leaders are white, married males who have held their positions for several years. A junior employee with six-months at the company is invited to a committee meeting to present on a topic, summarize a status report of specific work in process, and the committee will vote on the action items included in the presentation. This junior employee is a white female with approximately 15 years or more of their junior who is visibly active and exercises often. In the presentation, the junior member presents information about the inaugural health and wellness program the company will pilot later that year as one of the deliverables of this project. During the presentation, one of the senior leaders raises his hand to ask a clarifying question, and asks the junior member,

> so, I have a question. Tell me, you mentioned swimming as one of the program activities. Do you wear a bikini when you are swimming? Perhaps we can make up some flyers and get your picture at the pool for the marketing campaign because you clearly have the body to motivate people to join the program.

The comment is met first by long silence. The first person to speak is another female who is in a mid-level director position with 5-years at the company. She breaks the silence by laughing, then to say "ha, oh, that was funny! But, she's new here and doesn't understand our sense of humor. She doesn't get it" and then she laughs a bit more before silencing herself again.

In this example, the person who made the comment was in a position of power and privilege within the role in the company. The comment was an example that would be flagged by Human Resources as sexual harassment, if nothing else. The first person to speak attempted to minimize and justify the offensive comment using humor. Yet, the entire group was silent after the comment was delivered. It is easy to consider this scenario only affected the three key people in that verbal exchange; however, everyone in the group was affected. The extent to which each member and the group as a whole experienced the comment as offensive or a micro- or macro aggression may be different. POs are in a unique position as a part of the group while also being an external observer of the group's dynamics to point out this fact and help facilitate the conversation accordingly. Not addressing the event or creating the space for the consideration of the members to address the event may fuel continued oppressive and problematic behaviors for individuals as well as the larger culture and system. Ignoring the behaviors by not addressing them actually applauds public micro- and macroaggressions by those who make them, typically bullies. It reinforces a culture and system that tolerates bullying and harassment. It challenges those receiving and hearing these comments to speak up regardless if they are the direct recipient or a witness.

In this scenario, there are elements a PO must consider that are specific to the dynamics and process of the group as a whole, the dynamics and processes of the members within the group, and the specific communicators directly involved in the exchange. It is also just as critical for the PO to be mindful of their reaction as they are also a party to the exchange and experience that occurred. Part of the uniqueness in group (even task groups) is that space for process discussions are permitted and especially encouraged as a point of learning and growing when a PO is involved. None of this is meant to imply it is easy to cut through a very thick air of tension when triggering and disrespectful language or interactions are occurring in a group. It is hard work! And, still, POs may be in positions to assist. By doing so, the PO can influence the focus of how the group as a whole responds as well as the individuals involved in the exchange.

It can also be hard for a PO to confront the group and the possibility that what was said was in fact inappropriate. Perhaps the POs interpretation of the exchange was not the same as the experience the entire group had. Perhaps the PO was accurate in identifying the comments were offensive, but in so doing, the entire group erupts into a different direction than the focus of the task group. Or, perhaps a member attempts to offer a comment that may be viewed as a Process Observation, but does not appear to accurately capture the exchange and further reinforces the oppression, privilege, or power dynamics that were illustrated by the original comment. Regardless of who is offering a process-related comment – a PO or a member or the leader – it is important to remember, embedded within the comments offered is the specific perspective or lens in which each person uses to view the world and illustrate their values. Emotions and our individual backgrounds cannot be left out or covered up. This becomes a challenge recognizing how fast exchanges within groups occur – it's hard to keep up with the fluidity of the group dynamics happening every second.

Conclusion

Task groups may vary greatly in their scope, purpose, size, and timeline. They all can benefit from the insights and input of a PO who is able to provide the members and the group leader(s) with important feedback that can shape the group's efficiency and dynamics. Cultural factors must always be intentionally considered from the initial planning and conceptualization of any group as well as the addition of a PO, which adds another dimension to the experience overall. While it may not always be feasible for a group leader to hire or engage with a formal PO in a task group, we hope this chapter provides practical information to those interested to serve as group leaders or group POs.

References

American Psychological Association (APA) (2022). *Online Dictionary of Psychology* https://dictionary.apa.org/.

Bonaccio, S., O'Reilly, J., O'Sullivan, S., & Chiocchio, F. (2016). Nonverbal behavior and communication in the workplace: A review and an agenda for research. *Journal of Management*, *42*(5), 1044–1074. DOI: https://doi.org/10.1177/0149206315621146.

Coogan, T. & Steen, S. (2022). *Group counseling leadership skills for school counselors*. San Diego, CA: Cognella, Inc.

Hackman, J. R., & Morris, C. G. (1975). *Group tasks, group interaction process, and group performance* effectiveness: A review and proposed integration. In L. Berkowitz (Ed.), *Advances in experimental social psychology* (Vol. *8*, pp. 47–100). San Diego, CA: Academic Press.

Hall, J. A., Horgan, T. G., & Murphy, N. A. (2019). Nonverbal communication. *The Annual Review of Psychology*, *70*, 271–294. DOI: https://doi.org/10.1146/annurev- psych-010418–103145.

Sue, D. W., Alsaidi, S., Awad, M. N., Glaeser, E., Calle, C. Z., & Mendez, N. (2019). Disarming racial microaggressions: Microintervention strategies for targets, white allies, and bystanders. *American Psychologist*, *74*(*1*), 128–142.

Tuckman, B. W., & Jensen, M. A. (1977). Stages of small-group devel- opment revisited. *Group & Organization Management*, *2*, 419–427. http://dx.doi.org/10.1177/105960117700200404.

Chapter 11

Process Observation in Non-Therapeutic Settings

Christine Suniti Bhat, Ohio University

In virtually every organization, whenever a group of people convenes to accomplish a goal or a project, Process Observation (PO) can illuminate group dynamics to enhance efficacy and accomplish the goals of the group expeditiously. In all groups, the unique dynamics within it, the unique mix of members comprising the group, the ways in which they engage with each other, the sub-groups or cliques that might form, the leadership that is or is not exercised in the group, and the clarity of purpose of the group may all contribute to whether the group flourishes or fails. A PO can be an important asset to any non-therapeutic group, as someone who is not involved in the actual work of the group, but instead observes the group, and with a bird's-eye view, illuminates how process is helping or hindering the group's progress. Non-therapeutic groups, the focus of this chapter, exist in workplaces, factories, schools, or universities, and typically are task and goal oriented.

According to the Association for Specialists in Group Work (ASGW) *Guiding Principles for Group Work*, "Task groups promote efficient and effective accomplishment of tasks by a group of people typically assembled to achieve a specific and time-limited goal" (McCarthy, et al., 2022, p.12). Task groups do not aim to have members grow or change as a result of participating in them. However, change may happen, especially in groups that meet regularly over a longer period of time. For example, friendships may grow or deepen, and people may become more supportive of each other as the group "grows" together. What makes groups that have been created to accomplish a task or specific outcome successful? Below are some key elements of successful task groups in education or other workplaces.

Elements that Enhance the Efficacy of Workplace Task Groups

- Members feel that they are valued, that their contributions are worthwhile, and that they have a voice.
- Goals are clearly and operationally defined in as collaborative a manner as possible.
- Goal achievement is linked to specific people who will complete them, and timelines for completion should be clear.
- Members are invited to discuss roadblocks that they might be experiencing as they work towards accomplishing goals.
- Leaders set a positive, collaborative tone, and keep the group focused on accomplishing the goal/s of the group.
- Members see the value of the work they are doing, and do not consider it a waste of their time.

DOI: 10.4324/9781003281955-14

- Leaders provide positive feedback and encouragement to members who are helping accomplish goals.
- Leaders provide support, consultation, and encouragement to members who are struggling to accomplish goals.
- Members feel connected to the group and to each other.

Chapter 10 described task groups in detail, and in this chapter, I provide two case examples in non-therapeutic settings of how process observation might help a group improve its functioning. In the first case example, we will "observe" a task group at a university that got off to a poor start due to a lack of planning and a lack of awareness of process elements. Tips and strategies offered by a Process Observer to help right the course of the group are provided. In the second case example, we will see how an external consultant works with a small group in a manufacturing plant to begin to address issues of diversity awareness. POs of the positive interventions implemented by the consultant are offered. With both case examples, suggestions to assist with PO are provided in PO guides presented in tables.

Case Study One: University International Students Group

The helpful role of PO is highlighted in the following example about a task group at a university. The College of Education international student association at XYZ University, a predominantly white institution, is a newly formed task group. The leader of the group, Dolores, is a doctoral student in educational administration. Dolores' primary identities are: Puerto Rican, Catholic, heterosexual, ciswoman. She researches and writes about colonialism in higher education and in her current role as chair of the task force, she is invested in highlighting the challenges faced by international students from Central and South America.

The group is composed of volunteers who joined the group with great energy about two months ago. Group members and their primary identities are:

- Brooke, Ghanaian, Christian, ciswoman, lesbian, and able-bodied
- Greg, Polish, heterosexual, Catholic, cisman
- Mary, Irish, bisexual, Catholic, ciswoman, uses a wheelchair
- Lin, Japanese heterosexual, ciswoman
- Barry, French Canadian, gay, Buddhist, cisman
- David, Ethiopian, cisman, pansexual, Jewish
- Wong, Chinese American, heterosexual, Taoist, cisman

The broad purpose of the group is to highlight and celebrate the contributions of the large number of international students within the college, and to increase their sense of belonging within the college community. The impetus to develop the group was anonymous feedback that international students provided in an annual evaluation of college climate indicating that they often feel side-lined and sometimes feel invisible within the college. The group has been meeting every two weeks for approximately two hours for each session over the period of three months, and dissatisfaction has set in within the group. Some of the group members have complained to the faculty advisor that the group seems stuck and is not making any progress. The faculty advisor of the group, a white ciswoman has thus far maintained a hands-off approach, believing that the group is being led by a very competent leader. Dolores also happens to be her advisee. However, upon hearing the complaints she decides to sit in as a PO during the next meeting.

During the meeting the faculty member realizes several things:

- Dolores dominates the conversation and has very strong opinions about how the group should proceed
- Dolores does not seek input from her members
- The body language of the group members indicates that they disagree with many of the points Dolores makes. For example, Greg has pushed his chair back and has his arms crossed. Brooke is doodling, and rarely looks at Dolores. Mary and Lin often make eye-contact and Mary sometimes rolls her eyes.

The group has stalled and needs an intervention to address some of the difficulties that are apparent. Because group leaders and participants in non-therapeutic settings often lack training in group work, group processes and dynamics may not be apparent or understood by them. They also may not know how to intervene effectively when they do observe unhelpful group dynamics. Further, leaders in such settings are often too close to the group or too involved to be able to identify processes that may be hindering the achievement of group goals.

A trained and impartial PO can do what participants or leaders cannot do on their own. For example, task group leadership must be properly planned! It is important for the leader to have clear goals for what needs to be accomplished and obtain buy-in from members regarding the goals of the group. This might be as simple as circulating draft goals prior to the meeting and requesting members to come in prepared to discuss, add to, eliminate, prioritize, and finalize the goals of the group. In the case of this group, Dolores, with the best of intentions, has come into the group and presented the goals she developed to members, without attempting to obtain buy-in from them.

Another mistake that Dolores has made is to jump straight into business without doing anything to join with the members, to help them feel valued and heard. In her zeal to address the problem she has ignored the very people who can accomplish the goals of the group. As group members become more resistant to Dolores' leadership style, they engage less in the group, leading Dolores to experience anxiety, which causes her to talk more. A task group leader who is not attuned to the process that is unfolding before them can be doomed to failure.

The faculty advisor requests a doctoral student who has a group counseling cognate to work with Dolores to help her address some of the issues that have developed. While it would have been preferable for these issues to have been thoughtfully addressed before the group began, it is never too late to change course and get a group back on track. Process Observers can work closely with task group leaders to help them plan the group and they can provide PO at the mid-point or at the end of a group meeting (see Chapter 2 for more specifics). In some instances, they can provide written suggestions to the group leader during the group. For example, they may write a note such as "group seems stuck" or "perhaps a short break now might be helpful." If notes are being used, the leader and the Process Observer should inform the group members what they are doing so that group members do not become suspicious of secret communications they are observing. Having an open discussion of some of the suggestions made by the Process Observer would be appropriate.

Below are some PO suggestions that a trained Process Observer might offer Dolores. This should be done in such a way that Dolores does not feel threatened or chastened for her handling of the group. The Process Observer could highlight Dolores' passion and desire to see positive change, which are real assets in her leadership of the group. And the Process Observer could help Dolores understand that any interventions being offered are focused on helping the group function more effectively.

The Process Observer could help Dolores develop an opening statement for the next group meeting, sharing her desire to work effectively with them, and acknowledging that her desire to accomplish as much as possible in a short period of time coupled with nervousness might have led her to engage with the group in an unproductive way. Making such a statement requires a willingness on the part of the leader to be vulnerable to take responsibility for their actions. However, it is not only up to the leader – group members must also be willing to explore how they are standing in the way of the group accomplishing its goals.

The opening statement made by Dolores could be followed by her inviting members to join with her and each other, engaging with a renewed sense of purpose. Note that this type of redirection can be very challenging. It is better to spend time thoughtfully planning a group rather than having to do damage control after it has gone awry. However, damage control is preferable to continuing with an unproductive group that is not meeting its goals. Below are additional interventions that Dolores might utilize to improve the interpersonal functioning of the group.

Additional Suggestions to Get the Group Back on Track

- Begin the next group by inviting group members to share their reasons for joining this group.
- Have each member share one intention or attitude they bring to the task at hand.
- Have each member share a goal for the group to accomplish and write these on a whiteboard.
- Have members vote for the goals or ideas that they feel most strongly about moving forward on – this would likely lead to buy-in from group members.
- Break the priority goals into intermediate goals and identify a timeline to accomplish them.
- Structure meetings with an opening statement about how each person's ideas are valuable and state that it is important for all voices to be heard during the meetings.
- Help Dolores utilize supportive and facilitative comments so that members feel that their contributions are valued.
- When it comes to taking action, Dolores should be clear about a process to have people volunteer to complete specific tasks and she should be clear of the timeline.

Process Observation Guides

In addition to the suggestions provided above, once the group is back on track, a designated Process Observer might utilize specific group Process Observation (GPO) guides that allow the systematic observation and documentation of leader and member behaviors. Two such guides that might be useful in the current case example are offered below. Table 11.1 is an observation of process elements related to the leader. The PO may make brief notes related to each element listed (examples are provided), and then share these observations with Dolores for discussion and consideration of what she might need to change in order to lead while being more attuned to group process. The checklist has been filled out so readers can obtain an understanding of the type of comments a Process Observer might make. Table 11.2 is focused on POs of member behaviors and includes a simple rating scale for each element along with brief notes. Again, these could be shared with the leader. They may also be shared with the members and members could be asked to reflect on what specific ways they can enhance their engagement and participation.

Table 11.1 Process Observation of Leader/s

Process Observation Elements	*Notes*
Starting the meeting: (e.g., did the leader set a welcoming tone?)	*Leader began with opening remarks and thanked members for giving their time and energy to this work. Members seemed to respond positively to this.*
Providing an overview of what the group needed to accomplish in the meeting	*This continues to be a challenge – leader must work on being very clear about goals for each meeting and should not try to accomplish too much.*
Setting in place a process that invites input from each member	*Yes, leader paused regularly, asked for feedback, and did not begin talking again too quickly.*
Being aware of body language in the group	*Leader needs to work on this more. For example, leader never noticed that two members were looking down and not engaging at one point. Help leader with intervention strategies.*
Being aware of energy levels in the group	*Process Observer suggested a short break due to lower energy levels at the one-hour mark.*
Calling a short break if needed	*Leader should understand that calling a break is better than trying to push through when the group is tired.*
Being aware of when the group might be stuck	*Help leader with identifying that the group is stuck.*
Being aware of when the group might be "in the weeds"	*Leader did a good job of bringing the group back to higher-level issues.*
Being aware of how the group might be straying off topic	*Leader did a good job of bringing the group back to the task at hand.*
Being aware of time and ending a meeting in a timely way	*Leader was aware of time during this meeting.*
Using summarizing skills at the end of a meeting	*Leader did a great job of validating the efforts of members and in pointing the way forward to the next meeting. Leader requested members to think about one specific point prior to the next meeting.*
Pointing the way to the next meeting	*See above*
Thanking people for their investment in the group	*Yes, great job!*

Table 11.2 Process Observation of Individual Members: Member X

Process Observation Elements	*Rating Scale of 1 (low) to 5 (high)*	*Notes*
Engagement (non-verbal)	4	*Seems engaged, makes eye contact, nods head*
Engagement (verbal)	2	*Hardly speaks; may need to be invited to share thoughts*
Lulls in Energy	Note number of times this occurred	*Seemed to participate less around the 1-hour mark*
Peaks in Energy	Note number of times this occurred	*Seemed most energetic at the start of the meeting*
Non-verbal agreement or disagreement	Note number of times this was observed	*When was this noticed?*
Affinity for members	How many members does X feels close to	*Are there specific members that this person seems to listen to or value more than others?*
Affinity for leader	4	*Seems to value the leader's input.*

Case Study Two: Addressing Diversity-awareness in a Manufacturing Plant

In this next case study, we explore how a consultant is brought into a workplace to help set up a team with a specific purpose The purpose of the team in a small automotive parts manufacturing company in the midwest is to address issues related to a lack of awareness around diversity resulting in both racist comments and in microaggressions. The company is a family-owned business and has 76 employees, many of whom are first-generation, BIPOC, female immigrants. The organization has grown rapidly in the past 2 years, more than doubling the workforce from 30 to 76. The three-member leadership team is composed of White males.

Following several complaints about the culture within the organization, the leadership team has decided to set up a workplace task force, which employees have begun to call the WTF with much mirth. No one in the leadership team or on the task force is aware of the jokes about the acronym as they have not abbreviated the name of the task force. A first step might be to change the name of the team or task force! The task force is made up of five members, one from each division within the plant. The five members have been picked by their supervisors, and their only instruction has been to meet with an external consultant during a day-long retreat. During this retreat, their stated goal is to formulate a plan to address the culture within the plant.

The retreat is led by a consultant, S, a White ciswoman in her early 30s who has recently completed a master's degree in clinical mental health counseling and has established a diversity training practice. Members of the task force are in their 40s and 50s and two of the five have no college education. They do not appear to be invested in the task force, are not sure why they were chosen, or what the tangible outcomes might be. Members include:

- G, cisman, age 55. G immigrated to the USA from an Eastern European Country about 20 years ago and has worked with the plant for the past 12 years. He is outspoken and speaks negatively about the task force or the need for it.
- W, Chinese American cisman, age 32. W has worked at the plant for two years and came to the USA at age three. He has a college degree in math education but left a teaching position in a high school after consistently receiving poor evaluations from students. W's supervisor has noted that he is smart and has leadership potential.
- L, White ciswoman, age 27. L has grown up in the same town in which the plant is located and has worked for them since the age of 22, demonstrating a strong work ethic.
- T, White cis-man, age 51. T is gay and has expressed anger about homophobic slurs that have been used in his presence or within hearing distance.
- X, Mexican ciswoman, age 43. X is typically quiet but seems to have earned the trust of many of the immigrant women who have been employed in the plant in recent years.

As in the previous case, this task force will be doomed to failure if members do not understand why they are part of this team, if members are not invested in the work of the team, and if members do not respect each other. The consultant, S has her work cut out for her to empower and coach the task force to do the important work they have been asked to do. The consultant has been hired to set the team up with a day-long retreat and she will check in with the group on a monthly basis, meeting in person with them again during the 6th meeting.

Realizing the importance of building rapport and noting that each member of the task force is from a different division, with only a passing acquaintance with each other, S chooses to begin with some "low impact," rapport-building activities to help the group gain comfort with each other. She utilizes a get-to-know-you game with nine squares requiring members to get up, engage with each other and note down responses to questions, such as favorite sporting team, best beer, dream vacation, name/s of pets, favorite candy bar, etc. From a PO perspective, S is using a simple ice-breaker technique to diffuse tension that comes with the unknowns related to this new task with this newly formulated team. Groups where members do not know each other well often benefit from these types of activities.

Given the focus on diversity awareness, S goes on to an activity that allows for deeper reflection and sharing. S distributes a handout with a winding road and asks members to mark at least three pivotal moments on their road. She then asks each member to tell their story of how they came to be at this manufacturing plant at this point in time, allotting them 10–15 minutes each. From a PO perspective, this activity is designed to illuminate the diversity within the team, and to celebrate the life journeys of each member of the team. While each team member tells their story, S requests those who are listening to write down positive adjectives to describe the person who is speaking. Words such as gutsy, persistent, confident, strong, calm, permeate the room, and there is a visible shift with people in the room beginning to "see" each other as more than passing acquaintances in the workplace. In a day-long retreat, S has not been afraid to spend two or more hours on setting the right tone and creating the right atmosphere within the group for the work that has to be done.

Once this initial rapport and trust has been established, S determines that the team is ready to move forward and leads the group in some preliminary goal setting. She explains that these goals might change as the day progresses and she uses the metaphor of the winding road she used previously to help members understand that they cannot get to their destination by rushing. S engages the group in viewing three brief video case studies on diversity in the workplace, and after each case, she helps the team discuss and process what the companies in each case have done to address company culture. S makes sure that in the discussions of case studies, the group explores content, and she coaches them to become more aware of the process. She emphasizes that every voice in the team is important, and she encourages them not to fall into a pattern of team members speaking in a particular order.

After each case study, S leads team members through a summarization of what was the problem in the case study, and the steps taken to resolve them. She uses note charts on the walls and encourages the group to write down symbols or key words on each chart representing the solutions that were taken in each case study. She then asks the group to reflect on whether or not the issue in the case study is one that is pertinent to their own workplace and whether or not a tentative goal might be set that is similar to the one in the case study, but that is tailored to their own workplace.

In this phase of warming up the members to the topic, S freely acknowledges that some of the case studies may seem cheesy or not realistic to some of the group members. But she requests that they approach them with an open mind, to examine specifics in the case, to reflect on how the case might be similar or different to the culture in their workplace, and she asks members to reflect on whether the solutions proposed are workable. S emphasizes that every voice is important and reminds each member how their individual journeys allow them to bring to the table unique and important perspectives.

S teaches the group the five-finger consensus exercise. For each solution that is proposed in a case study, members are asked to raise one hand with one to five fingers showing.

5 = Love it
4 = Like it

3 = Could live with it
2 = Dislike it
1 = Hate it

S has team members close their eyes as they participate in the five-finger exercise in an effort to prevent some members from influencing each other. She then asks members to open their eyes and look around to see where their peers are. If there are 5, 4, 3 fingers raised, the group makes a note of that solution as having potential for them to implement. If there are 2s or 1s, group members are asked to explain their views and after a discussion a five-finger "vote" is taken again. From a PO perspective, S is paying attention to allowing decision-making to happen without more powerful members of the team influencing less powerful members of the team. She is also reinforcing the idea that everyone's opinions and views are needed and valued.

Once this work with case studies is completed, S has a starting point for what the team might begin to explore as interventions to address the culture in their workplace. She spends the remaining time helping the group formulate and refine three goals to enhance the culture at their plant. S helps the group develop timelines to accomplish the goals and facilitates a discussion of what might help or hinder the accomplishment of these goals. At the end of the day-long retreat, the group has formulated three goals and timelines, and commits to meeting for two hours every two weeks to discuss progress. S has paid attention to the process by gaining buy-in from team members and by not overwhelming the team with too many different ideas. With a clear path forward, the team is more likely to achieve progress.

A trained external PO would most likely conclude that S has paid attention to the process effectively. She has helped members join with one another and understand each other a bit more. In doing so, rapport has developed in the group, and members have been made aware of positive assets that each member possesses. Sensing that the group is not ready to look within, S engages the group in some "then and there" work, having them look outside of their environment with the case studies, and then she brings them back to a "here and now" assessment of strategies using the 5-Finger Consensus model. Through this model she is also teaching the group how to respectfully share dissenting views with each other.

As a leader, S pays particular attention to allowing those voices that are not heard as frequently as others to be heard. In this group, there are two members who are very verbal and are often opinionated. S makes space for those who are less verbal by having each member write brief responses and then utilizes a Round Robin format so that all voices are heard. S uses varied strategies with the Round Robin format to mix up the order in which people speak – for example, people may speak by height, by length of time in the company, starting with the newest employee, or by having members choose colors. S utilizes a guide to analyze an initial meeting that helps her identify group process and devise strategies to address them (Guide 3).

S encourages the group to have a member be identified as a process observer for each group meeting going forward and provides them with a checklist of PO. Overall, S has set up the team to have a greater chance of success in accomplishing the goals of the group. Going forward, S plans to check in with the group periodically and to have one final session with them during their sixth meeting. The plan is then to present the workplace culture intervention to the management and then implement it in the workplace, with each member of the task force serving as a leader in their own division.

In this chapter, we have looked at how PO can enhance the success of groups in non-therapeutic settings. With the case example from higher education, the role of a Process Observer to help re-correct the course of a group that is not meeting its goals is explored. In the second example, in a

Table 11.3 Group Process Analysis, Elements and Strategies

Group Process Element	*Notes*	*Strategies to Address*
Level of rapport among group members	Members do not seem to share great rapport with each other.	*Take time to "join" and help members begin to know each other at a deeper level.*
Body language	Body language indicates some distancing and defensiveness. Members W and X seldom make eye contact with speakers except when Member L speaks.	*Since Member L seems well-accepted by the 2 quieter members, devise ways for her to speak first.*
Frequency of speech	Members W and X do not speak very much. Members G and T dominate the initial session.	*Find ways to break this pattern. For example, use a writing exercise or use pair and share activities.*
Heightened emotion	Member T became emotional while telling his "story." Member L expressed support to him.	*Model advanced empathy statements. Reinforce statements L might make.*
Level of Engagement	Member W seems disengaged overall	*Look for ways to engage Member W early on as it might become more difficult for him to engage if he is left alone.*

manufacturing plant, the planning and actions of the consultant leading the workplace team during an initial day-long meeting are explored through the lens of how group process can help set up a group effectively and help group members have a better chance of successfully accomplishing the goals of the group. PO is a key skill for any group leader to develop. It is equally important for group members to learn about and pay attention to processes in groups, to understand how a lack of attention to process can derail groups that might have been set up with the best of intentions.

Reference

McCarthy, C. J., Bauman, S., Choudhuri, D. D., Coker, A., Justice, C., Kraus, K. L., Luke, M., Rubel, D., & Shaw, L. (2022). Association for Specialists in Group Work Guiding Principles for Group Work. *Journal for Specialists in Group Work*, *47(1)*, 10–21. doi: https://doi.org/10.1080/01933922.2021.1950882.

Chapter 12

Process Observation in Education and Clinical Training

Lorraine J. Guth, Indiana University of Pennsylvania
Marty Jencius, Kent State University
A. Michael Hutchins, Retired Counseling Practitioner and Consultant in Tucson, AZ

Part I of this book provides solid fundamentals of Process Observation (PO) in groups. This includes essential foundations skills such as Process Observer selection; ethics and professional issues; diversity, equity, and inclusion considerations; process of PO; effective observation; and processing the process. This chapter will focus on how to apply PO skills in education as well as in clinical training. The content of this chapter and relevant case examples will focus on higher education settings. However, the skills and strategies discussed can also be applied in elementary and secondary education settings.

"People do not mind being led when they are led well" (Jacobs, Schimmel, Masson, & Harvill, 2022, p. 23). This statement applies to group counseling, but can also be extended to classrooms in educational settings. Just like groups, classrooms are composed of students (group members) and a course instructor (group facilitator). Just like counseling settings, maximum learning and growth occur in the classroom when the group is optimally functioning. This includes setting the stage where rapport is built among group members. Course instructors can learn/enhance and utilize effective group skills to invite participation, facilitate discussion, and process the class interactions. These skills include basic skills for group leaders; skills to establish, hold, or shift the focus; and the use of meaningful rounds, dyads, and exercises (Jacobs, Schimmel, Masson, & Harvill, 2022; Page & Jencius, 2009).

Just as group leaders use many different techniques and skills, in educational settings teachers use a variety of teaching styles and techniques. A full description of effective teaching tips is beyond the scope of this chapter. However, readers can consult helpful teaching resources such as *McKeachie's Teaching Tips* (Svinicki & McKeachie, 2014); *Handbook of Counselor Preparation: Constructivist, Developmental, and Experiential Approaches* (McAuliffe & Eriksen, 2011); and *Teaching in Counselor Education: Engaging Students in Learning* (West, Bubenzer, Cox, & McGlothlin, 2013). McAuliffe and Eriksen (2011) shares key principles for adult educators that include creating a feeling of safety; ensuring the existence of sound relationships between the student and teacher; showing respect for learners as active participants; engaging learners; providing opportunities for immediate application; practicing equity; and encouraging teamwork. These engaging techniques can help to facilitate a creative balance of content and process in the classroom. These principles were written for educators who specifically teach adults, but also have general applicability to educators at all levels.

Process Observation in Education and Clinical Training

The use of PO can be thought of as a continuum where on one end there is no PO and on the other end there is a designated Process Observer for each class session. Additionally, in the middle there can be process comments, the use of an occasional Process Observer, and/or PO included

DOI: 10.4324/9781003281955-15

in assignments. This part of the chapter will focus on two aspects: PO in general education as well as PO in clinical training. Several case studies will be shared to show how these concepts can be applied in education and clinical training.

Process Observation in Education

PO can be used in a myriad of ways in education settings. Understanding the process of interactions among students can help to enhance the learning environment. Prior to the start of the semester, course instructors need to think about the optimal design of the course that involves identifying the student learning goals/outcomes; creating the syllabus for the course; preparing class session plans; choosing appropriate teaching methods, and selecting the appropriate technology (Svinicki & McKeachie, 2014). The course instructor also needs to determine how to best arrange the classroom (e.g., chairs in a circle, chairs in concentric circles, chairs in a U, etc.) and attend to the process in a classroom. The instructor can serve as a facilitator to make process comments when needed and/or process the class interactions with students in a meaningful way. In this scenario, the instructor will comment on the process to bring additional insight into the interactions among the class members but will not utilize a designated Process Observer. Alternatively, the instructor can utilize Process Observer(s) in the course to observe the process within the classroom and share observations with the class as appropriate. Consider the following case examples.

Case Example 1: Utilizing Process Comments in a Research Course

Teri is teaching a research course where there are 20 students. The content of the lesson today is exploring concepts of reliability and validity. Teri begins the class session by welcoming everyone back from the weekend. Teri states, "Today let's begin by having you all share some key learning or questions you had after reading the two assigned chapters." After this open invitation, Teri is aware that there is complete silence in the class that is followed by all students looking at the floor.

In this situation, Teri decided during the planning of this research course that they were not going to use a Process Observer in the classroom. However, Teri is a trained group worker and is aware in the moment that the "vibe" in the classroom is off and something is happening in the group. Teri has two choices: (1) ignore the process and continue with the lesson or (2) take some time to reflect and address the group process. Teri chose option 2 and said, "I am aware that when there was an open invitation to share insights from the readings, everyone looked at the floor." This process comment led into a meaningful discussion about a troubling situation that happened on campus over the weekend that got in the way of students completing the readings. Teri was able to briefly process the feelings in the moment and remind students that counseling services were available at the university counseling center if needed. The processing of the process conveyed that the instructor cared and then led to meaningful interactions about reliability and validity as the class moved into the content for the day.

Case Example 2: Using Process Observation in a Multicultural Course

Alex has taught an in-person multicultural counseling course for many years and feels happy about the course design that includes mini-lectures, guest speakers, counseling demonstrations, experiential activities, and case-study applications. Alex was getting ready to prepare for the semester and was just notified that the in-person course was changed to a synchronous Zoom course due to the COVID-19 pandemic. This course will also utilize an online-learning management platform to supplement the synchronous zoom component of the class. This was the first time that Alex needed to pivot to this blended instructional format and was not sure how this would impact the class content and process of student interactions.

Alex possessed exemplary group facilitation skills but was a bit "stuck" on how to proceed with the new course delivery. Fortunately, Alex's university offered a summer teaching academy to enhance online teaching skills and she actively participated. Alex received training and mentoring on how to adapt her course to best facilitate student engagement and growth. She also utilized the ASGW document, *Ten Tips for the Facilitation of Virtual Groups* (Guth, Pepper, Stephens, Pollard-Kosidowski, & Garrow, 2021). For example, Alex established norms for this blended instruction, attended to cultural and accessibility considerations, and monitored the group process during the synchronous meetings and asynchronous assignments.

Alex enhanced her course design and teaching skills due to what she learned in this academy. She thoughtfully designed engaging activities that were utilized in the synchronous and asynchronous components of this course. She was also intentional about the importance of the balance of content and process during the semester. An example activity that included POs was the use of an introductory nonverbal dice activity. As an adaptation to the in-person BARNGA simulation game that challenges participants to consider normative assumptions and cross-cultural communication (https://sites.lsa.umich.edu/inclusive-teaching/barnga/), Alex created a nonverbal dice game that was used during the synchronous zoom activity. Students were divided into breakout rooms and played this nonverbal game using a dice rolling app on their phones. The winners and losers from each breakout room were then moved to other breakout rooms and the nonverbal game continued for several rounds.

After the game was over, Alex processed the experience with the class members and the experiential game was used to explore intersecting identities and how the game was a metaphor for diversity issues in counseling. At the end of the activity, Alex asked students to reflect on the process of interactions that they observed during the activity. In this way, multiple students shared their observations regarding the process of interactions. This included how people reacted when they had different rules such as being passive and giving in to the majority or becoming angry and forcing the rules on others in a nonverbal way. The PO that took place among the class members brought new insights to the students regarding their specific interactions when faced with differences in cultures and expectations. In this situation, Alex applied the three phase model for task groups (Hulse-Killacky, Killacky, & Donigian, 2000) in this classroom setting that included the warm-up phase where the activity was planned and introduced to students; the action phase that included the performance of the task and observations of the student interaction during the activity; and the closure phase at the end of the activity where the students reflected on their experience. This section showcased how process comments and PO can be effectively used in content courses in higher education. The next section focuses on integrating these concepts in clinical training.

Process Observation in Clinical Training

PO has often been successfully used in clinical training in the counseling and psychology professions. For example, Rees and Maclaine (2016) discussed the efficacy of using a concentric circles approach where clinical psychology students learned about interpersonal process from the perspective of both a participant and an observer. Bieschke, Matthews, Wade, and Pricken (1998) found that "a process observer method that is ongoing an integrated into the system in which it occurs can be useful to trainers and trainees" (p. 64). This section will provide two examples of how PO can be utilized in group training. The concepts discussed can also be applied to other forms of clinical training such as individual and family counseling.

Case Example 3 – Using Process Observation in an Introductory Group Class

José is an instructor who is teaching an introductory graduate course in group work. Each week he observes students who facilitate groups within the class and he follows them as a Process Observer. Each week, José reports his observations but senses that the students are not receptive. The students do not see the same dynamics he sees while they are participating in the group. After giving didactic instruction regarding the PO role, José decides to take one person out of the group each week and have them perform PO. To prepare the students for the role of Process Observer, José provides a class lecture and a checklist for students in the first week of class to use when they stand in as the session's Process Observer. Each week, José has a different student sit out from the group as a Process Observer using the checklist he provides (see Appendix 1).

Students created a schedule where one designated student group member would sit out and serve as a Process Observer for each week of the group. Everyone in the class had the opportunity to process observe at least once. At first, students in the role of Process Observer were apprehensive about their ability to complete the task. The student in the Process Observer role for the week used the checklist (Appendix 1) as a guide, and with that tool, expanded on themes they observed in the session. The student Process Observer sat outside the group circle and quietly noted observations during the session. At the end of the group José had a didactic conversation with the co-leaders about their process for the group in the presence of the group and the Process Observer. Following that discussion, José had a conversation with the Process Observer, listening to their observations, asking questions of clarity, and discussing next steps for the group, all in the presence of the group and the co-leaders. Process Observers in this position often state they are surprised by what they were able to see in the group process, that they could not see while a being member of the group. When the Process Observer returns to the group in the next session as a member, they can contribute with a different level of understanding.

In subsequent sessions, student co-leaders draw upon the comments of Process Observers in planning the direction of the session. New Process Observers stepping into the role for the first time are less reluctant to observe, and some even cherish the opportunity to sit out for a session and focus on process. Alternating Process Observers through the course of the semester gives each student a chance to learn the role and each student brings a slight variation to the role and what they focus on.

How to Teach Process Observation in a Group Work Class

As mentioned in this chapter there has been little in the literature about the commonly used technique of PO, with even less written about how to use PO and teach it within a group-work course. Since José knows the important components that are part of PO, he can use those components as part of the students' experience. If the desired outcome of training in PO is having students that can act as Process Observers, engaging the students in the experience of PO while training them using in vivo groups seems to be the most effective method.

Most group-work training occurs in a time-limited instructional model that is commonly in a semester format. Predominant models of teaching include a weekly didactic portion of instruction and an experiential portion of group work (Ward, 2004; Hulse-Killack, 1996). The group work done during the experiential portion of the class includes a variety of options including instructor-led groups, student-led groups, or non-instructor-led groups. Groups within the class structure can be *contiguous groups* or *serial groups*. In this example, *contiguous groups* are groups within the class that start and end each week with the group session picking up from the previous week's topic. Each group has the same student members each week and can be centered around a particular topic e.g., growth groups, stress groups, work/life balance groups. *Serial groups* can have the same student members every week, but student leadership roles change with a differing topic or setting each week. One week might be a role play of an addictions group and the next week could be a role play of an adolescent group. In both group formats, leaders are changed every week to provide training in group leadership experiences. Both formats, contiguous and serial groups, can benefit from using a Process Observer.

In teaching PO, José structures the experience in a way where each week a member is selected to sit out of the group process and act as a Process Observer. Having rotating Process Observers provides the opportunity for each student to learn the PO role and take on an outsider's position for the group. From the authors' experience, having a student member in the role of Process Observer can support and strengthen the course instructor's observations and reduce the implication that the group process needs to please only the instructor's direction. As a result, members, once having been in the role of Process Observer, return to the group with a greater appreciation for the work to be done by the group.

Aspects of the Group for the Process Observer to Gather

The first part of assuming the role of a Process Observer is understanding the constructs that are to be observed. We view elements of PO in a counseling training group as falling into three constructs. The aspects of counseling training group PO are divided into *structural* components, *existent* components, and *projective* components.

Structural Components

Structural components are elements that describe how the group is structured. This group structure is established before the start of the PO. The structure of the group provides a context for what will happen in the counselor training group session to be observed. Structural components include *staging* and *continuity*. Staging is simply, what stage is the group at in their work together. The stage of the group gives the Process Observer some idea of what can be expected to be observed in content and themes. A group in the norming stage will have different engagement around trust and expectations than a group in the working stage (Jacobs, Schimmel, Masson, & Harvel, 2022). Each group will also be looking at different themes and expectations for future groups.

Continuity refers to how previous work is brought into the current observed session. Bringing previous work to the current group session (continuity) is easier and more relevant in contiguous groups because of the group's unifying theme across sessions, than in serial groups whose subject and member identity can change every week. Despite their weekly changing topics, serial training groups do have continuity elements. Most commonly, what is similar from group to group in serial groups, like contiguous groups, is the level of experience students have with the group process. Students in counselor training programs, whether engaged in serial groups of contiguous groups, typically have one or two opportunities to lead the group. A counseling student may not have the opportunity to lead a group from beginning sessions to ending sessions until they are in their practicum or internship.

Existent Components

Existent components are those PO components that are seen while doing the observation of the session. Existent components include both *evident* and *summative* aspects. Evident aspects are those that are more objective and emerge as supportive evidence for the Process Observer's comments. Evident aspects include *balance* in amount and reaction to member responses, the *topic of the session* and *changes in topic*, and *topic flow*. Balance is how often and in response to whom group members respond (Wilson & Conyne, 1990). Do observable dyadic interactions imply some meta-communication going on in the group? Changes in topic refer to the observer noting the topic being discussed, who introduced it, when the topic changes, and who changed it. Topic flow reflects the topic changes throughout the session and if there were patterns observed in the flow changes.

Summative aspects relate to larger questions of who seemed to be engaged and who seemed to be silent in the group throughout the whole session. Are there implications for what was discussed in this session or in future sessions? Summative aspects include emerging themes from the session that capture larger issues that the Process Observer may speculate.

Projective Components

The final component in PO is the projective component. Projective components include those aspirational ideas that emerge from the Process Observer's experience with the counselor training group. From the observer's point of view, what does the Process Observer think the group might consider for its next steps? Does the group have any ideas about how to balance member engagement in future groups? These observations posit challenges to the group in ways that they could alter their process for the best experience.

Incorporating a Student Process Observer into Group Simulations

With the aspects of what a process observer needs to look at defined, the next task is to propose a process for training process observers within the context of the group course. Elements include *selecting the observer* trainee, *providing instructions* to the observer, *doing the actual observation*, and the *end of session report-out process* to the group.

Selecting the observer should include rotating through students for each group session so each student in the group gets at least one or preferably multiple opportunities to be a Process Observer. Identifying a student who possesses group skills as the initial Process Observer provides a model for students who follow. In this model, it is important that every student gets an opportunity to participate in the Process Observer role. Giving the instructions to student observers can be done as part of the didactic portion of the class so everyone gets the instructions at the same time and questions can be answered as a class. The instructor needs to provide the concepts to observe as indicated in this chapter, perhaps by creating a checklist (like Appendix 1) to remind the trainee of the multiple aspects of observation. Before each session starts, inform, or remind the group of the purpose of the process observer and how the report-out process will occur for the group.

An example of using a checklist as a guide for PO could be in the third session of a 12-session graduate student growth group. Using the checklist found in Appendix 1, the process observer would note structural components such as what stage the group is in (staging) and what is included from previous work (continuity). In this example, the group could be in the norming stage, where they are still trying to define the rules and group norms. They may be carrying over work from previous group sessions of the introduction of members, trust exercises, and discussions on confidentiality.

During the session, existent components could emerge. This included things that are evident (behaviors seen during the session) and things that are summative such as themes that appear to be evident to the Process Observer as well as topics remaining to be discussed. As this group is a group for graduate student growth and early in its work, there could be a variety of evident issues arising such as an imbalance in conversation where a few members are monopolizing the topic discussion. The topic of stress in graduate school might come up and be dropped or changed when someone brings up the topic of multiple life demands. The Process Observer would follow who is speaking and where the topics flow as part of the existent/evident elements of the session. As part of the existent/summative components contained the checklist, the Process Observer would speak to themes emerging, perhaps one of graduate student self-efficacy or restructuring goals, that they heard but didn't voice.

In this case, projective components of the checklist would be the Process Observer's recognition of where they see the stage of the group and what work would be necessary for them to move further in the group-stage process such as what will be necessary for the group to move from a norming to a working stage. There may be other contextual pieces for this group to consider as the differences among members dependent on where they are in their life stages (young adult, married, parents, career changers) that the observer can see but members may not be aware.

For the observation process, the process observer and instructor should sit outside of the group circle and quietly take notes on the group process. Restrict conversation between course instructor and Process Observer so as not to distract the group while they work. There are no guidelines for how observers take notes; however, having some framework, like a list of aspects mentioned above, can assist the trainee in providing a rich and impactful report-out at the end of the session.

The report-out process can take many designs and the reader is encouraged to adapt as needed for the class conditions. One option is to use a fishbowl process where the student Process Observer and the course instructor meet in the center of the group and have a conversation regarding their observations. The instructor leads the conversation through expository questioning regarding what was observed and ideas on how the Process Observer developed those insights. Group members are only to listen during this time. When the conversation concludes, the instructor and student Process Observer leave the center of the group and the rest of the group is directed to discuss what they just heard. This discussion could be led by the group's designated leader for that evening. The group discusses reactions to what they have just heard from the PO and the steps for the next group session. At that point in the report-out process, the instructor and the student Process Observer return to the center of the group for final comments. The instructor and student Process Observer may include what they believe was heard from the group and what may have been missed from the initial report-out.

The report-out process may seem tedious at first, with a great amount of detail and specifics to be addressed from the checklist of the Process Observer. Experience with using a checklist and debriefing with the Process Observer demonstrates that it heightens the group experience and the training of group counselors. Students may rarely be asked to be Process Observers for other groups, but this process also teaches students to be in the moment with their group and provides a reflective leadership experience.

Teaching counselors in training in their first group work class how to do PO can be valuable, but it requires that future instructors have been trained in PO during their advanced degrees. Case Example 4 provides an example of how PO could be taught in an advanced group course.

The first three cases provide examples of "process observation in action." The following example engages participants in the creation of a group where the focus of learning is on PO as a skill and experience. This example provides ONE model for being involved in creating a situation where participants are involved in the integration of skills required for being an effective Process Observer. By being engaged from the beginning of the learning situation, participants can come to a fuller understanding of the impact of PO on individuals, relationships within the group, and the group as an entity. This case illustrates how the use of PO and related interventions can enrich the group on multiple levels.

Case Example 4: Using Process Observation in an Advanced Group Course

Hussein is responsible for an advanced graduate-level group counseling class that focuses on "process observation." The content for the class is group process. Hussein wants the participants in the class to learn the content by participating in the process and he hopes to facilitate experiential learning throughout the semester. Fifteen graduate students have enrolled in the course, and they expect a syllabus to be given to them at the beginning of the first class. Hussein has different plans.

Hussein developed the following process for the course that was guided by the vision, mission, and goals for the course:

- Engage all members of the community by having them actively participate in determining the path to learning.
- Have each student individually design a syllabus for the course by articulating what he/she/they wish to learn in the class.
- Bring the students together as a group and have the group design the vision for the course, integrating the designs created by the students individually.
- Have students articulate the similarities and differences they experienced when working individually and as a community.
- Formalize the acknowledgement of cultural differences and explore ways to strengthen the vision by integrating cultural dynamics. Historically, the course instructor would design the process of learning. How does a shared, integrated, vision differ from one created by the instructor? Explore ways for the instructor, facilitator, and students to focus on "how" they are creating a learning community, not solely on "what" needs to be learned. Explore ways to share "corrective feedback" and other dynamics within the group setting (Hulse-Killacky, Orr, & Paradise, 2006; Orr, J & Hulse-Killacky, 2006; Hulse, & Robert, 2014).

Additionally, there were three skill sets that the course instructor wished to develop during the semester. As part of the course design, Hussein introduced these concepts to the rest of the group as specific behaviors emerged. These skill sets include translation skills that included how the group worked to articulate the tasks and activities to meet the course goals; maintenance skills that included continual ongoing reflection and PO; and evaluation skills that included examining the effectiveness of the learning and group process. As the group matures, it moves back and forth utilizing these different skill sets and providing opportunities for group members to develop PO skills. At different stages of group development, different behaviors will emerge and recede. As the students experience this fluctuation, they will come to a fuller understanding of the patterns and dynamics of group process. The questions asked are the kinds of questions a Process Observer will be exploring when working in classes and other experiential group activities. These questions are amongst the questions a group PO may bring into processing situations. As the group moves forward, students are also encouraged to intervene during an ongoing session to provide process comments.

1. *Translation Skills:* Have the students work together to create the *specific* tasks/activities they will use to accomplish the goals or move forward with the vision they have created. As they work to articulate the path toward accomplishing the group vision, have members of the group reflect upon the process they are using to articulate and accomplish the identified tasks. (Do they need to work together to design specific "exercises" or is the translation of the goals into specific behaviors enough of an "exercise"?) Facilitate the interactions as the group goes through the group development stages. Have different students become Process Observers as the group explores this activity. Have the group provide feedback to the Process Observers.
2. *Maintenance Skills:* As the group moves through the semester, have them regularly reflect upon how their working together on the specifics they have designed are integrating into the vision they have developed for the community. Are there specific feelings, thoughts, and behaviors moving the group toward the stated vision? How is this being done specifically? Do changes need to be made to the individual activities or to the vision/goal? If so, how does the group go about creating the changes? Encourage group members to reflect upon individual growth, growth in relationships they have with other group members, and the group as a community. What changes (or lack thereof) are they experiencing in group themes, thoughts, feelings, behaviors, and other dynamics?
3. *Evaluation Skills:* As part of the design, the community needs to build in a system for evaluating the process of learning. How are individuals, relationships, and the group-as-a-community experiencing the ongoing process? How are cultural differences being integrated into the ongoing process? Is safety being enhanced? If so, how? What are the "difficult discussions" and how are they being addressed by individuals, sub-groups, and the community-at-large? Is technology having an impact? If so, how? How are community members going to be evaluated? At the end of the course, what would participants do differently and how will that impact them as they move forward in the field? What is the most effective way to measure that change?

It is hoped that these cases provided illustrative examples of how to use PO in education and clinical training. Instructors need to intentionally think about how to best use process comments and/or PO in the courses that they teach. It should be noted that often in higher education settings, peer observations of faculty teaching occur. A discussion of this type of evaluation is beyond the scope of this chapter. However, the PO concepts covered can be thoughtfully utilized by peer observers as well. The next session will offer some tips for how to meaningfully implement the concepts covered in this chapter.

Ten Strategies for Utilizing Process Observation in Education and Clinical Training

There is sparse literature on using PO in education and clinical training. This chapter concludes with ten strategies for utilizing PO in this context. These tips are nonlinear and can be applied in general education and/or clinical training courses.

1. **Set the Stage for Success:** Prior to the beginning of a course, preplanning is paramount. Course instructors need to determine the course learning objectives, teaching style, format, and mode of delivery. Planning of class activities that include attention to the delicate balance of process and content must be considered. The importance of norm setting (Corey, Corey, & Corey, 2018) is also key for the successful utilization of a process observer.
2. **Understand the Role of PO and How Best to Utilize a Process Observer in Content or Clinical Courses:** Instructors must understand the role of the Process Observer, which includes having an observer in the group disregard the content of the meeting, focus more on the processes of the meeting, and then reflect back what appears to be happening with the interactions of the group (Conole, 1978). This observation includes attention to verbal communication such as who speaks and who is quiet; nonverbal signals such as facial expressions and eye contact; roles that are adopted or assigned in the group; general behaviors such as how people get along, subgroups, and group roles; and group climate and atmosphere (Conole, 1978). The instructor needs to determine if there will be a designated process observer, if the class members will be invited to collectively observe the process, or if they will provide process comments during the class meetings. Ground rules for providing PO during the group session will need to be clearly articulated. For example, the course instructor may decide to include PO by the students (or by a designated Process Observer) as a regular component at the end of each class session and to include PO in the syllabus. In all these scenarios, explicit instructions and training need to be provided on PO so all are aware of the intent and usefulness in the classroom. Particular attention may need to be paid to language consistency (e.g., not using "feel" when I mean "think or believe") and to themes that may underlie the overt behavior (e.g., Is there a group member who consistently attends to the "bigger picture" behind the immediate behavior?).
3. **Embody a Culturally Responsive Approach to PO in the Classroom:** *The Multicultural and Social Justice Counseling Competencies* (MSJCC) (Ratts, Singh, Nassar-McMillan, Butler, & McCullough, 2016) emphasize the importance of understanding the intersection of identities, the influence of oppression on well-being, the exploration of the social environment, as well as balancing individual counseling and social justice advocacy. The MSJCC framework needs to be used as a guiding document in the classroom that is composed of students who have intersecting identities. Conyne (2008) adapted Hanson's *What to Look for In Groups* document to include multicultural considerations in PO. Readers are encouraged to access Conyne's adapted guide as a useful tool for Process Observers, which could also be further adapted today to include concepts from the MSJCC.
4. **Use Meaningful Group Activities that Include Processing:** Course instructors can design lessons that incorporate meaningful and experiential group activities that relate to the course objectives. These activities are designed to facilitate learning and need to include a process/processing component (Jacobs, Schimmel, Masson, & Harvill, 2022; Jacobs & Schimmel, 2013). As an example, an instructor who is teaching a group counseling course can start off the class session with a designated word or phrase round where students must

say "here, getting here, or not here" to assess students' attention in the group (Jacobs, Schimmel, Masson, & Harvill, 2022). After the round is complete, for the members who said "not here" or "getting here," the instructor could ask, "What would help to get you here?" This can then serve as an example for how to use rounds in a group and then the students can be invited to share POs that were noted during the round, which also serves to model the importance of group process.

5. **Utilize Process Comments:** There are times in a classroom where Process Observer(s) are not being utilized, but process comments from the instructor can be very meaningful as was illustrated in Case 1. Course instructors can be aware of the process of interactions of the students and, when appropriate, can make meaningful POs to help maximize the optimal functioning of the group. With some guidelines, practice, and instruction, students may also be encouraged to make process comments during a class.
6. **Balance Content and Process in the Classroom:** A skilled group facilitator and course instructor can effortlessly balance the content and process in the classroom setting. "Groups must focus on both the content (or purpose) and on the process-that is, how things happen in a group and how members participate" (Hulse-Killacky, Killacky, & Donigan, 2001, p. 9). Course instructors can "attend to the process by asking the following questions: Who am I?; Who am I with you?; and Who are we together? Content questions include: What do we have to do? and What do we need to do to accomplish our goals?" (Hulse-Killacky, Killacky, & Donigan, 2001, p. 9).
7. **Utilize Guiding Documents When Challenges Happen in the Educational Setting:** Challenges and conflict may occur in the classroom and instructors can be guided by helpful documents in the field such as *Ten Strategies to Intentionally Use Group Work to Transform Hate, Facilitate Courageous Conversations, and Enhance Community Building* (Guth, Pollard, Nitza, Puig, Chan, Singh, & Bailey, 2019) or the *Guiding Principles for Group Work* (McCarthy, Bauman, Choudhuri, Coker, Justice, Kraus, Luke, Rubel, & Shaw, 2022). The content of these documents provides useful tools for navigating conflict and acquiring key group skills.
8. **Evaluate the Impact of the Course and/or the Use of a Process Observer:** Course instructors need to use formal and informal assessments to evaluate the effectiveness of the course including the impact of using a Process Observer. Additionally, the course instructor can administer self-evaluations to obtain feedback on the class facilitation. Evaluation contributes to the continued growth of the group facilitator and members (Berg, Landreth, & Fall, 2013).
9. **Adapt to Changes in Technology in a Meaningful Way that Attends to Group Process:** Recent events such as the global pandemic have changed the way that groups and education are delivered. New technological advances now allow groups and classes to be delivered via a variety of technology platforms such as Zoom, Microsoft Teams, and Google Meet. Course instructors need to adapt and learn how to use these new electronic platforms to best facilitate the content and process interactions when delivering a class.
10. **Enjoy the Process:** Ursula K. Le Guin wrote "It is good to have an end to journey towards; but it is the journey that matters, in the end." This quote underscores the importance of having course instructors and students enjoy the process during their collective time together in education and/or clinical training courses.

In conclusion, this chapter provided an overview of using PO in education and clinical training. The content and cases in this chapter showcase the importance of utilizing PO in content courses such as research as well as clinical courses such as group counseling. PO or process comments when utilized in a classroom can help to facilitate engaging student interaction, enhance the learning process, and increase self-awareness. It is hoped that the readers will apply the *Ten Strategies for Utilizing Process Observation in Training and Educational Settings* in their work settings.

References

Berg, R. C., Landreth, G. L., & Fall, K. A. (2013). *Group counseling: Concepts and procedures*. Routledge.

Bieschke, K. J., Matthews, C., Wade, J., & Pricken, P.A. (1998). Evaluation of the process observer method: Group leader, member, and observer perspectives. *Journal for Specialists in Group Work, 23*, 50–65. https://doi.org/10.1080/01933929808411381.

Conole, L. (1978). Process observation. *Asia Pacific Journal of Human Resources, 16(2)*, 11–17. https://doi.org/10.1177/103841117801600202.

Conyne, R. K. (2008). What to look for in groups: Helping trainees become more sensitive to multicultural issues. *The Journal for Specialists in Group Work, 23(1)*, 22–32. https://doi.org/10.1080/01933929808411379.

Corey, M. S., Corey, G., & Corey, C. (2018). *Groups: Process and practice* (10th ed.). Cengage.

Guth, L. J., Pepper, E. L., Stephens, A. F. Pollard-Kosidowski, B. L., & Garrow, J. (2021). Ten tips for the facilitation of virtual groups. *Journal for Specialists in Group Work, 46*, 309–321. https://doi.org/10.1080/01933922.2021.1984620.

Guth, L.J., Pollard, B. L., Nitza, A., Puig, A., Chan, C. D., Singh, A., & Bailey, H. (2019). Ten strategies to intentionally use group work to transform hate, facilitate courageous conversations, and enhance community building. *Journal for Specialists in Group Work, 44*, 3–24. https://doi.org/10.1080/01933922.2018.1561778.

Hulse, D., & Robert, T. (2014). Preplanning for feedback in clinical supervision: Enhancing readiness for feedback exchange. *Journal of Counselor Preparation and Supervision, 6(2)*, http://doi.org/10.7729/52.1091.

Hulse-Killacky, D. (1996). Using the classroom as a group to integrate knowledge, skills, and supervised practice. *Journal for Specialists in Group Work, 21*, 163–168 https://doi.org/10.1080/01933929608412246.

Hulse-Killacky, D., Killacky, J., & Donigian, J. (2001). *Making task groups work in your world*. Merrill Prentice Hall.

Hulse-Killacky, D., Orr, J. J., & Paradise, L. V. (2006). The corrective feedback instrument-revised. *The Journal for Specialists in Group Work, 31(3)*, 263–281. https://doi.org/10.1080/01933920600777758.

Jacobs, E, & Schimmel, C. (2013). *Impact therapy: The courage to counsel*. Impact Therapy Associates.

Jacobs, E., Schimmel, C. J., Masson, B., & Harvill, R. (2022). *Group counseling: Strategies and skills* (9th ed.). Cognella.

McAuliffe, G., & Eriksen, K. (Eds.). (2011). Handbook of counselor preparation: Constructivist, developmental, and experiential approaches. Sage.

McCarthy, C. J., Bauman, S., Choudhuri, D. D., Coker, A., Justice, C., Kraus, K. L., Luke, M., Rubel, D., & Shaw, L. (2022). Association for Specialists in Group Work Guiding Principles for Group Work, *The Journal for Specialists in Group Work, 47*, 10–21. https://doi.org/10.1080/01933922.2021.1950882.

Orr, J., & Hulse-Killacky, D. (2006). Using voice, meaning, mutual construction of knowledge, and transfer of learning to apply an ecological perspective to group work training, *The Journal for Specialists in Group Work, 31*, 189–200. https://doi.org/10.1080/01933920600777824.

Page, B. J., & Jencius, M. J. (2009). *Groups: Planning and leadership skills*. Lahaska.

Ratts, M. J., Singh, A. A., Nassar-McMillan, S., Butler, S. K., & McCullough, J. R. (2016). Multicultural and social justice counseling competencies: Guidelines for the counseling profession. *Journal of Multicultural Counseling and Development, 44*, 28–48. https://doi.org/10.1002/jmcd.12035.

Rees, C. S., & Maclaine, E. (2016). Concentric circles therapy training: Clinical psychology trainee's reflections on participation in a revised interpersonal therapy training group. *Australian Psychologist, 51*, 231–237. https://doi:10.1111/ap.12167.

Svinicki, M. D., & McKeachie, W. J. (2014). McKeachie's teaching tips: Strategies, Research, and theory for college and university teachers. Cengage Learning.

Ward, D. E. (2004). Introducing a special issue on teaching group work. *Journal for Specialists in Group Work, 29(1)*, 1–2. https://doi.org/10.1080/01933920490275286.

West, J. D., Bubenzer, D. L., Cox, J. A., & McGlothlin, J. M. (2013). *Teaching in Counselor education: Engaging students in learning*. Association for Counselor Education and Supervision.

Wilson, F. R., & Conyne, R. K. (1990). Observing groups at work: Models, means, and methods (ED316809). *ERIC*. https://eric.ed.gov/?id=ED316809.

Part IV

Past, Present, and Future of Process Observation

Chapter 13

Foundational History of Process Observation in Groups

Madison Blaydes, University of Texas at Austin

Keshav R. Goud, University of Texas at Austin

Introduction

Over the last century, the notion of process observation has existed in, and influenced, a multitude of fields and disciplines, like ethnography, therapy, social, and organizational psychology. However, seldom has it been studied as a concept of its own entirety. In this chapter, we attempt to extract Process Observation from the vast literature and synthesize its journey through the years across various disciplines. We will present this journey mostly chronologically, highlighting the significant contributions to Process Observation literature made by both notable individuals and different disciplines. Throughout these various contexts, the term and purpose of Process Observation has been used and defined in a variety of ways. Our intention is to give a taste of the different key figures and disciplines that shaped our theoretical understanding of Process Observation, rather than a deep dive into all possible literature, disciplines, and definitions. We hope the references in this chapter can be used by curious readers to dig deeper into these histories. For additional information regarding empirical research related to Process Observation, refer to Chapter 15 of this book.

To begin, we will focus on ethnographic research, as that is where we first witnessed the extensive usage of Process Observation. The work of ethnography is vast and diverse. Within this chapter, we have focused on one specific subset of ethnographic work that relates more directly to Process Observation, which is when ethnographers observe small groups.

Ethnography

Ethnography is considered to have formally originated in the 1800s through the work of Lewis Henry Morgan, who observed Native American groups like the Iroquois (Ugwu, 2017). With ethnography, the researcher joins their subject's social setting in an effort to improve their understanding and interpretations of various phenomena (Gusterson, 2008). Understandably, observation is a central component of this research. In the case of ethnographic research with smaller groups, researchers typically observe the processes unfolding within the groups in the naturalistic settings. An example of Process Observation within this context is the book *Street Corner Society* by William Foote Whyte, which is considered to be a classic work in sociological research.

The focus of Whyte's book was on observations of the inhabitants of Cornerville, a low income district made up of predominantly Italian immigrant families in the 1940s. Whyte moved to, and lived in, Cornerville, soon befriending an important member of the neighborhood, "Doc." Doc introduced Whyte to others in the community and over time and repeated interactions, Whyte became a well-known member of Cornerville. During the time of Whyte's observations, many Americans had negative perceptions of Cornerville, which were often steeped in limited

DOI: 10.4324/9781003281955-17

knowledge outside the pervasive negative news stories about Italian immigrant communities. An example of this bias was the stereotype that folks from the Cornerville community were criminal defendants. No solutions existed at Whyte's time for ways of better supporting individuals from this neighborhood. Thus, Whyte sought to better understand the happenings and nuances of Cornerville. Whyte documented his observations of the Cornerville community, including folks determined to be dominant leaders, and their actions within his book.

Although Whyte didn't utilize the term Process Observation within his first edition of the book, his role within the group centered around his impressions of group dynamics and behaviors, much like the role of a Process Observer in a more traditional therapy group-like setting. In the second edition of *Street Corner Society* (1955), Whyte added in an appendix that explored the methods of his work, including a section detailing his training in Process Observation for the role. Early ethnographic and anthropological work didn't always include the same terminology for Process Observers; however, the field has recognized early works like Whyte's as using this method within their research.

A notable difference in ethnographic work like this, and what we typically see in contexts that utilize Process Observation in more traditional ways, is that the ethnographic researchers do not provide ongoing feedback on their observations to all members of the group. Within ethnographic work, efforts are often made to observe processes unfolding more organically, which would be disrupted with conversations and feedback on ongoing group processes (Gusterson, 2008). This experience diverges from a critical point of the process observer's roles, which is to provide consistent, timely, and non-judgmental feedback to the group (Barnlund, 1955). Another discipline that utilized Process Observation without always using that specific terminology was family therapy, which is explored below.

Family Therapy

Interventions to help families navigate problems have existed for centuries. In the 1940s and 1950s, the more formal practice of family therapy we are familiar with today took root after the formation of the American Association of Marriage Counselors in 1942 (Nichols Jr., 1973). Early on, psychoanalysis informed family therapy work, which was later joined by learning theory and behavior therapy (Goldenberg & Goldenberg, 2012). Within family therapy work, the therapist has historically served as an observer of family dynamics (Rivett & Street, 2009). Families are yet another example of a small group structure, like Whyte's work with individuals from the Cornerville community, which makes them a relevant fit for conversations about Process Observation.

Rivett and Street (2009) note that within family interactions there are important behavioral patterns to observe in the therapy room as these inform dynamics occurring outside the therapy space. The therapist takes note of important family interactive patterns they observe, like which family members are more active or passive in conversations, who helps children in the family settle, and who interrupts other speakers in the family most. It's important for the therapist to have conversations with family members about the role of observation and feedback early on as this process is an integral component to facilitating change within the dynamics of the family. The therapist must be thoughtful about the timing of presenting these non-judgmental observations to the family to preserve the therapeutic alliance and maintain a safe atmosphere for change. The role of the therapist in family therapy has had many similarities in the work of a Process Observer, including the role of non-judgmental feedback and watching interactions unfold from an outside perspective. However, the term Process Observer hasn't always been used to frame this role.

Training opportunities for graduate students have also provided opportunities to observe family dynamics in therapy sessions. Historically, graduate students have had the opportunity to observe family therapy sessions live or by videotape, giving them a chance to watch and note important emerging dynamics (Everett, & Koerpel, 1986). The perspective of students outside the therapy space can be beneficial as they are not confined to the therapy room in which entrenched interaction patterns are actively occurring. Now that we have explored Process Observation taking place as a part of naturalistic settings and therapy rooms – without being explicitly referred to as process observation, let us turn to a more formalized and structured understanding of Process Observation.

Robert Bales

One of the first notable individuals to discuss group processes and observations was Robert Bales. Bales was a social psychologist, a professor and director of the Laboratory of Social Relations at Harvard University where he specialized in interpersonal interactions occurring in small groups (Kagan et al., 2006). He established the foundation of this work over 75 years ago, by underscoring the versatility of group Process Observation across diverse disciplines. Bales (1950) helped start the conversation about differences between relationship-oriented behavior and task-oriented behaviors that arose within groups, which is an ongoing discussion we see today about understanding process versus content in groups. He also discussed the importance and process of training observers to record experiences within groups, and even created a protocol for doing so.

Bales (1950) formulated a structured and generalized method for Process Observation, striving to cut across the disciplinary boundaries of clinical psychology, social psychology, sociology, and anthropology. He was the first to conceptualize structured observation of small groups in a controlled environment instead of a naturalistic environment. He also strived to make a "transition from an individually centered frame of reference…to a larger framework centered on multiple-person systems of social interaction and their dynamics" (Bales, 2017, p. xiii). That is, instead of focusing on only individual behavior, he treated groups as a primary unit of analysis. By adopting this larger framework, he could shed light on interactions and conflicts that occurred between individuals while performing a task in the group. He aimed at creating more generalized procedures for observations and analyses that would be applicable over a host of group settings across larger social systems. Through conceptualizing these methods, Bales aimed at integrating the influence of social interactions and individual's personality factors on group behavior, which he captures in his social interaction systems theory. This theory was the culmination of his life's work and its origins will be explored more in the following section.

Social Interaction Systems Theory

Bales (1951), in his first seminal book, *Interaction Process Analysis*, theorized a method to observe emotional, intellectual, and behavioral interactions that occur in small face-to-face groups. He arrived at this method through studying interactions of individuals with alcohol addictions in group therapy settings. In this book, he clearly defined the categories of observable behaviors and set procedures to note their occurrence and frequencies. These categories ranged across both task-related and socio-emotional behaviors.

In the task-related category, Bales (1950) distinguished between behaviors that sought clarification through questions (e.g., asking for more information, opinion or suggestions) and behaviors that provided clarification through answering these questions. In the socio-emotional category, Bales differentiated between positive and negative reactions. Positive reactions involved showing solidarity, agreeable behavior, and efforts towards releasing tensions between individuals. Negative reactions, on the other hand, involved exhibiting antagonism, disagreement, and creating tension. He collated these behaviors into 12 categories and proposed ways to map and analyze the frequency of behavior observed to understand a group's functioning across different settings, from planning, policy-forming and problem-solving to training and therapeutic contexts (Bales, 1950). While his method of assimilating and analyzing group behavior continually evolved in sophisticated ways over the second half of the 20th century, we believe that his fundamental distinction between content (task) and process (socio-emotional) was a crucial step in the history of group process observation.

Bales' interaction process analysis eventually evolved into the SYMLOG model – systematic multiple level observation of groups – an observational method used for determining the effectiveness of social interactions in groups and larger social systems. The SYMLOG theory emphasizes the role of personal, interpersonal, group-level, and external context on the individual's behavior within the group (Bales, 2017). This method maps behaviors of group members onto a field diagram that captures how the members relate to each other on three dimensions: dominance vs. submissiveness, friendliness (group-oriented) vs. unfriendliness (individualistic), and acceptance vs. opposition of authority. These dimensions are captured in a 26-item value-based rating form. The dominance vs. submissiveness dimension captures the power, status, and personal influence of an individual in relation to other group members. An example of an item measuring dominance is "individual financial success, personal prominence and power" and submissiveness is "giving up personal needs and desires, passivity" (Bales, 2017, p. 10). Additionally, an item on the acceptance of authority dimension is "conservative, established, 'correct' ways of doing things" (Bales, 2017, p. 10).

The role of a Process Observer within this model is to rate the group members' behaviors on 26-item values stemming from the three dimensions. Every rating form begins with a rating question. A standard example of this question is, "In general, what kinds of values does this person show in his or her behavior?" (Bales, 2017, p. 14). Data is also collected in order to understand the values that a most effective leader would act by; the rating question for the same would look like, "In general, what kinds of values does the most effective leader of a task-oriented team you have known show in his or her behavior?" (Bales, 2017, p. 15). This question can be customized to any organizational role by replacing the term "leader" with any other role title. In this way, SYMLOG captures data about both the actual behavior of a group member and the behavior that is expected by the organization (or fellow group members) to be in the most effective profile of functioning. Bales does believe that there is a set of most effective values and behaviors for optimum functioning in a group. In fact, he provides suggestions for moving the individuals towards this optimum profile based on the data he collected from numerous organizations (Bales, 2000). With the advancement of systems theory in the late 20th century, this model has been evolved to observe and assess group functioning at different levels of an organizational system.

In the following section, we will focus on Dean Barnlund's contributions to our understanding of Process Observation from a communication perspective. His work helped shape understandings of interpersonal and intercultural communication within organizational contexts.

Dean Barnlund

Dean Barnlund was a professor in communication who focused on interpersonal and intercultural communication. His interests in communication were shaped by his travels and research in Japan

(Bennett, 2012), like the nuance and complexity of communication styles and cultural differences in the United States and Japan. Barnlund believed that group discussions could be improved by using feedback from one or two observers focused on the effectiveness of group interactions, which he elaborated on in his article, "The use of group observers" (1955).

Regarding process observation, Barnlund (1955) defined the Process Observer's role as closely watching and tracking attitudes and actions that emerge in group behavior within organizational contexts, with the intention to report that behavior back to the group. He felt the Process Observer should withhold judgment in favor of more factual reports to allow group members to come to their own conclusions. For example, the Process Observer would document specific attitudes and actions made by group members rather than their interpretations of events that unfolded in the group. Barlund also described how helpful it is for the group to hear descriptive information of the group processes from the Process Observer. This stream of descriptive data from the Process Observer, he argued, helps improve the group's discussion process. Barnlund also noted that the Process Observer can become more attuned to subtleties in human behavior with practice. In an effort to help guide the process observer's attention, he shared a list of questions to keep in mind while watching the group, like: "Did all the members of the group have an equal opportunity to participate? Did the group make the best use of its potential? At what points did interpersonal tension exist? Why? What brought it about? How was it released?" (Barnlund, 1955).

Notably, Barlund (1955) felt the roles and responsibilities of the Process Observer were different from the content observer. This conclusion compliments Bales' work as Barlund (1955) also felt content and process were distinctly different, but important components of group dynamics. Through Barnlund's perspective, the content observer watched and noted the effectiveness of a group's ability to address problems it was investigating. For example, the content observer would note how quickly decisions were made by group members. Barnlund provided a list of questions to help guide a content observer's attention. For example,

> Did the group ascertain quickly the exact nature of its problem? Was the problem investigated in a logical and systematic manner? If not, why not? At what points did digressions occur? How serious were they? Who was responsible for them? How did the group recover?
> (Barnlund, 1955, p. 47).

Barlund noted that it could be helpful to have two different individuals serve as the content or Process Observer given the quickly evolving nature of group conversations.

Barnlund later went on to develop the transactional model of communication (1970), which elaborates on how messages can be sent and received simultaneously between individuals. The model includes a multi-layered feedback system in which the sender and receivers of messages communicate through continuous feedback. For example, at the start of a job interview, a job candidate introduces themselves and while the candidate is speaking, the interviewer is reacting to the candidate's words and body language. Thus, the candidate and interviewer are sending and receiving messages at the same time (Cuofano, 2022). The model includes three main components: public cues (i.e., occur within the environment and can be artificially created), private cues (i.e., emotional or sensory experiences that are verbal or nonverbal), and behavioral cues (i.e., behavioral reactions that are verbal or nonverbal). This model can be used to understand the continuous and simultaneous process of interpersonal communication (Barnlund, 1970).

Like this model, much of Barnlund's work on interpersonal communication centered around the dynamic of process rather than content. The next two sections will explore these key concepts of Process Observation in organizational diagnosis and process consultation theory. Both these sections are situated in the field of organizational development that aims at facilitating organizational and personal change through knowledge in social and behavioral science (Anderson, 2019).

Organizational Diagnosis

Organizational diagnosis involves understanding the underlying processes that occur in various systems of an organization, to enhance its effectiveness (Alderfer, 2011; Paul, 1996). Diagnoses can be used to inform managerial decisions and recommendations by consultants to improve performance (Harrison, 2005). Harrison (2005) overviewed the three parts of organizational diagnosis: process, modeling, and methods. Process includes collaborating with an organization (e.g., a business) to plan a diagnostic study to assess the organization's current state and illuminate areas of improvement. Conceptual models are used to develop, gather, and understand feedback collected about the organization, which can inform interpretations of the diagnostic study's results. Different methods can be implemented to gather and summarize this data, including Process Observation.

Paul (1996) noted that Process Observation within organizational diagnosis could be achieved through one of two ways: systematic observation or observer-as-participant observation. In *systematic observation*, a Process Observer follows a structured procedure with pre-determined categories and specific behaviors to observe. For example, a Process Observer could observe an organization across an assigned period of time, using their defined procedure to note important details related to effectiveness and performance. Systematic observation helps in maintaining objectivity as there is a procedure to follow and can help inform future areas of study. On the other hand, in *observer-as-participant observation*, an individual outside the organization participates in the organization's group processes (e.g., meetings). The observer-as-participant can watch the group processes and intervene as needed, like noting important problems that haven't been addressed. The data collection process in observer-as-participant observation can be enriching for the group members as they receive real-time feedback.

Process Consultation Theory

Edgar Schien is an organizational psychologist and a Professor Emeritus at the Massachusetts Institute of Technology's Sloan School of Management. His research focuses on organizational culture, career development, and group process consultation. He made crucial contributions to the organizational development literature in the last six decades.

In the late 60s, when the discipline of organizational development was still in its nascent stages, a consultant was considered as an expert who provided task-based interventions (i.e., providing structure, optimizing the business process and time management; Woodruff, n.d.). Schein (1969), on the other hand, was focusing on the human side: how he could help human systems help themselves instead of providing them with solutions. He believed the key to achieve this self-sustainability was in paying more attention to *how* things are done rather than *what* is done. The underlying *process*, according to him, communicates a lot more about the group than the content of the task at hand. For instance, imagine a group working efficiently to produce outputs for an immediate deadline. Here the *content* of the task would be optimizing the means of production, time management, and quick decision making. On the other hand, the underlying *process* impacting the task would be the way team members are interacting with each other during this high pressure situation. For example, when one member's micromanaging or non-collaborative behavior translates into another member's lack of motivation to work.

Guided by the belief of significance of such processes, Schein conceptualized "Process Consultation" (PC), a holistic way of supporting groups and organizations. In his words, PC involves

> a set of activities on the part of the consultant that help the client to perceive, understand, and act upon the process events that occur in the client's environment in order to improve the situation as defined by the client.
>
> (1988, p.11)

PC centers on collaboratively working with the client to diagnose a problem by discovering the underlying process together. Schein believed in empowering the clients to tackle organizational problems instead of them relying on the consultants to solve it for them. In his words, "The ultimate function of PC is to pass on the skills of how to diagnose and constructively intervene so that clients are more able to continue on their own to improve the organization" (Schein, 1999, p. 18).

The skill of observation is crucial to PC, as it entails understanding how the group accomplishes its task and how the members navigate interpersonal issues. While focusing on the *task process*, the process consultant observes the group's way of solving a problem (both the discussion and action stage) and making a decision (authority, majority, consensus or unanimity). While focusing on the *interpersonal process*, the process consultant observes how a group defines and maintains its boundaries and the development of interpersonal relationships within the group. Schein (1999) highlights the importance of just observing these group processes without necessarily intervening. These observations act as an archive for the consultant to understand the group and not intervening in the moment helps to facilitate and deepen the awareness among clients.

Schein's emphasis on observation while withholding interventions and empowering the client with the skills of Process Observation is akin to the evolution of Process Observation in group therapeutic contexts. Yalom is a salient figure that valued these tenets, and his expansive work with groups continues to shape the focus and mechanics of group work in therapeutic contexts.

Irvin Yalom

Irvin Yalom is an existential psychiatrist that wrote one of the more definitive texts for group therapy, *The Theory and Practice of Group Psychotherapy* (1970), which is now in its sixth edition (Yalom & Leszcz, 2020). Yalom defined Process Observation as attention to the process of what is unfolding in a therapy group, including focus on factors that may lie beneath the surface of the group therapy members' interactions. In this case, the Process Observer is the group leader or therapist. The group leader or therapist may take notes on group processes, like how a group ultimately came to a decision (e.g., communication styles, deciding factors). They may also attend to content that emerges within the group, meaning what specifically participants said in the group. For example, a group leader may document a pivotal exchange between two group members about their experiences in the group.

Yalom (1970) describes Process Observation as an important tool for group leaders to use to better understand group dynamics. Group leaders can identify what is said or omitted in group dynamics using Process Observation, which can help clarify relationships and tensions arising within the group. Yalom also notes the value of an objective role for therapists, in which they withhold their judgment while observing group processes. The objective stance helps the therapist's noticings and commentary provide a "corrective" emotional experience as group members experience more satisfying reaction to their concerns than previous encounters. For example, the therapist may note that a group member seems to be having a difficult time talking about a topic, which may feel more approachable to the group member than previous reactions of frustration or confusion from friends and family about the specific topic. Yalom also noted that Process Observation by the leader can set an example for group members, who, as the group matures, can be prompted to independently remark on the processes unfolding in the group.

Also, individuals outside the group can watch dynamics unfold and comment on developments they see. This technique is called a "fishbowl": the group and therapist are on the inside nucleus while observers circle them on the outer edges (Kane, 1995). This technique has and continues to be used in therapy training settings, like opportunities for graduate students in training to observe group processes in classes (Kane, 1995; Castles, 2011). For example, in a group therapy graduate level course, the group members and therapist are seated in a circle, and the graduate students are seated in chairs outside the group watching and noting interactions that unfold within the group. The intention behind fishbowls is to provide helpful feedback on group processes and content as observing members are not confined within the emotional dynamics and structure of the group processes. For further details related to Yalom's research with Process Observation, visit Chapter 15 in this book.

Summary

Throughout this chapter we identified various disciplines, theories, and influential individuals who have contributed to our past and current understanding of Process Observation. Although the terminology for and understanding of Process Observation has evolved, some common threads remain relevant throughout its history, like discussions about observing process versus content and the importance of the Process Observer withholding judgment. As we can see, the use and relevance of Process Observation has occurred in a parallel fashion across a multitude of disciplines, denoting the versatility and usefulness of Process Observation in many contexts. We hope this brief history helps guide your experiences with other chapters of this book and raises curiosities about what Process Observation's future looks like.

For additional details about empirical research related to Process Observation, visit Chapter 15. Although Process Observation has been discussed theoretically in a variety of contexts, most of the empirical research with Process Observation has been completed within the counseling realm, like in group and supervision contexts.

Acknowledgments

We are deeply grateful to Dr. Kenwyn K. Smith and Dr. Flora N. Taylor for their suggestions on literature and thinkers in tracing the history of Process Observation. Their guidance in helping us understand and experience the beauty of group processes is beyond measure.

References

Alderfer, C. (2011). *The practice of organizational diagnosis: Theory and methods*. OUP USA.

Anderson, D. L. (2019). *Organization development: The process of leading organizational change*. Sage Publications.

Bales, R. F. (1950). A set of categories for the analysis of small group interaction. *American Sociological Review, 15*(2), 257–263.

Bales, R. F. (1951). *Interaction Process Analysis: A Method for the Study of Small Groups*. Addison-Wesley Press.

Bales, R. F. (2000). Social Interaction Systems: Theory and Measurement: Book review. *Group Dynamics: Theory, Research, and Practice, 4*(2), 199–208.

Bales, R. F. (2017). *Social interaction systems: Theory and measurement*. Routledge.

Barnlund, D. C. (1970). A transactional model of communication. *Language behavior: A book of readings in communication* (pp. 43–61). De Gruyter Mouton.
Barnlund, D. C. (1955). The use of group observers. *Communication Education*, *4(1)*, 46–48.
Bennett, J. M. (2012). The public and private Dean Barnlund. *International Journal of Intercultural Relations*, *36(6)*, 780–788.
Castles, M. (2011). Supervision with reflecting teams: A view from the fishbowl. *Journal of the Australian & New Zealand Student Services Association*, (*37*).
Cuofano, G. (2022). What is the transactional model of communication? Transactional model of communication in a nutshell. *FourWeekMBA*. Retrieved from https://fourweekmba.com/transactional-model-of-communication/.
Everett, C. A., & Koerpel, B. J. (1986). Family therapy supervision: A review and critique of the literature. *Contemporary Family Therapy*, *8(1)*, 62–74.
Goldenberg, H., & Goldenberg, I. (2012). *Family therapy: An overview*. Cengage Learning.
Gusterson, H. (2008). Ethnographic research. *Qualitative methods in international relations* (pp. 93–113). Palgrave Macmillan, London.
Harrison, M. I. (2005). *Diagnosing organizations: Methods, models, and processes* (Vol. *8*). Sage.
Kagan, Jerome et al. (2006, April 20) Robert Freed Bales. Faculty of Arts and Sciences – Memorial Minute, *Harvard University Gazette*. https://news.harvard.edu/gazette/story/2006/04/robert-freed-bales/.
Kane, C. M. (1995). Fishbowl training in group process. *Journal for Specialists in Group Work*, *20(3)*, 183–188.
Schein, E. H. (1969). *Process consultation: Its role in organization development*. Addison-Wesley Publishing Company.
Schein, E. H. (1988). *Process consultation: Volume I: Its role in organization development*. (2nd Ed.) Addison-Wesley.
Schein, E. H. (1999). *Process consultation revisited: Building the helping relationship*. Addison-Wesley.
Nichols Jr, W. C. (1973). The field of marriage counseling: A brief overview. *Family Coordinator*, 3–13.
Paul, J. (1996). Between method triangulation in organizational diagnosis. *The International Journal of Organizational Analysis*.
Rivett, M., & Street, E. (2009). *Family therapy: 100 key points and techniques*. Routledge.
Ugwu, C. (2017). History of ethnography: Straitening the records. *International Journal of Sociology and Anthropology*, *9*(7), 64–68.
Woodruff, Susan. (n.d.). 1960: Process Consultation: Its Role in Organization Development is published by Edgar Schein. In D. Schugurensky (Ed.), *History of Education: Selected Moments of the 20th Century*. http://schugurensky.faculty.asu.edu/moments/1969schein.html.
Whyte, W. F. (1955). *Street corner society: The structure of an Italian slum*. University of Chicago Press.
Yalom. (1970). *The theory and practice of group psychotherapy*. Basic Books.
Yalom, I. D., & Leszcz, M. (2020). *The theory and practice of group psychotherapy*. Basic Books.

Chapter 14

Research on Group Process Observation

Shing Yee Bay, University of New Mexico

Yiying Xiong, Johns Hopkins University

Kristopher M. Goodrich, University of New Mexico

Juan, a newly licensed counselor working at his first agency, was recently assigned a group as part of his practice. Juan was assigned to a drug court group whose leader recently left the practice for a different agency. Juan was excited for the first group, but also a little nervous because he hadn't had any experiences with groups other than his basic group course at the start of his masters' training program. When Juan arrived to the group, he was met with a number of members who appeared disengaged and disinterested, a longtime member who appeared to want to challenge Juan for leadership in the group, as well as a couple of members who appeared to be whispering to each other as Juan and others attempted to engage in the group process.

Juan felt exhausted after the group, as well as a bit disappointed. He noticed a number of troubling dynamics within the group but wasn't sure how best to intervene. Being the newest member of the group, as well as its new leader, he wasn't sure how much he should share or not in the group, and what should be confronted or acknowledged. He remembered his previous group instructor discussing the need for group processing after each group, but couldn't recall what that should look like, how honest he should be, or if that should even be his role. He really wanted his first group to go much better than it did but felt at a loss for how to make it better.

Juan decided that it was time to dust off some of his old university books and find out more about group processing. What do we know about group processing? Is it effective, and if so, what should it look like in the context of his group? How should Juan think about raising the issue of group processing within the group, and in what form should it take, if he should even do it? Juan decided to write down each of these questions to support him in his search of what we know about effective group processing.

Introduction

Although group Process Observation (GPO) is used frequently, and often anecdotally cited as an effective tool in group work, there has been limited empirical evidence surrounding its efficacy. While research studies have demonstrated support for use of PO, it is important for readers to be aware that there are many forms of GPO. Not all of these forms of group process observation have undergone the same level of scrutiny, particularly given the frequency for which PO is used within the field. The terms group leader and group facilitator, the persons who work with PO, are often used interchangeably. For the purposes of the chapter, we will utilize the term provided by the scholar as we address the articles reviewed.

The goal of this chapter is to introduce the extant research in the area of group process observation. The chapter is divided into three sections. First, we will explore the assumptions

DOI: 10.4324/9781003281955-18

surrounding GPO in the area of group work, and then examine what has been researched and supported within extant empirical articles. Second, we will review the literature surrounding the use of process observation in the training of group work, including the assumptions and empirical work surrounding the preparation of group leaders. We will end by offering our own insights into current strengths, opportunities for growth, and future directions that group processing research can take to more effectively support its successful implementation in groups.

Assumptions Surrounding Process Observation Based on Group Research

The Association for Specialists in Group Work (ASGW) guiding principles highlight the importance of process observation in creating therapeutic conditions and in helping members make meaning of the process (McCarthy et al., 2022). In addition, the guiding principles highlight the importance of process observation as a method of assessment, training, and therapeutic alliance.

Similar to the guiding principle, Ward (2014) highlighted the value of group processing. In doing so, he noted the work of Brown (2009), who described the significance of process commentary at a group level. PO allows the group to deepen their experience by being aware of how their own behaviors and contribute to the goals of the group. Some of the functions of a Process Observer, such as identifying what the group is or is not engaging, ignoring, and highlighting these and other dynamics allow the group to have a process-focused orientation and decide how to best navigate that to make sure everyone is valued in the process. Engaging the group in process commentary has been found to show positive individual and group outcomes (Johnson, Johnson, Stanne & Garibaldi, 1990; Yager, Johnson, Johnson, & Snider, 1986; as cited in Ward 2014). Participants whose treatments included group processing have better treatment outcomes than those without.

Although this and other (e.g., Yalom & Leszcz 2020) experience-based work has highlighted the fundamentals of process observation. One common condition cited in the research surrounding GPO is Process Observers focus on providing examples that highlight the present moment dynamics that the group is exhibiting. If you are interested to learn more about it or the historical context please refer to the previous chapter on the history of PO, which will cover it in more depth. It is also important to gain a better understanding of extant research into group processing to better understand how research supports the process observation process. Although truly comprehensive and in depth research is scant, there is research that supports the use of process observations.

Some scholars have situated their research in relation to the therapeutic factors of a group (Yalom & Leszcz, 2020) that contributes to change, utilizing process observation but not labeling it as such. Burlingame, Strauss, and Joyce (2013) conducted a meta-analysis of the studies that explored group cohesion and found it had a positive relationship with treatment outcomes across 40 studies. They noted moderators that suggest leader actions can have an increased impact on the cohesion and outcome findings. Findings from this study support that facilitating member interactions to support positive bonds in the group can facilitate positive treatment outcomes. A recent update of the meta-analysis completed by Burlingame et al. (2018) found similar findings; in particular, they found a significant cohesion-outcome relationship, which suggests the moderating effect of cohesion on members' improvement in the group.

While there are limited studies on PO, however, from these studies above, we can deduce that the application of Process Observation could contribute to therapeutic outcomes as PO facilitates the cohesion between the members of the group. When considering PO one concern is the receptiveness of member to the observer, however a study by Kacen & Rozovski (1998) did not find the observer intrusive to the group process. These findings lend evidence that the Process Observer may play a valuable role in the group process to potentially provide feedback on the group cohesion for the improvement of group cohesion and might indirectly contribute to better group outcomes.

Another factor found to impact group outcome is group alliance/therapeutic alliance, which describes the relationship bonds among the group members and therapist (Yalom & Leszcz, 2020). In Alldredge et al.'s (2021) meta-analysis of 29 studies, some evidence was found for the relationship between therapeutic alliance and later treatment outcomes for clients (weighted correlation of $r=.25$; effect size of $d=.34$), which highlighted the importance of attending to the alliance in the group counseling process. The greater the therapeutic alliance between members appears to translate to the greater the therapeutic outcome for members. Process Observers can provide functional and normative effects by providing feedback, regulating group dynamics, and socializing (Kislev, 2015). This case study completed by Kislev points to the use of feedback that can promote prosocial behaviors in the group by indirectly reinforcing the rules of the group, which would allow the group to be functional, social, and productive, thus, enhancing the group alliance through the process.

PO can be either active or passive. When they are an active part of the group, the process observer interacts directly with the group members. Alternatively, Process Observers can play a passive role by mainly interacting with group leaders after the session in their feedback. Findings on which are of most benefits to the group appeared to be mixed. Bieschke and colleagues (1998) assessed whether having an observer would be disruptive to the group and found that the observer was not distracting to the group and did not impact the group content and process significantly. However, Dies, Coché, and Goettelmann (1990) found that group participants found observers, in general, to be more intrusive than group leaders. The magnitude of the negative reports of the observers highlights the needs for careful consideration of the observer's impact on the group. Though leaders of the group were much less critical of the observer's impact on the group and many of the participants have reported some positive effects (i.e. increased cohesion) in the process. By being intentional in creating a positive environment through communicating feedback to members can help reduce the negative reaction toward the observers.

Zieman and colleagues (1981) utilized nonverbal, trained Process Observers for therapy groups, where only the summaries of their notes taken in the session were mailed to clients, and no verbal feedback was provided during sessions. In this study, their clients reported that the summaries helped reduce anxiety, while also helping to focus the group on important issues, enhance the continuity across sessions, and promote therapeutic work between sessions. The potential conclusion that can be drawn from multiple studies is that when a Process Observer is not intentional, this can interfere with the group process; however, when done right can have a positive impact on the group outcome as demonstrated by group member therapeutic alliance, as well as self-reported treatment outcomes. As it does appear that Process Observation can have a positive influence on group work process, it is important to know how we can train future group workers in how they may best apply these skills. As such, we will look to the research on group training surrounding Process Observation to better understand how this may be addressed.

Process Observation in Group Work Training

Juan conducts research into the group process, and notes that the role of a group process observer can be helpful for the group when they are mindful of group dynamics and how they interact with the group. He knows the impact of the process observer can help to facilitate group cohesion and increase positive treatment outcomes. However, Juan reflects that he had little instruction about the implementation of group process observers in his counselor education program, and still felt adrift in how best to effectively implement process observation within his group. He then reached out to his former professor, Dr. Belinda Yazzie, to see if he can gain additional training or information about this form of intervention. After Juan reached out to Dr. Yazzie, she couldn't help but think of the curriculum of the counselor education program she taught in, and how the intentional instruction about group process observation has (or has not) taken place. She knew that the curriculum for groups had to be revised, but had little awareness of the training literature that might inform this revision. As such, she engaged in her own literature review to better understand how other educators may have addressed process observation in their training programs...

Several recent studies of group counseling training within Council for Accreditation of Counseling & Related Educational Programs (CACREP) programs have reported a lack of training focused on group counseling skills (Vannatta & Steen, 2019; Xiong & Lu, 2021). Despite the limited emphasis on skills training, Process Observation has been employed as a frequently utilized method to train group facilitators with their skills (Corazzini & Anderson, 1980; Yalom & Leszcz, 2020) and has been noted as such within ASGW's guiding principle on similar issues (McCarthy et al., 2022). However, there is limited literature addressing the utilization of observation in training group facilitators (Weiss & Rutan, 2016).

Muehl (2009) reported that the origins of observation in training group facilitators began with skills training groups such as the Basic Skills Training group, a small ongoing group held in Maine from 1947 to 1948. Group observers would report their observations to the group to help reflect on the functioning of the group as a whole. From there, observation continued to be utilized in the training group (T-group) that was utilized to provide training in human relations (Benne, 1964). In T-groups, members acted as both participants and observers of the group process (Kislev, 2015) discussing the process and offered feedback on each other's behaviors (Coghlan & Jacobs, 2005). The T-groups were based on the finding that the group members demonstrated positive attitude change, increased performance, and greater commitment to individual action when participative methods are applied to small groups (Coghlan & Jacobs, 2005). These T-groups laid foundations for Yalom's interpersonal group therapy (Yalom & Leszcz, 2020). In particular, interpersonal group therapy incorporates a Process Observer and end-of-group review discussion, which were utilized in T-groups.

Bieschke and colleagues (1996) noted the distinction between observation and Process Observation. According to Bieschke and colleagues, observation refers to situations where the trainee (observer) is not directly involved in the group process. In such experiences, the observer may observe the group from a one-way mirror or on a videotape and seldomly attend group meetings. Conversely, Bieschke and colleagues noted that Process Observation is a more dynamic and ongoing process. In Process Observation, the Process Observer often attends all group meetings, sits within or outside of the group, takes process notes, debriefs with leaders, and provides group case notes (Bieschke et al., 1996). Research indicated Process Observation may have more positive effects on the group process and training outcome than observation (Bieschke et al., 1998; Dies, 1980; Hogan et al., 2006; Yalom & Leszcz, 2020). As such, Bieschke et al. (1996) proposed a Process Observation system may be a beneficial training tool for the group facilitators. In their proposal, the Process Observer is introduced to the group at the beginning of the group with their roles being explained to the group members. The same Process Observer then needs to attend all group meetings as a silent member, and the group leaders continue to incorporate the Process Observer into the routine functioning of a group (Bieschke et al., 1996).

With this Process Observer model, Bieschke et al. (1998) explored the group trainees' experience at a college counseling center at a Mid-Atlantic University via a survey. The group observer was assigned to a therapy group for students at the university and introduced to the group at an early stage, and they observed the group for the whole semester. The group leaders included senior staff, interns, and graduate assistants at the counseling center. The group observers were trainees from the psychology or counseling majors. The group observers took notes during the session and attended the post-group processing/supervision. Based on the survey results from group members, group leaders, and Process Observers, Process Observers were minimally disruptive to the group. Further, the group leaders shared their appreciation to the group observers regarding the assistance in deepening their understanding of the group process and help with the group notes. The Process Observers reported benefits in learning group counseling skills and knowledge and understanding clients and themselves. However, additional research is needed to better understand the client experience of this process (Bieschke et al., 1998).

Several other researchers have also evaluated various group training models that incorporated observation or Process Observation. Weiss and Rutan (2016) investigated the experience of 42 postgraduate trainees at the Boston Institute for Psychotherapy who observed an ongoing, weekly, open-ended psychodynamic therapy group in an outpatient mental health clinic. The observers sat in the group room during the group time and attended the debrief session with the co-therapists after the group session. The observers (trainees) reported multiple benefits from the observation experience, including

> the ability to bear affect and trust the group process; the ability to follow and use group themes, metaphors, and underlying dynamics; the ability to use techniques to highlight attachment themes; an appreciation for working in the here-and-now and promoting immediacy.
>
> (Weiss & Rutan, 2016, p. 252)

Trainees also reported valuing learning through direct observation about how the leaders can "use humor, handle confrontations, and navigate their mistakes" (Weiss & Rutan, 2016, p. 252).

Another study by Rees and Maclaine (2016) investigated the training effect of a Concentric Circles Therapy Training model with clinical psychology post-graduate students in a group therapy training class. The model was based on the interpersonal therapy training group (Yalom & Leszcz, 2020) where the group trainees participate in a group as both group members and observers, using the fishbowl strategy. One group of trainees attended the group session in the "inner circle," while the other group of trainees observed silently in the "outer circle." The two groups swapped over after a process of debriefs of the first round. By analyzing the trainees' reflection journals, the researchers indicated the trainees appreciated the opportunity to participate as both observers and direct participation in the group process (Rees & Maclaine, 2016). Likewise, Kislev (2015) employed a similar training model where the group participants also observed the group process. Their model added a report component where the observers needed to write a report about what they observed during the session and report their observations during the next group session. By analyzing the trainees' reflection journals and interviews, the researcher concluded that the participant–observer model is beneficial in training group trainees especially about their ability to reflect and learn the group process (Kislev, 2015). Based on those empirical studies, it seems that employing the process observation in group leaders' training is beneficial to foster their reflection skills, understanding of group process, and group counseling skills and knowledge.

Besides those empirical studies, there are also conceptual works about how to incorporate Process Observation into group work training. Hanson (1972) shared detailed guidelines about what to observe in a group, including participation, influence, decision-making procedures, task functions, maintenance functions, group atmosphere, membership, feelings, and norms. For each area to be observed, Hanson (1972) offered guiding questions or prompts for observers. For participation, the observer focuses on high or low participators, the shifts in participation, participators' reactions to silence, as well as the communication patterns among participators (e.g. who talks to whom? Who keeps the ball rolling?).

Hanson (1972) defined influence as the impact of group members on each other. The group observer needs to focus on group members who have high or low influence, the power struggles among group members, and how group members attempt to influence others. Decision-making procedures are aimed at observing how the group members and group make decisions, including decisions to drift topics, group members' reactions to others' suggestions, and the group's attempts to arrive at a consensus. Task functions were defined as the behaviors of group members and of the whole group that are geared toward accomplishing tasks. The observers may pay special attention to group members who ask for or suggest ways to proceed with problems, those who summarize, those who search for facts, ideas, feelings, feedback, or alternatives, and those who keep the group on target. Maintenance functions are about maintaining group morale and harmonious working relationships, and creating a safe and trusting atmosphere to ensure effective teamwork. For group atmosphere, the observers need to focus on the overall atmosphere of the group and group members who prefer a congenial or conflicting atmosphere and how group members get engaged and involved in the group. Membership concerns interaction patterns among group members, such as subgrouping and outsiders. Feelings are frequently generated by interactions. Even though the feelings are seldom talked about, the observer may observe group members' tone of voice, facial expressions, gestures, and other nonverbals to sense the feelings of group members. Last, observers also need to pay attention to the norms that are the standards, ground rules, and the group's morals to control group members' behaviors. The norms can be either explicit or implicit, such as areas to be avoided, members who are overly polite, how norms facilitate or hinder the participation of group members (Hanson, 1972).

Based on the guidelines addressed by Hanson (1972) above, Conyne (1998) added a multicultural sensitizer that addresses cultural issues in group counseling to support group trainees in facilitating multicultural issues in group work. For example, regarding participation, other than the areas that Hanson (1972) proposed to observe, Conyne (1998) suggested that observers need also consider the cultural similarities and differences that influence the amount of participation, how silence may be related to cultural differences, how group members from different cultures participate in the group, and how group members from different cultural backgrounds interact with each other. These conceptual thoughts provided detailed and hands-on guidelines for observers; however, this deserves further study to establish empirical support.

In summary, there are numerous models to incorporate Process Observation/observation into group-work training. Based on the empirical studies about those models, it seems that the incorporation of Process Observers/observers in group-work training is beneficial for the training outcomes. However, more empirical research is needed. Future research directions are described next.

Future Research Directions

Based on the limited literature on GPO, we have a few recommendations regarding the future directions in research. First, as there is a scant amount of research that actually explores GPO, whether it is occurring in the context of training in group work or group intervention, and we would suggest any form of research would be beneficial to better understand this phenomenon. However, in exploring what we currently know based on extant research, we would recommend future researchers use more quantitative methods and larger sample sizes to investigate incorporating observation or Process Observation in group work, as well as group work training. The majority of the current studies used qualitative research with a few participants. Although qualitative studies provide a richness of depth of participant experience, quantitative studies can help provide more generalizable knowledge to different samples; for these reasons we believe there needs to be a balance between qualitative and quantitative studies in this area to have a fully balanced understanding of the impact and usefulness of group processing.

Further, studies of group training are mainly based upon the perspectives of group work trainees (i.e. group process observers) but exclude any data from the non-trainee (clinical) clients that participate in these groups. It is important to better understand client responses to different training models, as these models appear to be more based around the preferences of instructors and trainees. As noted in the group counseling literature, clients have different responses to models of Process Observation (i.e., Bieschke et al., 1998; Dies et al, 1990; Zieman et al., 1981). Limited research has explored the nuances of client response, and how observer behavior and integration within the group might influence both client perception and later treatment outcomes; this is deserving of future research. The guiding principles of ASGW highlight the importance to continue moving forward in seeking to establish empirical support for group work and to continue to strive for continuous use of evidence-based approaches to improve practice (McCarthy et al., 2022).

In regards to potential avenues for future research, it would be important to consider comparative studies to explore the impact or differences between use of a passive, versus an active, Process Observer for a group. There are limited extant studies about the impact or differences, and many of them are more anecdotal or conceptual in nature versus empirical evidence (e.g., studies that utilize quantitative, generalizable data with fidelity across groups beyond the treatment condition, such as type of Process Observer). Data lending to better understanding the differences of group member engagement, cohesion, and treatment outcomes would be interesting to know for the future. Additionally, the timing (or schedule of feedback) of Process Observations is currently understudied in the field. How does timing, as well as the process of observation (e.g., written, to leader/facilitator only or group-as-a-whole) influence the impact of Process Observation in the group process? We currently have little information to understand the influence of these different conditions towards the later dynamics of the group.

Further, there is a similar limited amount of evidence in regards to the use of process observation for the training of group workers. Potential further investigations might include researchers utilizing experimental designs to compare the training effect on trainees who have observed group sessions and those who have not observed group sessions. Currently, there is anecdotal or conceptual support for use of Process Observation in group training, but limited evidence to demonstrate its actual impact, as noted in the training section above. In particular, more work is needed to measure the effectiveness of the training model incorporating process observation such as the models by Hanson (1972) and Bieschke and colleagues (1996). Moreover, we would also recommend researchers compare the effect of different ways of operating observations in group training. With the experimental design, researchers may contrast different ways that Process Observations may be used (similar to those addressed in group work above) and how the different ways may influence the training effect.

Last, even though several studies indicated that Process Observation is beneficial for group trainees, many have not measured the specific factors that promote the benefits of Process Observation in group counseling training. As such, researchers are invited to consider use of qualitative, quantitative, or mixed methods to explore the effective factors that contribute to the benefits, which has also been recommended by the ASGW guiding principles (McCarthy et al., 2022). Once a more considerable volume of empirical evidence is obtained, scholars are invited to create standards relating to GPO in group work, and its training, to support the continued growth and development of the field moving forward.

As we have seen in this chapter, the literature surrounding GPO, as well as the training of Process Observation, is still an emerging area within our field that is ripe for future investigations. Our current empirical base into group process suggests that Process Observation can work when the Process Observer is intentional, coordinates well with the group leader/facilitator, the group members understand the purpose and trust the group observer, and that observer is well trained. What we currently need to know is how different types of groups might lend to a more passive or active Process Observer, the impact that timing (or the schedule or process of feedback) may influence group outcomes, and how best to train process group observers to engage in this process. As the empirical evidence is scant across each of these areas, any empirical work, whether it be quantitative, qualitative, or mixed methods would be warranted and helpful in the future.

After reviewing the available literature out there on this topic, Juan and Dr. Yazzie noticed the gap in the literature. After further reviewing the guiding principles in group work, they both decided that it would be beneficial to utilize a process observer in the group process to aid the group outcome. Additionally, this would be a great opportunity to add to the literature for them to collect some additional evidence for how process observer might be able to aid the group counseling process in their setting. Furthermore, this would allow them to assess how their group is progressing and the general outcome of their group. Following the thoughtful execution of their plan, they began to craft future plans on how to disseminate their findings so that they might continue to move the field forward.

Group Processing Question

After reading this vignette, how are you relating to Juan and Dr. Yazzie?

What role or roles might you play in progressing this area in our field forward?

As you read the chapter, what research questions do you have, and what research questions might you want to ask, in relation to the gaps highlighted in this chapter?

References

Alldredge, C. T., Burlingame, G. M., Yang, C., & Rosendahl, J. (2021). Alliance in group therapy: A meta-analysis. *Group Dynamics: Theory, Research, and Practice, 25(1)*, 13.

Benne, K. D. (1964). History of the T group in the laboratory setting. In L. P. Bradford, J. R. Gibb, & K. D. Benne (Eds.), *T-group theory and laboratory method: Innovation in re-education* (pp. 80–135). New York: Wiley.

Bieschke, K. J., Matthews, C., & Wade, J. (1996). Training group counselors: The process observer method. *The Journal for Specialists in Group Work*, *21(3)*, 181–186. https://doi.org/10.1080/01933929608412250.

Bieschke, K. J., Matthews, C., Wade, J., & Pricken, P. A. (1998). Evaluation of the process observer method: Group leader, member, and observer perspectives. *The Journal for Specialists in Group Work*, *23(1)*, 50–65. https://doi.org/10.1080/01933929808411381.

Brown, N. W. (2009). *Becoming a Group Leader*. Pearson.

Burlingame, G. M., McClendon, D. T., & Yang, C. (2018). Cohesion in group therapy: A meta-analysis. *Psychotherapy*, 384–398.https://doi.apa.org/doiLanding?doi=10.1037%2Fpst0000173.

Burlingame, G. M., Strauss, B., & Joyce, A. S. (2013). Change mechanism and effectiveness of small group treatments. In M. J. Lambert (Ed.), *Bergin and Garfield's Handbook of Psychotherapy and Behavior Change* (pp. 640–689). John Wiley & Son Inc.

Coghlan, D., & Jacobs, C. (2005). Kurt Lewin on reeducation: Foundations for action research. *The Journal of Applied Behavioral Science*, *41(4)*, 444–457. https://doi.org/10.1177/0021886305277275.

Conyne, R. K. (1998). What to look for in groups: Helping trainees become more sensitive to multicultural issues. *The Journal for Specialists in Group Work*, *23(1)*, 22–32. https://doi.org/10.1080/01933929808411379.

Corazzini, J. G., & Anderson, S. M. (1980). An apprentice model for training group leaders: Revitalizing group treatment. *The Journal for Specialists in Group Work*, *5(1)*, 29–35. https://doi.org/10.1080/15496295.1980.11728594.

Dies, R. R. (1980). Group psychotherapy: Training and supervision. In A. K. Hess (Ed.), *Psychotherapy Supervision* (pp. 337–366). John Wiley.

Dies, R. R., Coché, E., & Goettelmann, K. (1990). The impact of observers on group process and content. *International of Group Psychotherapy*, *40*, 323–338.

Hanson, F. (1972). What to look for in groups: An observation guide. In J. Pfeiffer & J. Jones (Eds.), *The 1972 annual handbook for group facilitators* (pp. 21–24). Pfeiffer.

Hogan, C., Harris, R. S., & Cassidy, J. M. (2006). The impact of process observers on interpersonal group therapy. *Journal of College Student Psychotherapy*, *21*, 21–32.

Kacen, L., & Rozovski, U. (1998). Assessing group processes: A comparison among group participants', direct observers', and indirect observers' assessment. *Small Group Research*, *29*, 179–197.

Kislev, E. (2015). The use of participant-observers in group therapy: A critical exploration in light of Foucauldian Theory. *Group*, *39(1)*, 9–24. https://doi.org/10.13186/group.39.1.0009.

McCarthy, C. J., Bauman, S., Choudhuri, D. D., Coker, A., Justice, C., Kraus, K. L., Luke, M., Rubel, D., & Shaw, L. (2022). Association for Specialists in Group Work guiding principles for group work. *The Journal for Specialists in Group Work*, *47*, 10–21. https://doi.org/10.1080/01933922.2021.1950882.

Muehl, K. (2009). Experiences of post-processing in group psychotherapy. *Theses and Dissertations*. https://doi.org/10.25772/KRA3-HS67.

Rees, C. S., & Maclaine, E. (2016). Concentric circles therapy training: Clinical psychology trainee's reflections on participation in a revised Interpersonal Therapy Training Group. *Australian Psychologist*, *51(3)*, 231–237. https://doi.org/10.1111/ap.12167.

Thomas, R. V., & Pender, D. A. (2008). Association for Specialist in Group work: Best practice guideline 2007 revision. *The Journal for Specialist in Group Work*, 111–117. https://doi.org/10.1080/01933920801971184.

Vannatta, R., & Steen, S. (2019). Pedagogical practices in CACREP accredited group counseling courses: A content analysis. *The Journal for Specialists in Group Work*, *44(2)*, 138–150. https://doi.org/10.1080/01933922.2019.1599477.

Ward, D. E. (2014). Effective processing in groups. In J. L. DeLucia-Waak, C. R. Kalodner, M. T. Riva (Eds.), *Handbook of Group Counseling & Psychotherapy* (2nd ed., 84–94). SAGE.

Weiss, A. C., & Rutan, J. S. (2016). The benefits of group therapy observation for therapists-in-training. *International Journal of Group Psychotherapy*, *66(2)*, 246–260. https://doi.org/10.1080/00207284.2015.1111083.

Xiong, Y., & Lu, H.-T. (2021). Group counseling courses in CACREP-accredited Programs: A national survey. *Journal of Counselor Preparation and Supervision*, *14(4)*. https://digitalcommons.sacredheart.edu/jcps/vol14/iss4/11.

Yalom, I. D., & Leszcz, M. (2020). *The Theory and Practice of Group Psychotherapy*. Basic Books.

Zieman, G. L., Romano, P. A., Blanco, K., & Linnell, T. (1981). The process-observer in group therapy. *Group*, *5*, 37–47.

Chapter 15

Technology and Process Observation

Sam Steen, George Mason University

Priscilla Rose Prasath, University of Texas at San Antonio

There is no doubt that technology has impacted our society in many ways. Providing counseling services via distance counseling and telemental health are not new practices, although to some counselors this may be a new experience. Prior to the onset of the global pandemic – COVID-19 – many may have bristled at the thought of moving their individual therapy online, let alone a group practice. The pandemic made online work and technology far more central and crucial to group work. Within the context of counseling and mental health, many group therapists encountered moments of questioning and self-doubt at the onset of the COVID-19 pandemic regarding how they would be able to sense nonverbal information from clients given a flat two-dimensional image. You, like us, might have wondered how a screen could transmit subjective and objective countertransference, induced feelings, subtle body movements, and the endless emotional tics and hiccups that appear in face-to-face sessions.

Many people now, and in the future, will need to become more familiar and hopefully more competent with computers and all kinds of technology. There are a plethora of hardware, software, and multimedia platforms including cell phones, laptops, video conferencing, chat rooms, discords, discussion boards, social media, and other applications and technologies, both emerging and yet to be created. There is some literature suggesting that clinicians must follow technology trends and find strategies to integrate online tools within their professional identities or miss out on making substantial contributions to the communities being served (Mason et al., 2019).

While the use of Process Observers (POs) within groups offered virtually is emerging within the literature, telemental health – essentially mental health services conducted using various technologies – had been under study prior to the onset of the pandemic. For instance, telemental health affords counselors and clients to connect with each other no matter where they may reside or despite any barriers that could prevent sessions to ensure the clients are provided the help they need. Groups conducted virtually have the potential to serve those who are unwilling or unable to participate face-to-face. The pandemic made it impossible to meet in person for several months and during this time folks living in rural communities or places where counseling centers or clinical mental health resources were less prevalent, benefited from the burgeoning online groups as they have become a valuable resource to many. Some may seek group therapy online due to geographical or physical obstacles to in-person access, while others may seek out assistance due to their feelings of alienation from others or a possible stigma in seeking mental health services. Seeking out available group therapy sessions online may be because folks may live where there are limited options for these services or lack reliable or affordable means of transportation to the counseling centers, or they simply find it more convenient to participate from the comfort of their own home.

In addition, telemental health services allow for clinicians and patients to adjust to constantly changing schedules when necessary. In other words, telemental health counselors bring the

DOI: 10.4324/9781003281955-19

services to the clients virtually and therefore there is more flexibility in scheduling. Overall, with the blurring of physical space boundaries, accessing and joining an online group has increasingly become a way to experience a clinical service in a direct, immediate and synchronous way that adapts to the quickly changing nature of modern communication.

Technology and Process Observation

Technology, broadly speaking, influences everything about groups and Process Observation is not exempt. Within an online group, there are different ways a PO could potentially engage online with the group. The group components including membership, duration, dynamics, and so forth are common factors impacting the success of a PO. Within groups, technology platforms include, but are not limited to, Zoom, Google Meet, Teams, and Cisco. When using a camera, the technology platforms (i.e., video conferencing) allows the group leaders and POs to scan participants' faces constantly for any emotional shifts and evidence of unexpressed feelings. With or without the use of a camera, these platform examples also allow different modes of communication for both leaders and members (e.g., chat box, emojis, screen sharing) therefore offering alternatives to verbal processing.

In general, a PO can play a pivotal role in the quality of the group processing. For instance, from Hogan et al.'s (2006) study participants, we find that a vast majority of group members (92%) who participated in a clinical therapy group found Process Observation to be extremely helpful in enhancing their overall group experience. Participants of other research studies have also indicated the significance of Process Observation (Prasath et al., 2022; Xiong et al., 2023). What is unclear from most of the existing examples within research studies is the extent to which POs have engaged in their virtual groups, how they go about offering their feedback and insight, and the degree of benefit that accrues for group members and leaders in online groups.

Typically, the purpose of these observations is to provide the group leader and members a sense of where they believe the group is headed and offer suggestions that could help facilitate and guide the development of group dynamics that led members to experience the positive and constructive power of groups (Toseland & Rivas, 2009). This information that is shared can include direct observations, clinical hunches, self-disclosures, questions, challenges, prompts to stimulate further exploration, and opportunities for the leader and members to pose their own questions to the group and/or PO.

Less problematic, yet very common, is the hesitation that many members express about offering input or giving feedback in virtual settings. POs may have to help participants overcome a hesitation to unmute and share their opinion for fear of speaking over someone else or feeling like they are taking up too much time from the group experience. Nevertheless, POs can play an important role at calling attention to the opportunities afforded and importance of giving feedback that is affirming and focused on growth and development. Helping participants and the group leader improve effective communication can be a noteworthy contribution of POs and helping members know how to give and receive feedback is a necessary ingredient to successful group encounters.

Models of Group Process Observation

Model One: Synchronous Group Process Observation – The most common and highly recommended model of Process Observation used within online/virtual spaces is called *synchronous group process observation*, wherein POs join the group meeting as one of the session participants via the virtual video conferencing platform.

Model Two: Asynchronous Group Process Observation – It is important to note that technology also allows POs to asynchronously observe a group process and offer insights that may be considered for the following group session by the group leaders and its members. In this setup, called *asynchronous group process observation*, POs can serve as observers of group process that met face-to-face or online by reviewing the recording of the session.

Key Considerations in Process Observation Using Technology

The use of various forms of technology being used within groups who draw upon a PO is at a nascent stage of development. Ponder this: how do the online communities that have formed during the pandemic use POs and/or Process Observations? In particular, if and when a conflict arises, how might a PO be used in this work? Should a PO step in and interpret the process or would they be better suited to impose limitations, remove disruptive people, or challenge the group leaders and members to address the conflict in session, immediately after the session, or prior to the next session? These sorts of questions are yet to be answered.

Let's take a step back and look at some specific questions and brief possible italicized answers provided by the authors that need to be considered related to Process Observation that occurs using a virtual platform:

1. Is it necessary for the PO to be in the physical presence of a group therapist and/or the group members to provide Process Observation? If so, how do you address this when the experience takes place online, synchronously? How does this need change for an asynchronous group? *Ideally all of our interactions would be in person, personable, and accessible to all. However, the pandemic, amongst other world phenomena, allow us to benefit from challenges that emerge during crisis. Technological advances allow us to engage in meaningful ways despite the physical distance.*
2. Given that computer-mediated communications offer some sense of anonymity to the group members, what measures can the PO take to facilitate therapeutic 'closeness' with the group leader(s) or if applicable, among members from a safe distance? *In some ways these measures will need to be negotiated with all participants up front.*
3. To what extent is 'closeness' necessary between the PO and group leaders and/or group members? *Closeness enhances group experience.*
4. What can the PO do to promote creativity and energy and facilitate an instant outlet for emotion through their role in an online group session? *Encourage an openness to emotional expressions, ideas, and different and myriad ways of communication.*
5. Would it be helpful if the PO attended one or more sessions conducted virtually unannounced? *Sure, however, this must be negotiated up front and has the potential to add a bit of spontaneity to the experience.*
6. What are some considerations for the timing of the PO's entrance to the group that takes place synchronously online? For example, when and how should a PO make their presence known to the group? *As early and as often as possible.*
7. Within virtual groups, how should the PO broach race and culture if the group leaders or members do not? *Race, gender, class, and so forth, must be broached directly, with intention, grace and consistency.*
8. What are some technology related ethical and legal considerations that are significant for PO that impacts Process Observation? *Confidentiality and limitations based on technological implications, dual relationships, and practicing within one's limits of expertise.*

9. What technical skills should a PO acquire and possess to effectively utilize technology for Process Observation? *Professional development should be sought as often as necessary. Additionally, this learning must occur outside the group and ideally prior to engagement.*
10. What additional training is needed for individuals serving in a PO role that will be facilitated online? *The training and preparation needed will depend on the scope of work. As soon as possible, discover what the role of the PO will be and develop/find the right tools for the role that will be taken within this work.*
11. What boundaries of online group behavior, both verbal and non-verbal group processes, must a PO consider during their Process Observation? *At the onset, a set of boundaries, guidelines, or ground rules can be negotiated and discussed.*
12. When conflict arises between group leaders and members, who is responsible for identifying this conflict? When conflict arises between members, who is responsible for identifying this conflict? *Everyone involved. However, a strong influential group leader, PO, and member(s) can influence these interactions to ensure they are inclusive and appropriate for all.*

Best Practices in Process Observation Via Use of Technology

In Model One set up described above, it is recommended that the PO remain as an unobtrusive observer. In online video conferencing platforms such as Zoom, it may be helpful for POs to have their videos turned off and microphone muted while they observe and take notes of the observations of the group members' and leaders' group processes and dynamics. This is a unique feature that is not available to POs who would be working in-person. Turning off video and muting self, means the PO is still there and visible, but also not there. Such unobstructive presence of the PO in the session will enable them to take a step back and view larger trends and patterns of the group dynamics and interpersonal interactions within the online setting. In such a setting, POs can utilize the 'chat' option to communicate their observations subtly to the group leaders and/or group members individually and privately as needed. Using the chat could be done privately to individual members including the facilitator; sharing process comments in real time in the chat where members can react to a 'bug in the ear,' or post the group. The chat could also allow members to respond to the PO. This is possible only due to the online set up that allows for such anonymity in communication between two parties at the same time.

Additionally, whenever the PO intends to jump in to offer their insights/feedback, they may utilize options such as 'raising of hand.' In other cases, POs may also choose to utilize the 'emoji' and 'reactions' options to communicate their take on the group dynamics by offering this feedback in real time for others to ponder. Furthermore, there are some common technology features associated with video conferencing, which include the sharing of 'whiteboard' that enables POs to collaboratively engage with the group in brainstorming of ideas or sharing of insights relevant to the group process. POs in certain cases may also choose to share their screen using the 'screen share' option in order for them to share their notes, images, or feedback/comments so that it may be helpful for communicating their message with clarity as well as aid in ensuring accessibility for diverse users within the group.

For Model Two of Process Observation, mentioned in the previous section, we recommend POs also use the tools to record themselves sharing their insights from the group observations in addition to their written notes to the group members and leaders. This may aid in minimizing the room for misinterpretation and misrepresentations of intent and meaning in the nuanced messages of PO. In general, access, equity, and safety for participants must be discussed regularly. Technology itself is not race-neutral. This means those responsible for creating the tools and applications must be intentional about ensuring this far-reaching platform is inclusive (Benjamin, 2019). Co-creating ground rules that include exploring the intersections of identity and open and honest communication helps set the stage for different ways POs, group leaders, and group members interpret and address the group process. In addition, the user of the tools must also be intentional that the interactions cultivated by the technology facilitate the potential goodness of people to counter the racism embedded throughout every aspect of our society.

Furthermore, the group components including membership, duration, dynamics and so forth are common factors impacting the success of a PO. Similar to a faculty teaching courses (Koehler et al., 2004), a PO is expected to demonstrate expertise in not only the skills of observing group dynamics but also in effectively utilizing technology in dynamic ways. Another way to think about POs and their influence on the group process stem from the following questions like, should the Process Observer attend every session? Or should they attend occasionally, rarely or just once? What about the timing of the process observers' entrance? Which is more likely to produce a better outcome and why? The beginning planning phase, or during a time of difficulty?

A group's cohesion level will also likely have an impact on the level of influence the PO has. In other words, the PO is not recused from the typical aspects of any group. However, a PO's skill set might be more narrowly focused on observation, communicating feedback, and offering recommendations. That said, a PO might not readily be accepted or valued for their potential contributions. In fact, they may likely begin as an outsider, especially considering that their job is to observe and evaluate the group's functioning. And the Process Observation role may elicit additional anxiety initially; this is another aspect that is common within any group experience. Now think about this information above and the impact of technology that has been burgeoning within the field of counseling.

Case Illustration

Below, we offer a tangible example of a PO providing feedback to the group facilitators and group members within a group counseling course. The example includes the use of Zoom technology for a group conducted online.

Case Scenario Background

Teena is a PO in an online group where Dorsa and Tomas are co-facilitators. The group is promoted as a social and communication skills group for teenagers. Members are referred by the school to the partnering community agency where Dorsa, Tomas, and Teena serve as licensed professional counselors. By the fourth session, there were ten teenagers who were actively engaged in the discussions and had moved beyond the forming stage.

Session Description

It was the fourth session, scheduled in Zoom for about 60 minutes. Teena turned off their camera after logging on. This session essentially began with checking in, followed by a topic-based activity, and finally a processing component. During the time group leaders were facilitating an initial check in, Teena was behind the scenes identifying group dynamics as they emerge during the group activity and interactions. Teena was also paying attention to the impact of group dynamics for both the members and the group. Here we offer two observations Teena made.

First, Teena noticed two members talk over each other at least twice during the processing of the activity. They also noticed the same members not using the 'raise hand' button as indicated during the first session. Teena makes note of the emerging pattern, but carefully waits for another instance when this behavior was repeated in order to highlight it in their feedback to the members. However, Teena seemed uncertain if it was genuinely a foresight of members to utilize the Zoom function or if they intentionally trespassed the established norm due to their existing defiant attitude toward authority (which Teena knew from their personal sharing during the first session).

On another occasion, Teena found three members turned their camera off one after the other. Quickly Teena made note of the content to see if there was a connection between what was shared and their actions. Teena observed the duration between when those members turned their cameras off and turned them back on. Teena made note of this to bring up their observation to the members at the end during processing.

Following the session, Teena turns their camera on and joins the group more directly to share their observations of the group. This observation and feedback period takes place at the end (almost about 20 minutes before the end of the session). For example, Teena brought up their observation on how three members turned off their cameras right at the same time when a topic was brought up. Teena invited members to share their response to their observation. It was found that paying attention to some subtle withdrawal behaviors, as seen through turning off of one's video feed, was indicative of the members' reservations with that particular content and shutting off their camera was their individual way of distancing from expressing their emotional reactions (which one member termed as 'mad' and the other two as 'extremely angry').

With regard to the observation about a few members (without mentioning their names) talking over each other, Teena first stated this observation. Leaving no moment to waste, the two members jumped in and apologized for not remembering to do that and moreover it being a topic they were passionate about (due to which they seemed eager to share). This explained to the PO as well as the rest of the group members who immediately showed signs of relief gained from the understanding. Then, Teena opened it up for sharing of ideas on how the group would like to resolve the concern potentially arising in the future where some members may accidentally step over others' ideas while being shared or not utilize a feature that the group had agreed upon in the beginning.

Finally, here are some important considerations for Teena in the role of PO - How might a PO recognize when members are beginning to disconnect and notice whether this is due to the topic or the online environment interacting? How might a PO recognize and distinguish Zoom exhaustion and resistance? Do we invite you to think about what other process comments might emerge that are squarely related to the fact that the session occurred online? Also, we encourage you to reflect if there were other process comments that would be less applicable if the session took place in person.

Conclusion

Major ideas in the chapter reinforced the fact that technology is constantly emerging within our society and this too impacts the counseling profession. In this day and age, the emerging opportunities are intriguing and quite complex. The impact of technology on the group process that is noted and explored with the input from the PO is still under study. But at this point of technology's infancy stage and integration within counselor training and group leader preparation, having tools to leverage a PO within various graduate training experiences is tremendous.

Process Observation in a group setting is still under investigation. The use of avatars and other simulations and gaming technologies in counseling clients is already in the horizons. The use of artificial intelligence has not been explicitly discussed, but virtual reality will impact counseling and group counseling in more and more ways. These alternatives offering safe and controlled 'shelter' (Riva & Vincelli, 2001, p. 52) for exploration and demonstration of one's emotional states as well as their identity will no doubt soon be within mainstream discourse related to PO and groupwork literature. Furthermore, the case illustration allows the reader to consider and to begin to draw one's own conclusions about the impact of technology and the intricacies of Process Observation. Finally, a critical discourse of the application of Process Observation and ideas for the future in terms of technology is captured.

References

Benjamin, R. (2019). *Race after technology: abolitionist tools for the new Jim code*. Polity Press.

Hogan, Harris, R. S., & Cassidy, J. M. (2006). The impact of process observers on interpersonal group therapy. *Journal of College Student Psychotherapy, 21(1)*, 21–32. https://doi.org/10.1300/J035v21n01_03.

Koehler, M. J., Mishra, P., Hershey, K., & Peruski, L. (2004). With a little help from your students: A new model for faculty development and online course design. *Journal of Technology and Teacher Education, 12*, 25–55. https://pdfs.semanticscholar.org/4df3/3eb2f0b7e70dcf3358ccbf25fb6f2583ea9f.pdf.

Mason, E. C. M., Griffith, C., & Belser, C. T. (2019). School counselors' use of technology for program management. *Professional School Counseling 22(1)*, 1–10. https://doi.org/10.1177/2156759X19870794.

Prasath, P. R., Xiong, Y., Zhang, Q., & Jeon, L. (2022). Self-efficacy development of graduate student leaders in facilitating groups for international students. *International Journal of Group Psychotherapy, 72(4)*, 331–357. https://doi.org/10.1080/00207284.2022.2107529.

Riva, G., & Vincelli, F. (2001). Virtual reality as an advanced imaginal system: A new experiential approach for counseling and therapy. *International Journal of Action Methods, 54(2)*, 51–64.

Toseland, R. W., & Rivas, R. F. (2009). *An introduction to group work practice*. Boston, MA: Pearson/Allyn and Bacon.

Xiong, Y., Prasath, P. R., Zhang, Q., Jeon, L., & Pillay, Y. (2023). A Phenomenological Study of Group Facilitators' Experiences: A Mindfulness-based Wellbeing Group for International Students During the COVID-19 Pandemic. *The Journal for Specialists in Group Work*, 1–25. https://doi.org/10.1080/01933922.2022.2158971.

Chapter 16

Conclusion

Congratulations on having acquired the first ever stand-alone text on Process Observation (PO) in groups! If nothing else, we hope it has proved the point we started with, that PO is a highly valuable, complex, and multidimensional endeavor. The seemingly simple label of PO, when unpacked, describes a variety of functions that range from the professional and ethical necessities, required skills, integration of theoretical perspectives, as well as the group needs, leader needs, and various settings in which it could play a valuable role. While the variety of aspects might seem daunting if you were only looking for a simple how-to on observing a group, it can also be inspiring. Let us take you through some of the implications of the work contained in this book.

Importance of PO

If there is a primary idea that we want to leave you with, it is the critical importance of PO to healthy group functioning. We have all heard about people's relief about having less in-person work meetings during the pandemic, and being able to attend on zoom and pretend to be listening. This is a sign that there are many poorly led group meetings out there, crying out for a PO to inject some energy into the life of their group. Chapter 13 describes the many ways in which PO has been around for some time, in many different types of work and clinical settings. In group work, it is clear that PO is not just for new group leaders in training or groups that have gone off the tracks. Yet we suspect in many settings, those who lead groups (say in business or even education) would have a hard time giving up control of those meetings. Leaders who are unaware of the opportunity for enhanced functioning might see sharing airtime with a PO as a distraction at best and an impediment at worst. If the goal is members who feel valued and therefore are more productive, resilient, and effective as a group, this needs to change.

In a helping setting, we suspect group leaders are more than willing to benefit from a PO, but likely do not know enough about how to find one, or use one, to really experience the full benefits of one. Therefore, in settings where there is a staff of helpers available with group training, such as a community agency or college counseling center, more emphasis could be placed on making PO a normal part of the process. As noted in Chapter 12, this already happens in education settings when it comes to teaching, in which an observer sits in on a class and provides feedback to a teacher (i.e., leader of instruction). In our experience as college teachers, this type of observation can be incredibly valuable as well as idiosyncratic, since guidelines and structures for these types of observations vary widely. In addition, they can be high stakes when included as part of the promotion process, which place unintended consequences on the nature of the observations. For example, how honest can you be about your feedback when the person being observed is also being evaluated? Of course, in K-12 settings the process of teaching and observation is much

DOI: 10.4324/9781003281955-20

more normalized and integrated into the daily lives of teachers. In order for PO to become more commonplace, it must also become more professionalized, a topic we turn to next.

Professionalization of PO

The chapters in Part I of this book ("Essentials of Process Observation") make a compelling case for the need to professionalize PO. Quality PO, as we note above, is complex and multifaceted, and requires advance planning, a unique set of skills, and ongoing engagement with the group and its leaders. Simply asking a person to observe a group and provide feedback is unlikely to yield as many benefits as following the steps recommended in these chapters. When the proper ethical and professional issues are attended to, PO's can have a tremendous impact on the functioning of a group, particularly when it comes to observing for equity and inclusion.

A number of concrete recommendations therefore are necessary for the field. PO needs its own professional standards for practice, intersections with equity, inclusion, and social justice, framework of ethics conduct, and intersections with equity, inclusion, and social justice. PO should involve a consent form with the group, and include documentation of the PO role, what is observed, and resulting reports and recommendations for the group. It is also likely that credentialing will be necessary in the near future for PO, similar to the type of credentialing necessary for the supervision of clinical work. Supervisors are recognized as possessing the clinical skills being practiced by the persons they are overseeing, as well as an additional layer of expertise necessary to be an effective supervisor. Similarly, a PO needs to have fundamental knowledge of group theory and practice, as well as the unique skills of being a PO. We recommend that POs be taught as a separate set of skills in group intervention courses.

Future Research

Chapter 14 describes the existing state of PO research, which is quite scarce, and the need for future research aimed at better understanding effective PO. As noted in this chapter, most of the research that has been done is in graduate training settings, and even here, best practices are far from settled. As a baseline, we do not even have data on how often POs are used and for what purposes. As noted in Chapter 15, the role of technology in PO is likely to increase, and it is here that future research could be particularly important in shaping the field.

A Note About Our Process

We worked with our co-authors over the course of a year to develop and write this book and in doing so enacted our own group process. In Fall 2021 we convened potential contributors to discuss the state of PO and what contributions each author would make to the project. We recommend this highly for edited books in the future – our discussions about our experiences with PO were highly illuminating, and helped us establish what needed to be included in a book about PO, where essentially nothing currently existed. Attention to Diversity, Equity, Inclusion was a common theme of our discussions, since the topic is both at the forefront of societal discussions and in the helping field. We also came to consensus on writing a book that was practical and used as many examples and provided the reader with as many tools as possible. And of course we cast ourselves in the role of PO whenever possible when the group met. We hope the result of our work is useful to you and that you continue to advance the field in this important area.

Appendix I

Sample Process Observation Checklist

Group Goals and Objectives

- Did there appear to be a general understanding of the group's objectives and consensus among members of the same?
- Do members appear confused about the group's objectives? Or their personal goals for the group?
- How well did the leader respond to the questions or concerns raised regarding group goals and objectives?
- How well did group members respond to each other's questions on the same topic?
- How well was each member able to articulate their own personal goals and their hopes for the group?

Patterns of Group Interaction

- Based on observation of interaction patterns, what is the pattern of engagement and interaction within the group?
- Are all members engaged, or are some more engaged than others?
- Is there a silent member or an overactive group member that the leader needs to manage?
- What is the participation level for the group as a whole?
- Is the group is generally well engaged or is the group struggling to engage with each other in addressing the focus of the group?
- How is the leader or other members contributing towards leveling group member participation? How is the leader performing with regarding to encouraging group participation?

The Nature of Group Discussions

- Was there consistency in the discussion of the subject matter?
- Are members' dialogue expanding conversation on the group core focus or deepening discussions on the group's core purpose?
- Was the discussion arbitrary, meaningful, and insightful, or was it focused and cohesive?
- Were members able to conclude discussions on emerging concerns or are most discussion not concluded?
- Do members appear to be favoring certain subject matters while ignoring others, or are members consistent in addressing all emerging concerns with the same focus, emotional investment, and consistency?

- Which topics are members avoiding discussing? Are topics related to social-cultural factors and identities emerging within the group? When they do, are they named, acknowledge ad engaged with or are they ignored? Is race, gender or sexual identity playing a role in member interactions within the group or the reactions of the leader or other members in the group?

Group Interpersonal Dynamics

- How are members interacting with each other and how are they interacting with the leader?
- Is the relational dynamic amicable and connective, or is it conflictual and disagreeable? When disagreements emerge are they addressed or ignored?
- Are members joining with each other, and if so, who is joining with whom? And who is left out of group interpersonal connections and discussions?
- Are leaders/members responding to interpersonal dynamics, such as sub-grouping based on discussion content, or sub-grouping driven by social cultural norms of alignment within the context in which the group is contextualized?

Worksheet 1

Process Observation Reflection Form

Group Topic: ______________________

Role of the PO, as discussed with the leader:	Purpose of the group, as discussed with the leader:
Date:	Session Number:

Group Development

Given the number of sessions the group has had, where would you expect it to be developmentally?

Beginning Transition Middle End

Based on your observation in this session, how would you characterize where the group is developmentally?

Beginning Transition Middle End

Is developmental stage an area in which you wish to provide feedback?

Yes No

Group Norms

What are the facilitative (helpful) norms you see in the group?

What, if any, norms do you observe that get in the way of the group's process?

Are norms an area in which you wish to provide feedback?

Yes No

Conflict

Was there conflict observed in this session?

Yes No

If yes, was the conflict handled appropriately by the leader(s)/ members?

Yes No

Were there -ist or other aggressive/ microaggressive comments observed in the session?

Yes No

If yes, were the comments addressed appropriately by the leader?

Yes No

Are conflict or -ist comments an area in which you wish to provide feedback?

Yes No

Interpersonal Process

What do you notice about how members relate to one another?

What do you notice about how members relate to the leader?

Are there interpersonal process issues on which you would like to provide feedback?

Yes No

Energy

The energy of the group seemed to be

High Moderate Low

Is the energy of the group an area in which you would like to provide feedback?

Yes No

Unfinished Business

What, if any, unfinished business remains?

Debriefing With Group Leader – Questions

Date: Session #:

Participants present:

- What was the tone of the group tonight?
- What topics/themes were covered?
- What norms are starting to form?
- What techniques did you use?
- Did anyone dominate? Who, Why? How did you handle it?
- Did anyone not participate? Who, Why? How did you handle it?
- What are some of the differences or commonalities that were at play in the session?
- Were there any significant developments? What were they and how did they present?
- Was there anything that occurred either positive or challenging?
- Was there anything that came up in tonight's session that you would consider a challenge either on an individual basis or in terms of the group?
- Was there anything that came up in tonight's session that you consider a success either on an individual basis or in terms of the group as a whole?
- Anything else?

Process Observer Group Notes

Leaders:____________________ Session #:__________ Date: __________

Members: ____

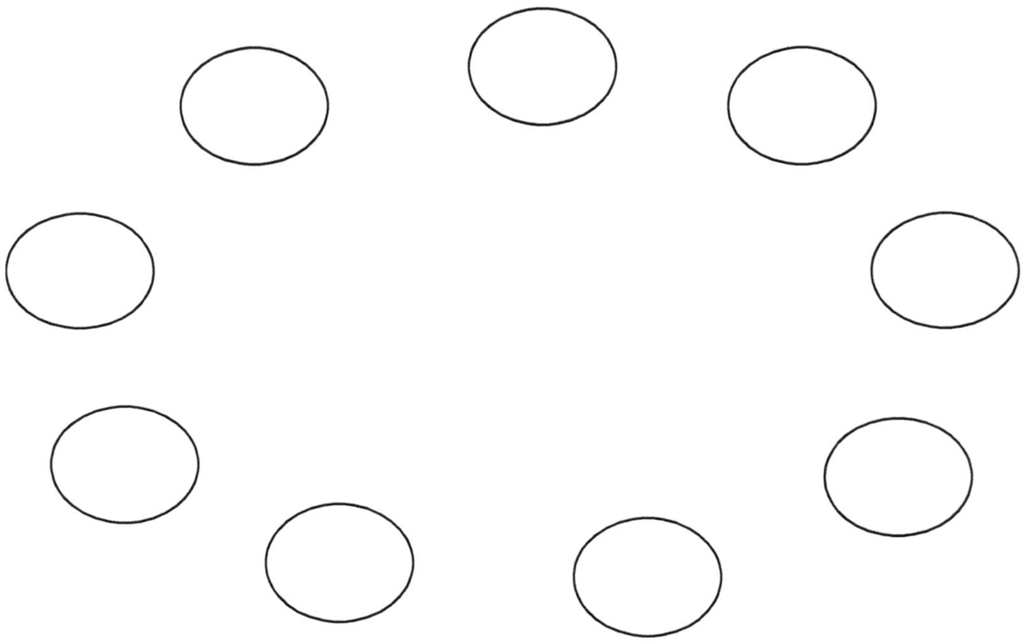

Process Observation:

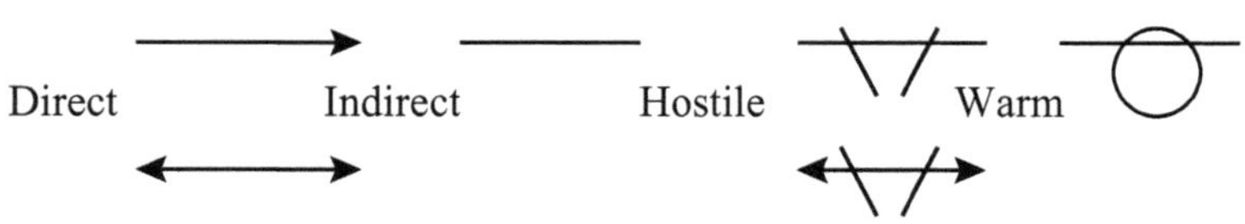

Process Observer Checklist

1. Structural Components

   a *Staging* – What stage is the group at in their work together?

   b Continuity – How does the group include previous work in the current session?

2. Existent Components

   a Evident

      i. Balance in group member responses – How often, and in response to whom, do group members respond? Is there meta-communication occurring and when did the Process Observer recognize it?

      ii. Change in the topic – Note the topic being discussed, who introduces it, when the topic of discussion changes, and who introduces the change in the topic?

      iii. Topic flow – Provide a complete session view of topic changes and ideas about when and how they changed.

   b Summative

      i. Themes emerging – What emerging themes from the sessions are noticed?

      ii. Remaining topics – What topics were brought up and dropped during the observation?

3. Projective Components

      i. Developing group stage – What does the group stage look like after this observation?

      ii. Succeeding group tasks – From the observer's point of view, what might the group consider for the next steps?

      iii. Contextual pieces – What are some final considerations for this group that are specific to the members and context of the group?

   Additional Process Observations and Notes:

Training Notes on Process Observation

During each group/meeting, take turns in the role of the Process Observer and make notes.

The purpose of writing these process notes is to analyze the process of events that occur in each group. In other words, describe not WHAT happened, but HOW AND WHY it happened. To get at the "process" underlying what occurs, you need to "read between the lines."

1. Consider the following questions:

    - What sequence of events occurred? What does this reveal?
    - How did people communicate? What did they communicate?
    - How much did each person participate?
    - Who were the leaders? What alliances were present?
    - How does this session compare to previous ones?
    - Was the group productive? Stuck? Why?
    - What direction is the group taking?
    - Pay attention to how the group changes over time.
    - Be sure to describe your thoughts and feelings and if you participated in any way in the group.

    Observe and make notes on the following issues:

    - leadership patterns
    - alliances and subgroups
    - communication patterns
    - how problems are solved
    - how decisions are made
    - how emotions are expressed
    - how disclosure and vulnerability is responded to

    Final analysis:

    - What changes occurred in the group over time? What were critical events in its history?
    - Draw a sociogram of the group. How did the socio-emotional factors of the group affect its task performance and its communication patterns?
    - What obstacles did the group confront? Did it succeed? How could its performance have been improved?
    - What role did you play in the group? What are your personal thoughts and feelings about the group?

Process Observer Notes – Training

Name: ____

Date: ____________________

Use the following areas to make notes on what you observe. Please note any feelings or sense of belonging or exclusion as well. Be prepared to share themes from this report with the whole group at the end, though you will turn it in only to the instructor.

E.g. 1. We seemed to live up to (or challenge) our norm of __________ when we… 2. Some patterns of communication I noticed… 3. The nonverbal communication seems to be indicating… 4. Frustration seemed to increase when… and decrease when… 5. People seemed more engaged when…but less engaged when… Patterns of engagement I noticed were… 6. We seemed to get stuck when…

Did the group appear to have a purpose? How well does the group adhere to its agreements and where does it veer from them?

Did everyone appear to have clarity about the group goals? Were they implicit or explicit?

Record/tally the positive, negative, or neutral comments made during the group activity. Suggestions, directions, encouragers, can all be comments.

Task Roles	*Interactive Roles*	*Self-Oriented*

If you had to assign roles to any members, what might you label?

Positive Comments (e.g. great idea; I love that; thanks; appreciate you)	*Negative Comments (e.g. I know it's silly; brutal; ouch; I don't feel heard)*	*Neutral comments (e.g. ok; what do people think of this; how shall we start; say more)*

How would you describe the energy level across the group?

What was the atmosphere (relaxed, tense, competitive, resistant)?

Did everyone participate? Explain.

Did conflict arise? How was it resolved if so?

Overall impressions:

Vignette – Process Observation of a Group Dynamic

[You can decide the context of the group, the leader, the age of the group, and what kind of group it is.]

The group consists of eight persons. Roughly similar in age, they include:

- Brooke, who identifies as a Black Christian lesbian ciswoman, and temporarily able-bodied
- Greg, Polish American, heterosexual, Catholic, cisman
- Mary, Irish American, bisexual, Catholic, ciswoman, uses a wheelchair
- Lin, Japanese American, heterosexual, Christian, transwoman
- Barry, French Canadian, gay, Buddhist, cisman
- Dolores, Puerto Rican ciswoman, heterosexual, Catholic
- David, Ethiopian American, cisman, pansexual, Jewish
- Wong, Chinese American, heterosexual, Taoist, cisman

As the group begins to get started, Brooke, one of the group members cuts off the leader who was starting to speak. "Hold on," she says, "I know you want to get started and we don't want to waste daylight, but we've got an issue that keeps coming up, and for the last four meetings we've dismissed it as not having enough time. So, I want us to start with it!"

The leader cuts in, "I know, and I was going to make time today, but we really have to return to the issues we were working on last time. I think those are more important."

Another group member, Greg, says, "Um, not to be difficult, but I have no idea what you are talking about. What's this concern?" they ask as they turn to Brooke, who throws up her hands in exasperation, and responds, "Are you serious? I feel like I'm invisible here when I've been trying to get this on the agenda for the last five meetings!"

Lin nods in agreement, "Yes, I'm with you there Brooke. It's really silencing to get this confusion every time."

Barry says, "Well, that's not helpful!" Indicating Greg who had asked the question and looks downcast, "now you're just making people feel bad."

Several people start speaking at once, and voices get raised, until the chaos abruptly ends as people realize what's happening. Everyone subsides into silence looking frustrated and a couple of group members pat each other on the arm to comfort or give sympathetic looks.

Index

Note: Locators in **bold** refer to tables and those in *italics* to figures.

For Product Safety Concerns and Information please contact our EU
representative GPSR@taylorandfrancis.com
Taylor & Francis Verlag GmbH, Kaufingerstraße 24, 80331 München, Germany

www.ingramcontent.com/pod-product-compliance
Ingram Content Group UK Ltd.
Pitfield, Milton Keynes, MK11 3LW, UK
UKHW050234200926
475702UK00020B/3033
9781032251806